JOHN BROWN

JOHN BROWN

QUEEN VICTORIA'S HIGHLAND SERVANT

RAYMOND LAMONT-BROWN

SUTTON PUBLISHING

First published in the United Kingdom in 2000 by
Sutton Publishing Limited · Phoenix Mill
Thrupp · Stroud · Gloucestershire · GL5 2BU

Reprinted in 2000

British Library Cataloguing-in-Publication Data
A catalogue record for this book is available from the British Library.

ISBN 0 7509 2252 4

Typeset in 12/13.5pt Bembo Mono.
Typesetting and origination by
Sutton Publishing Limited.
Printed and bound in England by
J.H. Haynes & Co. Ltd, Sparkford.

CONTENTS

CHRONOLOGY

THE LIFE AND ROYAL ASSOCIATIONS OF JOHN BROWN

1819

24 May   Princess Alexandrina Victoria is born at Kensington Palace, only child of Prince Edward, Duke of Kent and Strathearn (1767–1820), and Princess Victoria Mary Louisa of Saxe-Saalfeld-Coburg (1786–1861), widow of Emich Karl, Prince zu Leiningen.

26 Aug   Prince Francis Albert Charles Augustus Emmanuel of Saxe-Coburg is born at Schloss Rosenau, Coburg, youngest son of Ernest I, Duke of Saxe-Coburg and Gotha (1784–1844), and his first wife Princess Louise of Saxe-Gotha-Altenburg (1800–1831).

1826

8 Dec   John Brown is born at Crathienaird, Crathie parish, Aberdeenshire, second of the eleven children of tenant farmer John Brown (1790–1875) and his wife Margaret Leys (1799–1876).

1830

John Brown begins his education at the local Gaelic-speaking school at Crathie and at home.

1831

The Brown family move to The Bush, a farm at Crathie.

1838

28 Jun   Queen Victoria is crowned at Westminster Abbey.

1839

John Brown works as a farm labourer at Crathienaird and helps out at The Bush; he also works as ostler's assistant at Pannanich Wells.

1840

10 Feb   Queen Victoria marries Prince Albert.

1842

John Brown becomes a stable boy on Sir Robert Gordon's estate at Balmoral.

Queen Victoria's first visit to Scotland (1–15 Sep).

1844

Queen Victoria's second visit to Scotland (11 Sep–2 Oct).

1847

The royal family visit Ardverikie and tour the west coast of Scotland (11 Aug–19 Sep).

1848

Queen Victoria is advised to visit Deeside for her health by her Physician-in-Ordinary, Sir James Clark.

8 Sep   Queen Victoria visits Balmoral for the first time.

1849

11 Sep   First mention of John Brown occurs in Queen Victoria's *Journal*.

John Brown is promoted to gillie at Balmoral.

Typhoid sweeps Crathie; two of John Brown's brothers and one sister die.

1851

John Brown takes on the permanent role of leader of Queen Victoria's pony on Prince Albert's instigation.

1852

Prince Albert buys the 17,400 acre estate at Balmoral for 30,000 guineas.

1853

28 Sep   Foundation of a new castle at Balmoral to the designs of Prince Albert.

1855

7 Sep   The royal family take possession of the new castle at Balmoral.

1857

26 Jun   Prince Albert is created Prince Consort.

1858

John Brown takes Archibald Fraser Macdonald's place as personal gillie to Prince Albert.

1860

First 'Great Expedition' by the royal family to Glen Fishie and Grantown, with John Brown in attendance (4–5 Sep).

1861

Second 'Great Expedition' to Invermark and Fettercairn, again with John Brown in attendance (20–21 Sep).

Third 'Great Expedition' to Glen Fishie, Dalwhinnie and Blair Atholl (8–9 Oct), again with John Brown in attendance.

Fourth 'Great Expedition' to Ca-Ness (16 Oct), with John Brown in attendance. 'It was our last one,' Queen Victoria wrote poignantly in her *Journal*.

14 Dec Death of Prince Albert at Windsor Castle.

1862

1 Jun John Brown travels south (with other gillies) to the Second International Exhibition.

Aug John Brown goes to Germany in Queen Victoria's entourage.

1863

7 Oct Carriage accident involving Queen Victoria, Princess Alice and Princess Helena en route from Altnagiuthasach. John Brown 'indefatigable in his attendance and care', writes Queen Victoria in her *Journal*.

1864

Oct In conversation with Princess Alice, the Keeper of the Privy Purse Sir Charles Phipps and Royal Physician Dr William Jenner discuss Queen Victoria's sustained depression and reluctance to appear in public since Prince Albert's death. It is suggested that John Brown be brought from Balmoral to help remind the Queen of 'happier times' on vacation in Scotland.

Dec John Brown arrives at Osborne as groom.

1865

3 Feb Queen Victoria decides to keep John Brown 'permanently' on her immediate staff.

2 Jun Dr Robertson prepares a memorandum of John Brown's ancestry at the Queen's instruction.

Aug John Brown is in the royal entourage at Darmstadt, Germany.

1866

30 Jun   *Punch* ridicules John Brown.

Aug   Ridicule is followed up in *John o'Groats Journal*.
          John Brown's salary reaches £150 p.a.

1867

May   *Tomahawk* lampoons John Brown.
          The Royal Academy Spring Exhibition includes a picture of
          John Brown and Queen Victoria by Sir Edwin Landseer.
          Queen Victoria's 'Tour of the Borders' (20–24 Aug), with
          John Brown in attendance.

1868

          Stories circulate about John Brown being beaten up at Balmoral.

1872

29 Feb   Queen Victoria is attacked by Arthur O'Connor. John
          Brown assists in restraining assailant and is rewarded with a
          'Faithful Service Medal' and a 'Devoted Service Medal', plus
          an annuity of £25 p.a.

17 Nov   John Brown is designated 'Esquire'.
          John Brown's salary reaches £400 p.a.

1875

          John Brown's portrait is painted by Heinrich von Angeli for
          Queen Victoria, from a photograph as Brown refuses to pose.
          Queen Victoria's trip to Inveraray (21–29 Sep), with John
          Brown in attendance.

18 Oct   Death of John Brown Sr, at Wester Micras, Crathie.

1876

          Queen Victoria gives John Brown a substantial cottage at
          Balmoral.
          Queen Victoria approves the Bill that will make her Empress
          of India.

2 Aug   John Brown's mother dies at Craiglourican Cottage,
          Balmoral.

1877

1 Jan   Queen Victoria is proclaimed Empress of India.

1879

          Queen Victoria visits France and Italy. Brown is in
          attendance, but suffering from erysipelas.

1881

John Brown is awarded a ten year service 'bar' to his 'Faithful Service Medal'.

1882

2 Mar   Queen Victoria is attacked by Roderick Maclean at Windsor. John Brown is upstaged by Eton scholars assailing the culprit.

1883

27 Mar   John Brown dies at Windsor Castle.

5 Apl   John Brown is interred at Crathie churchyard.

1884

Feb   Queen Victoria publishes *More Leaves from the Journal of a Life in the Highlands*. The Prince of Wales is indignant at references to John Brown.

Mar   Queen Victoria abandons her 'memoir' of John Brown and publication of extracts of their correspondence and his diary. Queen Victoria erects a plaque to John Brown at the royal mausoleum at Frogmore.

1887

20 Jun   Queen Victoria's Golden Jubilee Year begins. The Queen sustains contact with John Brown's siblings.

1897

20 Jun   Queen Victoria's Diamond Jubilee. John Brown's brothers are still in royal service.

1901

22 Jan   Death of Queen Victoria at Osborne. She had reigned for sixty-three years.

4 Feb   Queen Victoria interred in the royal mausoleum at Frogmore; in her coffin are placed mementoes of John Brown.

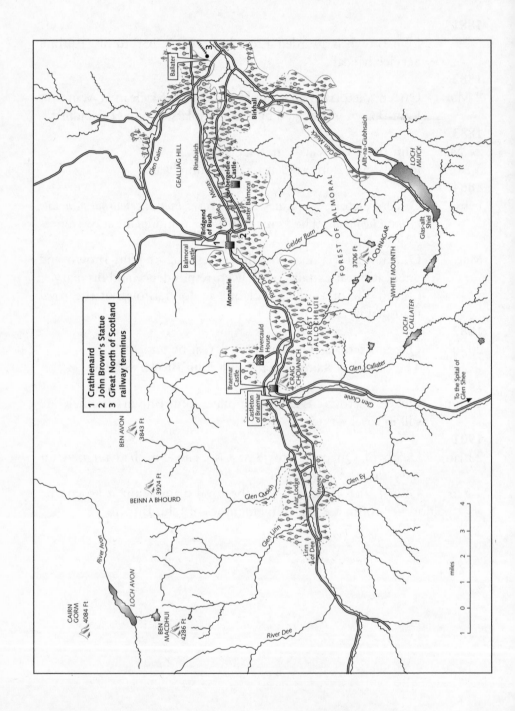

1 Crathienaird
2 John Brown's Statue
3 Great North of Scotland
  railway terminus

CAIRN GORM 4084 Ft
LOCH AVON
RIVER AVON
BEN MACDHUI 4286 Ft
River Dee
BEN AVON 3843 Ft
BEINN A BHOURD 3924 Ft
Glen Quoch
Glen Linn
Mar Lodge
Inverey
Linn of Dee
Glen Ey
Ballater
Birkhall
Glen Cairn
GEALLIAG HILL
Rinabaich
Abergeldie Castle
Easter Balmoral
Crathie
McCrae
Bridgend of Bush
Balmoral Castle
Monaltrie
River Dee
Invercauld House
Braemar Castle
CRAIG CHOINICH
Castleton of Braemar
FOREST OF BALLOCHBUIE
Gelder Burn
FOREST OF BALMORAL
Glen Muick
LOCH MUICK
Glas-allt Shiel
Allt-na-Giubhsaich
LOCHNAGAR
3706 Ft
WHITE MOUNTH
LOCH CALLATER
Glen Callater
Glen Clunie
To the Spital of Glen Shee

miles
1 0 1 2 3 4

BIRTH OF ROYAL RUMOUR

At last King Edward VII could take his revenge. It was petulant, infantile and undignified, but it was immensely satisfying. Not many months after his mother's death at 6.30pm on 22 January 1901, at Osborne House on the Isle of Wight, HRH Albert Edward, Prince of Wales, now King Edward VII, ordered his obliteration, or forced removal, of all the artefacts, busts and statues of Queen Victoria's favourite Highland servant John Brown.[1] On the morning of the Queen's death shepherds on the hills above Balmoral noticed that the cairn of stones the Queen had had raised to the memory of John Brown was flattened and the stones spread around. Such desecration was too much even for the gales on these airy slopes, and all who saw the site believed that new royal orders from Osborne had been carried out.[2] At Windsor, the Keeper of the Royal Pictures received an unequivocal order. Carl Rudolph Sohn's lifesize portrait of John Brown in black coat, dark brown tweed kilt and brown horsehair sporran, which had been commissioned by Queen Victoria in May 1883 (two months after John Brown's death), was to be removed from its place of honour, deleted from the inventory at Windsor Castle and sent gratis to John Brown's brother William at Crathie.[3] Queen Alexandra testified to her husband's wrathful revenge and expunging of all sentimentality in a letter to her sister-in-law the Empress Frederick of Germany: 'Alas! during my absence [in Copenhagen] Bertie had had all your beloved Mother's rooms dismantled and all her precious things removed.'[4] King Edward's ultimate insult to Brown's memory was the conversion of his apartment at Windsor Castle into a billiard room.

As hammers smashed plaster busts, scissors rent keepsakes and photographs buckled and hissed on bonfires, no one in the inner royal circle had any doubt about the reasons for the new sovereign's ire against the famous Scot. Those with the longest memories recalled stories of how John Brown had smacked the backside of the errant young Prince of Wales. Surely these vicious attacks on the memory of John Brown by a sixty-year-old man could not be traced back to such a minor indignity, however painful? No, there was more to it than that. King Edward had been deeply humiliated by his mother's taking Brown's side in the quarrels he had had with the Highland servant. Yet there was a deeper insult in Edward's eyes. After Prince Albert's death in 1861, Queen Victoria looked upon her family as having 'no Male head', thus degrading her son's position.[5] The fact that John Brown was 'discreet' gave him manly qualities in Queen Victoria's eyes and won him a position of virile gentlemanliness in her household. A deeply insecure man, King Edward was further blisteringly offended that his mother should consider a servant to have finer qualities than himself.[6]

Although Edward was more than aware that his mother was 'amazingly indiscreet', he had been very dismayed at her impropriety, as he saw it, in 'expressing her private life to the world' in her volume *More Leaves from the Journal of a Life in the Highlands*.[7] He even told her so in a letter of 1884 thanking her for an advance copy of the book, and alluding to the mention of Brown in the text.[8]

Edward had long been irritated by his mother's attitude towards servants. Queen Victoria had spent a large part of her life among servants, and held most of them in great esteem – higher than she did many of her friends and family. Edward looked upon his mother's regard for servants as a part of her eccentricity, but he thought that in rebuking her offspring, and members of her immediate household, for being haughty to servants she was going too far. He had some sympathy with his brother Prince Arthur, whose Governor Sir Howard Elphinstone had been constantly bombarded with terse and lengthy letters from the Queen about 'the boy's offhand manner [to servants]'.[9] Edward's own epistolary tactlessness over the Queen's *More Leaves* revelations sprang as much from his fear that the public would deride his mother's sentimentality about servants in general, and John Brown in particular, as from his active hatred for Brown. Despite his own serial adultery as Prince of Wales, Edward was always stung by the rumours that persisted for decades about his mother and John Brown.

Queen Victoria had been brought up with sexual tittle-tattle in her mother's entourage. Had she not herself once glimpsed the tender whispering, the touched hands, the arm around the waist, that had suggested intimacy between the Duchess of Kent and her Household Comptroller Sir John Conroy? It was a scene that she had described to her devoted German friend Baroness Späth, her mother's Lady-in-Waiting.[10] And then there was all the 'horrid gossip' about her randy Hanoverian uncles, the sons of her grandfather King George III. Now it was her turn.

Queen Victoria was well aware of the scandalous rumours that circulate about her and John Brown. In a letter to her equerry Lord Charles Fitzroy, she wrote about 'those wicked and idle lies about poor, good, Brown which appeared in the Scotch provincial papers last year'.[11] The Queen was referring to one paper in particular which circulated in the Balmoral area.[12] It had run this story:

THE GREAT COURT FAVOURITE

The London correspondent of the *John o'Groats Journal*[13] says: 'I suppose all my readers have heard of the great favourite John Brown. His dismissal some weeks ago was generally talked about at the time, and I observe that the fact has now found its way into print, coupled with the suggestion of John Brown's probable restoration to power before long. The reason assigned for his dismissal is an inordinate indulgence in the national taste for whisky, and the restraining of that appetite is mentioned as a likely condition of his re-admission to favour. Far be it from me to question Mr Brown's power of suction . . . [yet] it is easy to suppose that a Highland gillie, who has achieved a practical realisation of his compatriots' with 'a Loch Lomond of whisky' will certainly not be a teetotaller. But Brown's fall has been more commonly ascribed to Mr Punch than to any shortcoming of his own. A few weeks ago *Punch* gave us the following as 'Court Circular':

"BALMORAL, Tuesday.

Mr John Brown walked on the slopes.
He subsequently partook of a haggis.
In the evening Mr John Brown was pleased to listen to a bag-pipe.
Mr John Brown retired early."

Those few lines gave rise to an immense deal of gossip and in a few days we heard that Brown was discharged. It is said his insolence to every person he came in contact with about the Court was latterly quite intolerable, and some friends of mine, who were near Windsor fishing, not long ago, who frequently saw the favourite, not then disgraced, gave me the benefit of a good deal of local gossip about the lusty gillie.

Queen Victoria was suspicious about who was spreading gossip about John Brown and herself, and she concurred with her Prime Minister Edward George Stanley, 14th Earl of Derby, who believed that certain courtiers were leaking anti-Brown comments to such journals as *Punch* and *Tomahawk*. He cited names to the Queen, including George Villiers, 4th Earl of Clarendon, and Sir Edwin Landseer.[14]

Scandalous rumours about Queen Victoria were nothing new. Soon after her accession to the throne she had become increasingly dependent upon her Prime Minister, William Lamb, 2nd Viscount Melbourne. He became her 'indispensable father figure'. Yet, although 'there was never the least impropriety' between them, Queen Victoria was soon gossiped about as 'Mrs Melbourne'. And there was another soubriquet. The pre-Raphaelites, that group of 'natural form' painters and others, were to call her 'Empress Brown'.[15]

An anonymous American visitor noted:

Englishmen do not scruple to sully the fair name of their Queen . . .
    Soon after my arrival in England, at a table where all the company were gentlemen by rank or position, there were constant references and jokes about 'Mrs Brown' . . . I lost the point of all the witty sayings, and should have remained in blissful ignorance throughout the dinner had not my host kindly informed me that 'Mrs Brown' was an English synonym for the Queen . . .[16]

Rumours that John Brown and Queen Victoria had a sexual relationship were well established during her reign and there is a curious royal link which gave them substance. Tradition had it that from time to time the Prince of Wales shared the bed of the Victorian trollop Catherine Walters, known in loose society as 'Skittles' because she had once worked in a Liverpool bowling alley. She was 'kept' for many years by Spencer Compton Cavendish, Marquess of Hartington, the eldest son of the 7th Duke of Devonshire. 'Harty Tarty' – as the peer was known in the Prince of Wales's set – was a prominent procurer of society ladies and tarts for the Prince's bed and was privy to his indiscretions – as was Skittles.

The Prince of Wales was devoted to Skittles and commissioned the Austrian-born sculptor Joseph Edgar Boehm to prepare a bust of her for his collection. During her sittings Skittles gossiped with Boehm about Brown, as the sculptor had been commanded to Court around 1869/70 to create a bust of Brown for the Queen. John Brown referred to the sculptor thereafter as 'Herr Bum'. Historians believe that Boehm was the main informant – spiced up with pillowtalk from 'Harty Tarty' and the Prince of Wales – via another of Skittles' lovers, the diplomat, traveller and poet Wilfred Scawen Blunt, who himself kept a very indiscreet private diary.

Blunt recorded:

Brown was a rude unmannerly fellow . . . but he had unbounded influence with the Queen whom he treated with little respect, presuming in every way upon his position with her. It was the talk of all the Household that he was 'the Queen's Stallion'. He was a fine man physically, though coarsely made, and had fine eyes (like the late Prince Consort's, it was said), and the Queen, who had been passionately in love with her husband, got it into her head that somehow the Prince's spirit had passed into Brown, and four years after her widowhood, being very unhappy, allowed him all privileges. It was to be with him, where she could do as she liked, that she spent so much of her time at Balmoral, though he was also with her at Osborne and elsewhere . . . She used to go away with him to a little house in the hills where, on the pretence that it was for protection and 'to look after the dogs', he had a bedroom next to hers, ladies-in-waiting being put at the other end of the building . . . [There could be] no doubt of his being allowed every conjugal privilege.[17]

Blunt made no attempt to substantiate any of his comments.

Because Queen Victoria's life was largely hidden from the public, it was hardly surprising that a whole range of myths about her were given undue credence and had some plausibility, being apparently based on sound sources. Four rumours in particular were given regular airings in scurrilous pamphlets such as *Mrs John Brown*.[18] The first was that Queen Victoria and John Brown were married; second, that a child had been born to the Queen and John Brown; third, that John Brown was a spiritualistic medium who helped the Queen to keep in touch with her beloved Prince Albert; fourth, that the Queen had gone insane and John Brown was her 'keeper'. The first two of these calumnies were given credence in the Swiss publication *Gazette de Lausanne*. Under an anonymous hand the offending paragraphs read:

> *On dit* [They say] . . . that with Brown and by him she consoles herself for Prince Albert, and they go even further. They add that she is in an interesting condition, and that if she was not present for the Volunteers Review, and at the inauguration of the monument to Prince Albert, it was only in order to hide her pregnancy. I hasten to add that the Queen has been morganatically married to her attendant for a long time, which diminishes the gravity of the thing.[19]

The British Minister Plenipotentiary, the Hon. E.A.J. Harris, based at Berne, made an official complaint to the Swiss Federal Council about the paper's allegations. The Swiss did nothing but Harris's complaint inevitably gave the scurrilous nonsense a wider audience than it would have otherwise achieved.[20] By and large the British press left the Swiss paper's gossip alone, and even the socialist radical weekly *Reynolds Newspaper*, certainly no supporter of Queen Victoria, refused to follow up the story. Yet from such as the Swiss gossip branched a whole tree of slander and innuendo, and not just on the tongues of the lower classes.

These rumours are as alive today as they were in Queen Victoria's own lifetime, and the 1998 film *Mrs Brown* gave them a new lease of life. What was the truth behind these persistent rumours? This book endeavours to unravel fact from fiction against the background of Queen Victoria's courts at Windsor, Osborne and Balmoral.

QUEEN VICTORIA'S SCOTTISH INHERITANCE

Early in the morning of Thursday 24 March 1603, Queen Elizabeth I of England died. Within eight hours of her death, 36-year-old James Stewart was proclaimed King of England in London. He had reigned in Scotland as King James VI ever since his mother, Mary, Queen of Scots, had been forced to abdicate on 24 July 1567. On 5 April 1603 James disappeared down the road to Greenwich, with his 'gowff clubbis', to be at the hub of his new United Kingdom. Thereafter royal visits to Scotland became rare for some 220 years.

James VI and I returned to Scotland once, in 1617, in an attempt to impose Anglican ritual upon the recalcitrant Scottish Kirk; he stayed for seven months. James's second son Charles I, who was born on 19 November 1600 at Dunfermline, Fife, visited Edinburgh as monarch and on 18 June 1633 was crowned with Scotland's own regalia. During June 1650 Charles II landed in Scotland and on 1 January 1651 was crowned King of Scots at Scone; he never returned to Scotland after his Restoration in 1660. In 1679 James, Duke of York, later King James II, stayed at Holyrood Palace, to the disgust of strict Presbyterians who loathed his religion and his predilection for drama and court entertainments. Nevertheless James returned to Edinburgh in 1680 as Lord High Commissioner, bringing with him his wife Anne Hyde and his daughter Princess Anne, who was to rule as Queen Anne, the last of the Stewart monarchs.

There were no further royal visits to Scotland until 1715, when Prince James Francis Edward Stewart, the only surviving son of James II landed at Peterhead in an attempt to win back the British throne from the grasp of the Hanoverian succession. Again in 1745, Prince James's son Charles Edward Stewart, great-grandson of Charles I, took up the cudgels against George II, but all his hopes were strangled at Culloden field on 16 April 1746, when Charles's Jacobite army was utterly destroyed by the forces of his cousin, the Hanoverian Prince William Augustus, Duke of Cumberland. Prince Charles's desperate flight to France from the shores of Loch nan Uamh aboard *L'Heureux* on 19 September marked the end of this phase of royal visits to Scotland.

Almost seventy years later, the Scots were startled to learn that their new monarch King George IV, who had succeeded his father George III in 1820, intended to visit Scotland. The Scots aristocracy were sent into a flurry of consternation and activity as no one could remember how a royal progress should be organised. As royal pageant-master, Sir Walter Scott dug and delved in the nation's archives in order to create a tartan panorama to welcome the monarch. His efforts were based mostly on invented Highland mythology, customs and dress, but the jubilation, processions and presentations lasted for ten days from Tuesday 13 August. The Scots would never see their like again.

Twenty more years passed before Scotland received another visit from a British royal personage. In the meantime the exiled royal Bourbons of France, Charles X, Comte d'Artois and King of France, Louis and Marie Theresa, Duc et Duchesse d'Angoulême, Charles and Caroline, Duc et Duchesse de Berri, and Henri, the titular Henri V of France, along with his sister Princess Louise, were all state guests at Holyrood Palace variously during periods in 1796 and 1830. Five years after her accession to the throne of Great Britain, after the death of her uncle King William IV at twelve minutes past two in the morning of 20 June 1837, Queen Victoria herself decided to take an early autumn holiday in Scotland.

During June 1842 Queen Victoria asked her Prime Minister Sir Robert Peel to set in motion the arrangements for her Scottish jaunt. To the Queen's great surprise she was told that Peel and the Tory ministers in the Cabinet did not advise such a journey. They noted that the areas of northern England through which she would have to travel were rife with 'Chartist sympathisers'. These were the agitators who demanded a 'People's Charter' of parliamentary reform; only a few years previously, in 1839, they had signed a petition in the major towns of England towards this end and riots had broken out when Viscount Melbourne's Liberal government had supported the rejection of the petition. No, the Queen was told, a Scottish trip was neither feasible nor safe. However, backed by Lord Melbourne, the Queen persisted with her wishes. After a lengthy discussion with Sir James Graham, the Home Office Secretary, Prime Minister Peel agreed that the trip could take place if the initial leg of the journey was by sea. Thus on Monday 29 August 1842 Queen Victoria embarked on the royal yacht, *Royal George*, at Woolwich, and her squadron, led by the 36-gun vessel *Pique*, set sail for Scotland.

By 1 September the little fleet was anchored off Leith. The Queen was met at Granton Pier by Walter Francis Montague-Douglas-Scott, 5th Duke of Buccleuch and 7th Duke of Queensberry, joint Lord President of the Council and Privy Seal, Captain-General of the Royal Company of Archers, and Lord Lieutenant of Mid-Lothian and Roxburghshire, along with Prime Minister Peel. Her visit was to last until Thursday 15 September, with trips as far north as Taymouth Castle in Perthshire, the home of John Campbell, 2nd Marquess and 5th Earl of Breadalbane, Lord Lieutenant of Argyllshire. During this visit, the Queen recorded later in her *Journal*, at the Duke of Buccleuch's home, Dalkeith House, she first enjoyed real Scottish 'oatmeal porridge' and 'Finnan haddies' – the latter being split and smoke-cured haddock, named after the village of Findon in Kincardineshire.[1]

Queen Victoria was to make two more visits to Scotland before her great love affair with the country and its people really began at Balmoral. In September 1844 she landed at Dundee for a month-long expedition to Blair Castle at Blair Atholl, hosted by George Augustus Murray, 2nd Lord Glenlyon, nephew of the mentally disturbed estate owner John Murray, 5th Duke of Atholl. While driving by the River Tummel Queen Victoria tasted 'Athole Brose' for the first time at the inn at Moulinearn. This was a local drink made from a mixture of honey, whisky and milk.[2]

> *On Prince Albert*
> 'It's very pleasant to walk with a person who is always content.'
> **John Brown**

Between 11 August and 19 September 1847 Queen Victoria and Prince Albert made a tour of the west coast of Scotland aboard the royal yacht *Victoria and Albert*, paying a visit to Ardverikie in Inverness-shire, where the Groom of the Stole to Prince Albert, James Hamilton, 2nd

Marquess and 1st Duke of Abercorn, had rented a deer forest and holiday house. During these early visits Queen Victoria was able to see something, and learn more, of the Scottish inheritance she had received from her Stewart and Hanoverian forebears. Throughout her life Queen Victoria sustained her pride in the (albeit-very-diluted) Stewart blood that ran in her veins and felt as happy in Scotland as a Jacobite as she was in England as a fluent German-speaking Hanoverian.

At Queen Victoria's accession to the throne Scotland was calculated by geographers to cover some 30,200 square miles, some nineteen million mostly uninhabited acres; its north–south length was nearly 280 miles, and its east–west breadth around 150 miles. It was divided into 33 counties, with 948 parishes.[3] The 1831 Scottish census showed that Victoria ruled over 1.11 million males and 1.25 million females in her northern realm. The largest number of male employees in any single industry was among shoe and bootmakers at 17,307, while domestic service was the major employment for women at 109,512.[4]

The Scotland that Queen Victoria fell in love with had developed into two distinct regions by 1837. To the north lay the Highlands, where a separate culture had grown differently from that of the Lowlands. For centuries the Highlanders had lived in close-knit, Gaelic-speaking communities, with a strong loyalty to their (mostly) Tory chiefs, linked together by their proud heritage and all sustained by their Roman Catholic or Episcopalian faiths. The Lowlands were centred upon Edinburgh and favoured England in both speech and trade, their political and religious faiths being old Whig leaning to new Liberal and Presbyterian. As the nineteenth century progressed the Lowlands were more and more Anglicised, with the upper classes being educated to an increasing extent in English public schools and universities, with Scottish capital and industry falling under the influence of English boards of directors.

By the time Queen Victoria died in 1901, Scotland's alignment had changed from north–south to east–west, with the industrialisation and 'Hibernianisation' of Clydeside. Yet the Victorian Age for Scotland was more than a regal division. The Queen brought to Scotland a truly British Age – she was the first monarch since the Union of the Parliaments in 1707 to achieve this. She also brought greater harmony to the Scottish and English nations and was instrumental in the wider acceptance of Scots south of the border, without automatic ridicule. Her Court in Scotland reflected all these influences.

Strictly speaking, Scotland had not had a royal court in residence for over two centuries, since that April day in 1603 when King James VI of Scotland, newly proclaimed James I of England, crossed the border at Lamberton Toll, just north of Berwick-upon-Tweed, on his long journey to London. Yet when Queen Victoria inherited the throne of what she called her 'wicked uncles', she became heiress to a ceremonial court of Scottish Officers of the Crown, Officers of State and a Royal Household whose functionaries jealously guarded their hereditary places. There were six Officers of the Crown under the Hereditary Grand Constable and Knight Marishal, William George Hay, 18th Earl of Erroll of Slains Castle, Aberdeenshire. This position was granted initially by King Robert I, the Bruce, to Sir Gilbert Hay, 5th Lord Erroll in 1306. It was made hereditary in 1314 after the Battle of Bannockburn. The duties were simple: to safeguard the sovereign's person on Scottish territory. The other Officers of the Crown were the Lord-Justice General, James Graham, 4th Duke of Montrose; the Lord President, the Rt Hon. Charles Hope; the Vice-Marshal, William Schaw Cathcart, Viscount Cathcart; and two Standard Bearers.

The Hereditary Bearer of the Royal Banner of Scotland in 1837 was H. Scrymgeour-Wedderburn of Birkhall. Sir Alexander Scrymgeour had carried the royal banner for Robert I in the Wars of Independence. When he became king, Robert I conferred the hereditary aspects of the position on the Scrymgeour family who became Earls of Dundee in 1660. The banner was defined by its armorial device of 'lyon rampant'. The Hereditary Standard Bearer at this time was James Maitland, Earl of Lauderdale, of Thirlestane Castle, Berwickshire.[5]

The Officers of State were led by the Commissioners for the Custody of the Regalia, whose senior member was the Keeper of the Great Seal, George William Campbell, 6th Duke of Argyll. The Royal Household in Scotland was led by the Duke of Argyll as Hereditary Master, with two Deputy Masters in the shape of the Hereditary Usher, Sir Patrick Walker, and the Hereditary Carver, Sir William Carmichael Anstruther. The office of Master of the Household was given to Archibald, 2nd Earl of Argyll, in 1494. The position was made hereditary in 1528, and the Master was responsible for 'below stairs' and state function arrangements.

The Grand Constable and Standard Bearer were joined by Lady Seton-Steuart of Touch-Seton, the Hereditary Armour-bearer and Squire of the Royal Body, making up the three Marshals of the Royal Household. The Household was composed of twenty-two further appointments, ranging from the Falconer (Thomas Marshall Gardiner) to the Tailor (William Fraser). Many of these appointments were of great antiquity: the position of Dean of the Chapel Royal dated from 1120, while the Royal Limner (painter) was a later introduction in 1703. In 1837 forty-nine persons held warrants as suppliers to the court, ranging from the Royal Baker (James Aikman) to the Royal Wine Merchant (Alexander & Sons). Among the warrant holders for Scotland ranked the Queen's Surgeon-in-Ordinary, Sir George Ballingall, and her Surgeon-Extraordinary, Mr John G.M. Burt. In the medical household they were joined by two Surgeon-Dentists, Robert Nasmyth and D.W. Johnston.[6]

Another important group within Queen Victoria's Scottish ceremonial court were the still extant Royal Bodyguard, the Royal Company of Archers. Administered from Archers Hall, Edinburgh, they still appear at important royal occasions in their braided green doublets and Kilmarnock bonnets decorated with eagle feathers. Their Company was formally constituted in 1676, although tradition says they carry on the spirit of the archers who fell protecting King James IV of Scots when he and the Scottish army were routed at Flodden Field, Northumberland, by the English army under Thomas, Earl of Surrey, in the Anglo-Scots Wars of 1513.

Queen Victoria also inherited the 'Honours of Scotland', the Scottish Regalia or Crown Jewels, which themselves had had a colourful history, with bold adventures keeping them out of the hands of rapacious Englishmen like Oliver Cromwell. After the Act of Union of the Parliaments of 1707, the Honours were walled up in a vaulted chamber in Edinburgh Castle's palace buildings; they were finally 're-discovered' and placed on display by a warrant of the Prince of Wales (later King George IV) in 1818. The Honours comprise the crown, the sceptre and the sword of state. Tradition has it that the Scottish Crown incorporates the 'circlet' of King Robert I, the Bruce; made some time after 1314, it is known to have been used at the coronation of the five-year-old son of Robert the Bruce, King David II, in 1329. This crown has been subsequently altered at the behest of succeeding monarchs, and was 're-made' for James V in 1540. The sceptre was presented to James IV by Pope Alexander VI in 1494; it was melted down and refashioned by James V. The Italian-wrought sword of state was a gift to James IV from Pope Julius II in 1507.

Scotland retained its own Order of Chivalry in the Most Ancient and Most Noble Order of the Thistle, which had been revived and promulgated by statute of King James II on 29 May 1687. Tradition has it that the Order was founded in 809 by Achaius, King of Scots, to honour the Patron Saint of Scotland, the Apostle and Martyr St Andrew of Bethsaida in Galilee. The Order fell out of use in James II's reign but was revived by Queen Anne on 31 December 1703. The purpose of the Order was to give Scotland an equivalent to the Most Noble Order of the Garter founded in England in 1348. When Queen Victoria came to the throne none of the sixteen Knights of the Thistle ranked below Viscount, and one of their number was her 'wicked uncle' Prince Augustus Frederick, Duke of Sussex.

> *On Society*
> 'Me and the Queen pays nae attention to them.'
> **John Brown**

All matters heraldic and armorial in Scotland were (and still are) under the jurisdiction of the Lord Lyon King-of-Arms, who settles questions of family arms in the Lyon Court. The office of Lord Lyon first appeared in the fourteenth century and historians aver that it was a successor to the Celtic *sennachies*, the tribal genealogists and reciters of family lore and history.

Queen Victoria's Court always retained a rather stuffy formality of dress, particularly at levées, 'drawing rooms', presentations and state occasions. This meant that each special event saw a glittering assembly of court dress, wherein many of the men outdid the women in the splendour of their lace, gold braid, medals and feathers. Ministers of the Crown, lawyers, Lords Lieutenant, Governors General, officers and functionaries all wore special Court dress and colourful uniforms, each designed according to custom. In Scotland a specific court dress was formulated for Highlanders. It was thus formally gazetted in the Victorian *Dress Worn at Court* Guide:

Black silk velvet Full Dress DOUBLET. Silk Lined.
Set of Silver CELTIC or CREST BUTTONS for Doublet.
Superfine Tartan Full Dress KILT.
Short TREWS.
Full Dress Tartan STOCKINGS.
Full Dress long SHOULDER PLAID.
Full Dress white hair SPORRAN – silver mounted tassels.
Patent leather and silver chain STRAP for SPORRAN.
Full Dress silver mounted DIRK with Knife and Fork.
Full Dress silver mounted SKEAN DHU with Knife.
Patent Leather SHOULDER BELT, silver mounted.
Patent Leather WAIST BELT, silver clasp.
Silver mounted SHOULDER BROOCH.
Silver KILT PIN.
Lace JABOT.
One pair BUCKLES for instep of SHOES.
One pair small ankle BUCKLES for SHOES.
Full Dress BROGUES.
Highland CLAYMORE.
Glengarry or Balmoral [bonnet], CREST or ORNAMENT.

The Skean Dhu was the Highlander's short-bladed, black-hilted sheath-knife or dagger. The Claymore reference is an error: a Claymore is a two-handed sword but the English author of the *Guide* meant a 'basket-hilted' sword.

The castles, palaces and houses of Queen Victoria's Scottish inheritance which were dubbed 'royal', or had played some part in royal history, were myriad; they ranged from Dumbarton Castle, rising precipitously on its rock at the junction of the Rivers Clyde and Leven in Dumbartonshire, to Tarbert Castle, its walls already ruined by Queen Victoria's day, standing 60 feet above sea level on the shores of the small creek called Loch Tarbert on the west side of the Loch Fyne, Argyllshire. From her forebears Queen Victoria inherited four palaces, at Dunfermline, Linlithgow, Falkland and Holyrood, but it was only at Holyrood that Queen Victoria ever occupied the royal apartments. She first stayed there in 1850, but in later years she often made Holyrood a resting place on her way to and from Balmoral. Prince Albert designed the modern approaches to the palace, which superceded the ancient processional way through Edinburgh's Canongate thoroughfare. Albert also caused the area to the east of the ruined abbey church, abutting the palace, to be levelled and laid out in garden form. In 1854 the palace's 'Historical Apartments' were opened to the public and much restoration work was undertaken by 1872, when a private suite was established for Queen Victoria's visits.[8]

Two of the palaces and seven castles had hereditary Keepers who were required from time to time to appear at Queen Victoria's Scottish Court. The Keeper of Holyrood in 1837 was Alexander, 10th Duke of Hamilton and Brandon, the premier duke of Scotland. The office had been bestowed on the 1st Duke in 1646. The Keeper still 'maintains order' through the blue-coated, top-hatted High Constables of Holyrood, who are in turn answerable to the Bailie of Holyrood. At the Palace of Falkland the Keeper in 1837 was Mr Oneisiphorous Tyndall-Bruce. The royal castle of Dunstaffnage, the fifteenth-century fortress commanding the entrance to Loch Etive in Argyllshire, was in the Keepership of the 6th Duke of Argyll, who also held in his remit the ruined castles of Dunoon and Carrick. Rothesay Castle, founded in the eleventh century on the Isle of Bute, had been in the Keepership of the Stewarts since 1498, with John Crichton-Stuart, 2nd Marquis of Bute, as Keeper in 1837. At Lochmaben Castle, the Keeper was Mr J.J. Hope-Johnstone of Annandale. Edinburgh and Dumbarton castles were deemed military buildings with a tradition of soldier governors.[9] Despite all these properties at her command Queen Victoria established a new royal estate at Balmoral, further north than the ancient royal properties.

Today the estate of Balmoral runs to some 50,000 acres in total, plus 7,000 acres of grouse moor; there are a further 10,000 acres rented from a neighbour, with 190 acres farmed and 272 acres let. The castle itself sleeps in excess of 100 people, attended by 56 full-time staff. A further 100 or so work part-time during the visitor season, when 80,000 people view the castle and its policies.[10] The 1998 film 'Mrs Brown', about the relationship between Queen Victoria and John Brown, has increased the number of interested visitors to the area.

While Queen Victoria and Prince Albert were visiting the west coast of Scotland in the lashing rain of 1847, across the Cairngorms Balmoral was basking in a prolonged spell of sunshine. John Clark, the 27-year-old son of the Queen's physician Sir James Clark, was convalescing on Deeside from a long illness; he was a guest of the diplomat Sir Robert Gordon, brother of George Hamilton-Gordon, 4th Earl of Aberdeen, who had been British Ambassador to Vienna and was now lessee of the Balmoral estate. Young Clark reported to his father how his health had improved through the purity of the air. Sir James, an expert on the influence of climate on health, mentioned this to the Queen who, together with Prince Albert, was seriously considering establishing a 'Scottish home'. Deeside, Sir James continued, would be a good place for the Queen to rest from her frequent twinges of rheumatism.

Prince Albert ordered a report on Deeside, its environs and climate. He was informed that it was 'one of the driest areas in the country'. Coupled with Aberdeen artist James Giles's sketches of the surrounding

---

On John Brown

'Remember John Brown? Aye, that I do; and a very good fellow he was too. Sometimes when I was a-mowin' the lawns – it used to take me fourteen days to go right over all of 'em – anywhere near the house if he seed me, he'd put up his hand in the air an' call "Hi, Jackman," and then he'd say when I come up: "Don't you stay thirsty out in the sun an' heat; you just go in the hall and say I sent you in for a good draught."

'Ah, the servants lost a good friend when John Brown died. You've seen the granite chair what the Queen put up in memory of him in that side walk just before you comes to the House, haven't ye? Well it was put there in that particular spot, because Mr Brown used to walk up and down there reading his letters from home. I don't rightly recollect the inscription on the seat. I know there's when he was born and when he died, and I think it goes on something like this: "To the truest and most faithful servant and friend that any monarch ever had . . ." But the granite that it is made of was brought all the way from Scotland. Yes, I liked John Brown. He was a bit hasty and outspoken, but always just and kind he was. Fine voice he had, an' a very fine-looking man in his kilt.'

William Jackman,
Osborne Estate worker

scenes, also commissioned by Albert, this report persuaded the royal couple that their autumn holiday should be spent on Deeside. And here fate took a hand. On 8 December 1847 Sir Robert Gordon collapsed and died at the breakfast table at Balmoral. Learning that the Queen was in search of a Deeside residence, Sir Robert's brother, Lord Aberdeen, suggested Balmoral, which still had twenty years to run on the lease from the Earl of Mar.

James Giles was dispatched to do some further drawings – 'I never made any money working to royalty', he grumbled. Queen Victoria was delighted with the pictures and immediately agreed to take the lease sight unseen. On 5 September 1848 Queen Victoria and Prince Albert arrived off Aberdeen aboard the royal yacht *Victoria and Albert*. The next day they disembarked to a civic welcome and processed through triumphal arches of evergreens, heather, thistles and wild flowers. They breakfasted at Cults and lunched at Aboyne, and cannon welcomed them at Ballater. At Crathie there stood a triumphal arch which proclaimed: 'Welcome to your Highland home, Victoria and Albert', and at 2.45pm they arrived at Balmoral.

On Friday 8 September Queen Victoria made the first entry in her *Journal* concerning her new home:

> We arrived at Balmoral at a quarter to three. It is a pretty little castle in the old Scottish style. There is a picturesque tower and garden in front, with a high wooded hill; at the back there is wood down to the Dee; and the hills rise all around.

After lunch they made their first exploration of the policies. All that they saw was delightful: the hills surrounding Lochnagar and the glen towards Ballater were given the royal seal of approval as it reminded them of Thüringerwald.[11]

The servants at Balmoral also more than passed muster. John Grant, the Head Keeper – an employee of Sir Robert Grant for over twenty years – was approved for his 'fine, intelligent countenance', and 'singular shrewdness and discreetness'; William Paterson, gardener, was more than acceptable, while gillie Macdonald made a fine figure in his kilt. Somewhere in the stables worked one John Brown. Many of Sir Robert Gordon's retainers were kept on, as well as his dog 'Monk'.

While Prince Albert was piecing together the history of their new home, Queen Victoria was learning about the subtleties of the *gillie* system of Highland society. Gillies were first introduced into general literary parlance thanks to the popular novels of Sir Walter Scott. In *Waverley* (1814), he refers to the barefoot Highland lads as 'gillie-wet-foots'. The word gillie, gilly or ghillie had started to appear in general Scots vernacular in the seventeenth century to describe a youth. But by the eighteenth century it had developed into a term meaning specifically a male servant, especially an attendant on a Highland chief.

Prosperous chieftains would have a *gillie-casfliuch* (Gaelic for the man who carried the chief over fords and burns), a *gillie-comstrain* (who led the chief's horse over difficult places), and perhaps even a *gillie-trusharnich* (a baggage carrier). Most respected of all was the *gillie-more*, the chief's armour bearer. Victoria and Albert's growing penchant for the sturdy Highland gillie they first encountered at Balmoral gave these retainers a new role in the nineteenth century as sportsmen's attendants for both deerstalking and angling.

As they relaxed in their sitting-room – formerly Sir Robert Gordon's drawing-room, as Queen Victoria noted in her *Journal* – Prince Albert recounted what he had found out about the history of Balmoral. The estate first appears in written records in the fifteenth century as 'Bouchmorale'.[12] When the estate was let to Sir Alexander Gordon of nearby Abergeldie Castle, at £8 18p p.a. in 1484, it was known as 'Balmorain'. It was the Gordons who first built a small castle at Balmoral, but by 1662 the family had fallen so deeply into debt that the Crown allowed the Farquharsons of Inverey to foreclose on the mortgaged Balmoral. In their turn, however, the Farquharsons were themselves to be financially embarrassed, largely because of their support of the Jacobite cause in the risings of 1715 and 1745, and in 1798 the estate of Balmoral was bought by James Duff, 2nd Earl of Fife, for letting. The 2nd Earl died in 1809 but there were no heirs of his marriage to Lady Dorothy Sinclair and he left his whole estate to an illegitimate son. The ensuing legal challenge to the will caused the estate, including Balmoral, to be invested in the Fife Trustees. Balmoral was leased first to Captain James Cameron, who became a friend of Prince Albert, thence to Sir Robert Gordon and his sister Lady Alicia Gordon. Sir Robert spent much time improving the estate; he established a deer forest in 1833 and made many alterations to the house during the period 1834–9. On 20 May 1848 the Fife Trustees assigned the lease of Balmoral to Prince Albert.

Prince Albert now began a programme of acquisition in Deeside. The process of estate purchase (or leasing) was a slow one. First, the royal family purchased the 6,500 acre Birkhall estate, at the head of Glen Muick, with its house built in 1715, for use by Albert Edward, Prince of Wales, then aged eight. The Gordons refused to sell their early fourteenth-century property at Abergeldie, which abutted Balmoral, but Prince Albert accepted instead a forty-year lease. This was to be the home of Queen Victoria's mother, also Victoria, Princess of Saxe-Saalfeld-Coburg and Duchess of Kent, from 1850 to 1858; from 1858 until her death in 1861 illness prevented the duchess from making the long journey north. It was not until 22 June 1852 that Prince Albert signed the papers of purchase for the 17,400 acre Balmoral estate, for £31,500.[13] Prince Albert had also had his eye on the Forest of Ballochbuie, owned by the Farquharsons; they were unwilling to sell and Queen Victoria had to wait until 1875 to acquire it. Three years later she bought Abergeldie for around £100,000.[14]

Then, in August 1852, a fortuitous event took place. On the death of the miserly and eccentric barrister James Camden Neild (b. 1780), it was found that he had left his entire fortune of £500,000 to Queen Victoria. This greatly helped to fund developments at Balmoral.[15] A lengthy programme of alterations was set in motion, from stables and cottages to workshops and even a prefabricated ballroom. William Smith, the City Architect for Aberdeen, whose 1847 design for the Trinity Hall of that city had so impressed Prince Albert, was summoned to prepare plans for the new schloss the prince wanted at Balmoral.

The planned schloss comprised two rectangular blocks, united corner to corner by a five-storey square tower. Queen Victoria and Prince Albert spent much time deciding what materials to use for the buildings, both outside and in. For the main structure a fine-grain Glen Gelder granite was chosen and specially quarried from the Balmoral estate by local labourers overseen by surveyor James Forbes Beaton, who matched slates from the Foudland quarries at Strathbogie. For the interior decorations Prince Albert invented the Balmoral Tartan – black, red and lavender, on a grey background – for use in the new Balmoral colour schemes; to this Queen Victoria added Victoria Tartan for the furnishings, interlarded with Royal Stewart (red and green) and Hunting Stewart (green, with red and yellow stripes) tartans.[16] Prince Albert designed everything from curtain ties to door knobs and the whole was dubbed by courtiers a 'feast of tartanitis'. On a number of occasions John Brown helped Queen Victoria to pin her tartan shawl around her shoulders. If she fidgeted while he was doing so, he would upbraid her with 'Hoots, wumman, canna ye hold yer head still?' At other times he would be disparaging about her dress: 'What are ye daeing with that auld black dress on again? It's green-moulded!' He was also stern with her when she couldn't decide what to wear: 'Ye dinna ken yer ain mind for two minutes together.'

The development of a 'Scottish home' at Balmoral – which Prince Albert regarded as a *Jägersrühe* (hunting lodge) – was not welcomed by the dismayed courtiers. Balmoral was a long and tedious 567½ miles from London, and thus an inconvenient place from which to rule an empire. There was therefore a reluctance to visit. Arthur Ponsonby remarked: 'Lord Salisbury [Robert Arthur Talbot Gascoyne-Cecil, 3rd Marquis of Salisbury, three times Prime Minister], unlike some other ministers did not "attempt to conceal his disgust with the place" and was "heartily glad" when the time came for him to get away. Campbell Bannerman [Sir Henry Campbell-Bannerman, Liberal Cabinet Minister], in a letter to his wife wrote, "It is the funniest life conceivable: like a convent. We meet at meals and when we are finished, each is off to his cell."'[17] Lord John James Robert Manners, later 7th Duke of Rutland, averred of Balmoral: 'Yes, this is a very curious place and more curious things go on here than I should have dreamt of . . .'[18]

The English diarist Charles Cavendish Fulke Greville, erstwhile Clerk to the Privy Council, was nervous about the lack of security at Balmoral: 'There are no soldiers and the whole guard of the sovereign, and of the whole Royal Family is a single policeman who walks about the grounds to keep off impertinent intruders or improper characters.'[19] And Sarah Spencer, Lady Lyttleton, the royal governess commented: 'Scotch air, Scotch people, Scotch hills, Scotch rivers and Scotch woods [are] all far preferable to those of any other nation in or out of this world [to the Queen] . . . The chief support to my spirits is that I shall never see, hear or witness these various charms.'[20]

The construction of the new Balmoral Castle was a slow process: a fire broke out in the workmen's wooden barracks; the building granite was difficult to quarry; and the labourers were quarrelsome, downing tools at regular intervals for increased wages. Good relations seem to have been restored with the appearance of Charlie 'Princie' Stewart with 'ankers' of illegally distilled whisky for the workers' refreshment.[21] Soon *The Scotsman* was able to report:

The Queen's residence at Balmoral is making considerable progress, and promises, without great pretensions, to be a place of solid and real construction. A correspondent comments on the circumstances, that the Highlanders seem to have a contempt for scaffolding, ropes, or windlass. He says that every block of granite – from two to three feet long – is transported singly on a Highlander's shoulders. Up a narrow platform of boards and tressels to the place where it is to be set, and with considerable celerity, larger blocks are conveyed by four Highlanders, on a couple of poles. Primitive certainly.[22]

With a libation of oil and wine bringing to a close the ceremonial part of the programme, Queen Victoria laid the foundation stone of the new Balmoral Castle on 28 September 1853. By September 1854 a journalist from the *Morning Chronicle* filed this report:

The last portion of the main building . . . is now ready for being roofed. On the ground floor of the west and north sides are the public rooms, and over them are the principal bed-rooms and other accommodations for the Royal Family. The other two sides are three stories in height, and will be reserved chiefly for the accommodation of the suite. [That is, Queen Victoria's courtiers.] On the east side, a wing is being built seventy feet in length, and in connection with a very prominent part of the edifice, viz., a tower forty feet square, which will be about eighty feet high, with a circular staircase on one angle, making the height 100 feet. It will be surmounted with a flag staff . . . The south and west fronts especially are very handsome, there being some very fine carving and moulding in the details. There are very fine oriel windows for the principal rooms . . . The whole is to be fireproof, according to Barrett's patent.

The new Balmoral was occupied by the royal family on 7 September 1855, although many of the courtiers and servants still had to live at the old house or rough it in cottages on the estate. One Court lady took a dim view of the fact that her breakfast was delivered to her cottage accommodation each morning in a wheelbarrow. Queen Victoria recorded: 'An old shoe was thrown after us into the house, for good luck, when we entered the hall.' The throwing was done by the French steward in charge of the house, François d'Albertançon, who had filled the same role for Sir Robert Gordon. To enhance the royal family's privacy, a new bridge was opened over the Linn of Dee on 8 September 1857, thus diverting the old road which used to pass close by Balmoral. By 1859 Prince Albert's improvements for the gardens and grounds were complete, with new cottages for retainers and beds of roses flanked with white poplars from Coburg.

In time Balmoral was to formulate its own 'Court'. Day-to-day administration, while the Queen was in residence on her twice-yearly visits, was carried out by the Lord Chamberlain and his staff, supplemented by a Commissioner and Factor at Balmoral. They would all regularly cross swords with John Brown in the future. Brown became an expert in Queen Victoria's 'Balmoral routine', any variation of which made her cross. She was an early riser and often preferred to take her breakfast at 9am in a former gardener's cottage near the castle. Here she would scan the albums of newspaper cuttings, trimmed and pasted in each day by her wardrobe maids. Lunch was at 2pm, tea at 5.30pm and dinner at 8.45pm, with pipers playing outside the windows at all meals. Interspersed with the meals were morning, afternoon and evening drives as the Queen fancied, with the outside staff meeting her after the latter with flaming torches in winter.[23]

Although at Balmoral she was hundreds of miles from the heart of government, Queen Victoria was a stickler for detail in preparing her letters and dispatches. Two extra trains ran from Aberdeen to Ballater for this purpose at 11pm and 4pm, and there was always a Balmoral courier waiting at the station to meet the trains, with a distinctive yellow gig.[24] Before the railway system was developed it took two days for dispatches from London to reach Balmoral; a twelve-hour journey by train carried the mail and couriers to Perth, before another half a day's journey by postchaise brought them to Balmoral.[25]

There were many reasons why Balmoral became a special place for Queen Victoria and Prince Albert. It was a place of refuge and recreation, in the latter's true meaning of being refreshed and fashioned anew. At Balmoral they could be themselves without the constant fear of giving offence by making the wrong move publicly. Certainly in the early years of their marriage, Queen Victoria was aware that her German consort was not popular. At Balmoral they were away from the sneering glances of criticism; at Balmoral they had no necessity to be always circumspect. More than that, it was a place that they had found themselves, in a home they had created themselves, with a household they had formed themselves, with no age-old traditions to be adhered to under the creakingly archaic control of the Royal Household at Buckingham Palace or Windsor. Balmoral gave them an escape from the awful world of lackeys-in-waiting who were more keen to be ladies and gentlemen than servants. The Scots staff at Balmoral were willing, honest and openly sincere, and were not shocked by what the southern courtiers might regard as the Queen's eccentricities.[26]

It was Charles Greville who first noted Queen Victoria's delight 'in the simplicities and sincerities that she found in Scotland'.[27] This was to lead to a certain naivety in her acceptance of all things 'Highland', but Balmoral gave her much-needed relief from the ceremonial and court routines. She loved the lack of obsequiousness on the part of the Highlanders: one gillie's mother – Old Mrs Grant – welcomed the Queen to her home with the words 'I am happy to see you looking so nice', which made the Queen glow with affection. At Balmoral then, Queen Victoria had a sense of *gehören* (belonging).

CHAPTER ONE

CHILD OF THE MOUNTAINS

John Brown was born at Crathienaird in Crathie parish, Aberdeenshire, on 8 December 1826, the second son of John Brown (1790–1875), a tenant farmer, and his wife Margaret Leys (1799–1876), who also came from farming stock.[1] They married at Crathie on 25 August 1825, when Margaret was five months pregnant.[2] John and Margaret courted and were betrothed through the old Highland custom of 'bundling', a practice in which the sweethearts slept together, without undressing, in the same bed or couch. According to the tradition, should the 'bundling' prove fruitful and the baby seemed likely to go to full term, the couple married.[3] So John and Margaret Brown already had a year-old son, James, born on 15 November 1825, when John arrived.[4]

When John Brown was born his future royal employer and friend had entered her eighth year; Victoria was born on Monday 24 May 1819 at Kensington Palace. Her father Prince Edward, Duke of Kent and Strathearn, died on 23 January 1820, just six days before his blind and insane father King George III. So little Alexandrina Victoria, the new heir to the throne, was brought up in reduced circumstances by her affectionate but impulsive and quarrelsome mother, the Duchess of Kent, the former Princess Victoria Mary Louisa, widow of Emich Karl, 2nd Prince zu Leiningen.

In 1826 Princess Victoria, along with her mother and eighteen-year-old half-sister Princess Feodore of Leiningen, made her first visit to Windsor to call on her uncle King George IV, who lived at Royal Lodge. 'Give me your little paw', he had said on their first meeting, and Victoria remembered him as 'large and gouty but with a wonderful dignity and charm of manner'.[5] The next day Victoria was out walking with her family from their apartments at Cumberland Lodge when they were overtaken by a royal phaeton in which rode the King with his sister Princess Mary, Duchess of Gloucester. 'Pop her in', he ordered, and to the Duchess of Kent's no little anxiety – she feared that the monarch would kidnap her daughter – they sped away with Victoria for a visit to 'the nicest part of Virginia Water'.[6]

Because of their straitened finances Princess Victoria's early years at Kensington Palace were not luxurious. She remembered:

We lived in a very simple, plain manner; breakfast was at half-past eight, luncheon at half-past one, dinner at seven – to which I came generally (when it was no regular large dinner party) – eating my bread and milk out of a small silver basin. Tea was only allowed as a great treat in later years.[7]

Victoria was to remain a stickler for the exact timing of her meals when John Brown served her, but while the Princess enjoyed tea as a 'treat', that beverage was hardly seen at Crathienaird.

In all, the Brown family of Crathienaird increased to eleven children: nine boys and two girls. The eldest son, James, emigrated to Australia; on his return he became a shepherd on the Balmoral estate and married Helen Stewart (1824–1904). After John came Francis (b. 1828), who died aged three, and then Anne (1830–67). Charles (b. 1831), Margaret (b. 1834) and a second child named Francis (b. 1839) all died in the typhoid epidemic that swept through this part of Deeside in the winter of 1849. They were buried together at Crathie churchyard and John Brown raised a stone to them years later.[8]

Donald, the sixth child, was born on 9 September 1832. He went on to become a porter at Windsor Castle and Keeper of the Queen's Lodge, Osborne. William, the eighth, was born on 18 March 1835 and was gifted the tenancy of the farm of Tomidhu by Queen Victoria; he married Elizabeth Paterson (1838–1900) in 1869 and died at Torridoes, Crathie, in 1906. Hugh Brown was born on 21 December 1838 and emigrated to New Zealand; on his return he became Keeper of Her Majesty's Kennels at Windsor and Extra Highland Attendant after his brother John's death. Hugh was succeeded in this position by his nephew William. Hugh Brown married Jessie McHardy (1840–1914) in 1863 and died at the East Approach Lodge, Balmoral, in 1896. Queen Victoria insisted that nothing be made of the fact that the main cause of his death was alcoholism.[9] The last sibling of John Brown was born on 6 September 1841 and christened Archibald Anderson Brown; he became valet to Prince Leopold and thence Page of the Royal Presence. He died in 1912.[10]

The Browns of Crathienaird had originated within the Highland clan grouping of Lamont (Gaelic, *MacLaomainn*). A clan of great antiquity, the Lamonts owned considerable parcels of territory in Argyllshire, but owing to the encroachment of the Campbells of Argyll and other clansmen, their territories were confined mainly to Cowal, that large district of Argyll which includes lands between Loch Fyne and the boundary with Perthshire; of this area John Lamont became 'Bailie' in 1456.[11] At Toward Castle, in South Cowal, north-east of Rothesay, Sir John Lamont of Inveryne entertained Mary, Queen of Scots, in 1563.

During the seventeenth-century outbreaks of civil war in Scotland, the Campbell chiefs ravaged the lands of the Lamonts and destroyed their main bases at the castles of Toward and Ascog on the Isle of Bute, and in 1646 they treacherously massacred two hundred Lamont leaders at Dunoon. When Toward Castle was sacked the principal clan residence became Ardlamont, near the Kyles of Bute and Loch Fyne, and the dispersed clansfolk became connected by marriage to many titled families of Scotland. John Lamont, 19th Chief of the Clan Lamont, commanded the Gordon Highlanders at Corunna in 1809.

As the Lamont clansmen scattered from their foes, the rapacious Campbells of Loudoun, they adopted new disguising names, Black, White and Brown being popular. They settled in safe havens, such as those in south-west Scotland. John Brown's forebears, though, are likely to have been among the clansmen who settled in the Highland area of Strathspey, that broad lower valley of the River Spey just the other side of the Cairngorm Mountains from Crathie. Some time in the early eighteenth century John Brown's immediate forebears moved from Strathspey to become tenants of the Ogilvys, Earls of Airlie, who lived at Cortachy Castle, Angus. The Browns now farmed Ogilvy land in the neighbourhood of the old hand-weaving town of Kirriemuir.

The Ogilvys were descendants of the ancient Earls of Angus. They were Royalists and Jacobites who engaged actively in Scotland's civil wars and the Jacobite Risings of 1715 and 1745. During the latter rising John Brown's great-grandfather and his brothers joined the Forfarshire Regiment led by David Ogilvy, 5th Lord Airlie (the son of John, 4th Earl of Airlie), in support of the Jacobite leader Charles Edward Stewart. He had landed in Scotland in order to help win the throne of Great Britain from the Hanoverian succession for his father, Prince James Francis Edward Stewart (whom the Jacobites dubbed King James VIII & III). Consequently the Browns were with David Ogilvy at the Battle of Culloden in April 1746 when Prince Charles Edward Stewart's cousin, Prince William Augustus, Duke of Cumberland, vanquished the Jacobite army. Along with the whole Clan Ogilvy, David Ogilvy was attained and fled to France; he would not return until he was pardoned in 1783.

As with hundreds of other clansmen who survived the slaughter at Culloden, the Browns returned to their tenancy in Angus to 'lie low'. For years though, Hanoverian government troops harassed the clansmen, burning and pillaging their homes. The Browns, who suffered similar difficulties, decided to seek a more peaceful area in which to rebuild their shattered lives.

In the 1770s John Brown's grandfather, Donald Brown (*c.* 1750–1827), who married Janet Shaw (c. 1751–1836) of Badenoch, left Angus and took the road north through the Capel Mounth Pass to take up a new tenancy at Rhinachat, a small part of the Monaltrie estates of the Farquharsons of Invercauld, an estate in the Dee Valley about 1½ miles from Braemar.[12] There they raised their family, which included six sons, one of whom, 'Old' John, was John Brown's father. He became a prominent character at Crathie.[13]

Deriving its name from the Gaelic word *Creathach* (brushwood), Crathie lies on the main road from Braemar to Ballater and is situated about a mile from the modern Balmoral Castle.[14] The hamlet of Crathie grew out of an early Scottish ecclesiastical site. In his historical notes the Revd Ronald Henderson Gunn Rudge, Minister of Crathie from 1964 to 1971, opined:

The story of the Christian Church in Crathie goes back through the long years to the misty records of the 6th century when the Celtic or Brithonic Saints, St Colin and St Monire, brought the Christian Gospel north into Deeside. A famous pool in the River Dee, near

Balmoral Castle, is known as Polmanaire – "the pool of St Monire" – so called because in this pool the Saint of old is said to have baptised his Christian converts.

The earliest Chapels are reputed to have been erected at The Lebhall (on the north Deeside Road); at Balmore (in Aberarder Glen); and at the Mains of Abergeldie (on the south Deeside Road). In the 15th century a new Church was built beside the River Dee, where the ruins can still be seen in the old Churchyard. This was the centre of worship until 1804, when it was replaced by a larger, but austere, Church built on the site of the present Church – dedicated in 1895. It was in the 1804 Church that Queen Victoria [and the Brown family] worshipped during the greater part of Her Majesty's residence at Balmoral Castle. The Queen laid the foundation stone of the new building on 11 September 1893, and two years later was present at its dedication.[15]

The area around Crathie is very hilly, with the principal peaks being Lochnagar, Cairntoul and Ben Macdhui. Their presence gave rise to the gossiping Lord Clarendon referring to John Brown, unkindly, as a 'Child of the Mountains'.

When Old John Brown settled into his tenancy at Crathienaird, the area had already been substantially improved by the 'model landlord' Colonel Francis Farquharson, who himself had fought in the Jacobite Army.[16] He introduced new agricultural methods, repaired old buildings and established new ones, built roads and bridges, and even developed the four mineral springs which had been known since the thirteenth century at Pannanich in the nearby united parish of Glenmuick, Tullich and Glengairn.[17]

The house at Crathienaird where John Brown was born has now vanished. In his day Crathienaird was a *clachan* (hamlet) of some eighteen heather-thatched houses built of mud and unhewn stone. Each was a two-roomed cottage built in the Highland style of 'but and ben'; in some of the poorer households the inhabitants shared their dwelling with their cattle.[18] Within, the floors were of hardened earth which became damp and muddy in winter. The large Brown family slept in a series of traditional 'box beds', which were curtained off or shut off with doors. The younger members of big families generally slept around the peat-burning hearth, wrapped in blankets or plaids. For light the house had small unopening windows with four to six panes of glass. Quite often, on leaving such a 'bothy' (house) for a new job, the family would take the windows with them as personal property. The focal point of the Brown's main living area was the hearth, with its cooking pots supported on a '*swee*' (a movable iron bracket) over the fire; a cauldron of water was kept permanently heated on a three-legged trivet. Light from the fire supplemented the oil-burning *cruises* (boat-shaped rush-wick lamps). In 1831, when John Brown was five years old, the family moved to larger accommodation at The Bush Farm, Crathie, where he spent his childhood days.[19]

Around this time the Duchess of Kent was giving attention to her daughter's education. In 1824, when Victoria was five, she had been transferred from the care of her nurse Mrs Brock to her German governess Fräulein Louise Lehzen, whom King George IV had appointed a Hanoverian baroness in 1827. Yet it was now time for Victoria to move on from nursery stories to a proper education. Towards this end the duchess consulted Charles James Blomfield, Bishop of London, and John Kaye, Bishop of Lincoln, about the current state of the princess's education and how it should be developed. The result was a recommendation for her to continue with the tutorship of the evangelistic clergyman Revd George Davys, whose languages and history lessons were now supplemented by a music teacher, a singing master, a dancing instructor and a drawing master.

Victoria was a quick if somewhat unwilling pupil, but she had a flair for languages and drawing. Her love of riding made her an accomplished horsewoman, and she terrified the ladies-in-waiting with fast gallops through Windsor Park. Victoria's destiny, however, was beckoning: on Saturday 26 June 1830 King George IV died and was succeeded by his brother Prince William Henry, Duke of Clarence, as King William IV. In the shadow of the throne which was now destined to be hers, Princess Victoria developed a distinct character and temperament. As Arthur Benson and Viscount Esher were to remark:

She was high-spirited and wilful but devotedly affectionate, and almost typically feminine. She had a strong sense of duty and dignity, and strong personal prejudices. Confident, in a sense, as she was, she had the feminine instinct strongly developed of dependence upon some manly adviser. She was full of high spirits, and enjoyed excitement and life to the full. She liked the stir of London, was fond of dancing, or concerts, plays and operas, and devoted to open-air exercise.[20]

Herein were clues that were to make her an enthusiast for Scots outdoor pursuits and the devoted friend years later of the red-headed lad who ranged over the hills at Crathie. Yet there was more in her character that would bind her to John Brown. She hated change; she looked upon herself as a 'deserted child' (after her father's death); she was blisteringly truthful, admitting to 'fearless straight forwardness', and Lord Melbourne was to comment that she was 'the honestest person I have ever known'. Further she showed firm loyalty to friends; her trust once given was not withdrawn. And her 'nervous shyness' made her cling to the people she knew and liked; as she said herself: 'I am terribly shy and nervous and always was so.' These traits of truthfulness, honesty and loyalty were all recognisable too in John Brown's developing character. Open-air activities, especially, were to be an important factor in John Brown's upbringing, for his education had a much more practical aspect than Princess Victoria's.

John Brown attended a few *raithes*[21] at Crathie school. Crathie's first parish schoolmaster had been appointed in 1710, but his post had fallen out of use.[22] By 1719 a charity school had been set up by the Society for Promoting Christian Knowledge[23] and this was one of the thousand parish schools still extant at the time of the Scottish (Education) Act of 1803. At Crathie it cost the Brown family 3*s* 6*p* per quarter for a high standard of primary education. At school the Brown children learned the Gaelic language in parallel with English.[24]

Most of John Brown's education was conducted out of school. He learned the arts of deerstalking, fish spearing, rowing, swimming, shooting, and riding the Highland breed of ponies known as garrons, which were used for rough hill work. He learned how to walk the mountains, climbing and tackling gradients at speed. He became an expert on the flora and fauna of the area and learned how to forecast the weather. Victoria came to pay close attention to his weather lore;

On John Brown

'John Brown stands out as a striking figure of a man in my boyhood memories. Often as I was playing with other children on the green slopes in the Castle grounds Queen Victoria would come along in her chair drawn by a pony.

'A groom sometimes attended the pony, but by the Queen's side there always seemed to be John Brown with his rich Scots brogue. The Queen would always smile and say a few words to us, then pat the head of the nearest. On several occasions that was me. John Brown might also say "Good-day" but he was just a little too stern to get really friendly with us.

'Wherever the Queen went, in the castle grounds or about the rooms, John Brown was always at her side. When he died the Queen had a two-foot high brass plate erected in memory of her "true and faithful" servant in the Royal Mausoleum at Frogmore. But when King Edward came to the Throne he had the plate removed, and I never heard what happened to it. Everyone about the Royal house knew that the Prince of Wales disliked John Brown.

'Brown was popular with the servants at Windsor, although they went in awe of him. He was just in settling disputes and obtained for them many little extra comforts and privileges.'

**H.L.F. Gale,
son of a Queen's Messenger at Windsor Castle**

she always averred that if Brown said it would rain or snow, even on the finest day, then it would. He was fluent, too, in the Gaelic names of the glens and mountains, the shepherds' greetings and their whistle calls to their dogs. And all this information he shared with Victoria as he walked at her horse's head from the early days of his royal appointment.

While John Brown was learning his trade and adopting the lifestyle of a Highland laddie, Princess Victoria was going through a very emotional part of her life as heiress presumptive to her septuagenarian 'Uncle King'. The stress led to mental exhaustion. As part of her education the Duchess of Kent took her on 'royal progresses' to various towns and historical sites, much to the annoyance of the King, who believed that his sister-in-law was deliberately keeping his niece from his court, where Princess Victoria was already being groomed in royal protocol by Queen Adelaide. It was true. The Duchess, supported by Sir John Conroy, her ambitious Comptroller of the Household, was attempting to influence Victoria in case the King died before she came of age. In such an event the Duchess would probably be declared Regent, with Conroy as her chief adviser; the prizes would be rich for both.

During one of these tours the Duchess gave her daughter a book of blank pages in which to record her impressions. Thereafter she was to keep a daily record of events for the rest of her life. By the time of her death in 1901, her writings stretched to several dozen volumes. From her accession in 1837, though, the extant *Journal* is the truncated version prepared from the original sheets by Princess Beatrice, Victoria's youngest daughter and co-literary executor, who removed 'anything which might cause pain'. Thus much (innocent) information about Queen Victoria and the early life of John Brown was 'sanitised'.

In 1836 Princess Victoria was seventeen and as her legal majority approached there was increased talk of her marriage prospects. Pools of suitors were divided into rival Court groups. At St James's Palace King William was keen to introduce her to eligible young men of his choice, particularly if they were not favoured by the Duchess of Kent whom he now detested. So he invited the Prince of Orange, the eldest son of the King of the Netherlands, to visit, along with his sons William and Alexander. In Brussels, Princess Victoria's uncle Leopold, King of the Belgians (and King William's bête-noire largely because he was the Duchess of Kent's brother), cherished his sister's hope that Victoria would form a liaison with her cousin Prince Albert of Saxe-Coburg. This would mean a German alliance, a move which King William deprecated. First, though, came the Dutch brothers whom Victoria found 'plain'. Then arrived the Coburg princes, Albert and Ernest, whom she found 'amiable, very kind and good . . . Albert is very handsome.'[25] Although Albert was ill during his trip and did not take to Court life, Princess Victoria wrote thus to her Uncle Leopold:

I must thank you, my beloved Uncle, for the prospect of great happiness you have contributed to give me, in the person of dear

Albert. Allow me, then, my dearest Uncle, to tell you how delighted I am with him, and how much I like him in every way. He possesses every quality that could be desired to render me perfectly happy. He is so sensible, so kind, and so good and amiable too. He has besides, the most pleasing and delightful exterior and appearance you can possibly see.[26]

Other foreign suitors came and went but by the next year Princess Victoria's mind was occupied with more serious matters. On 20 June 1837 King William IV died and Princess Victoria succeeded to the throne. Styled 'Victoria, By the Grace of God, of the United Kingdom of Great Britain and Ireland, Queen, Defender of the Faith,' she was crowned at Westminster Abbey on Thursday 28 June 1838. She settled down to learn the profession of monarchy against a background of political intrigue. On 12 October 1839 Queen Victoria wrote again to her Uncle Leopold:

The dear cousins [Albert and Ernest] arrived at half past seven on Thursday, after a very bad and almost dangerous passage, but looking both very well, and much improved . . . Albert's beauty is most striking, and he so amiable and unaffected – in short very fascinating.[27]

The outcome was that Queen Victoria finally made up her mind and proposed marriage to Prince Albert. He accepted, and on 23 November she informed the Privy Council of her intention to marry. On 16 January 1840 she officially announced to the country her betrothal in a speech from the throne. She married Prince Albert on 10 February at the Chapel Royal, St James's Palace. On 21 November 1840, nine months and eleven days after the wedding, Princess Victoria ('Vicky') Adelaide Mary Louisa, the Princess Royal, was born at Buckingham Palace.

By 1840, at the age of fourteen, John Brown had finished with formal education and had become a member of the workforce at Crathienaird. Like many of his Scots contemporaries, despite his poor circumstances, John Brown was a keen reader. Old John had encouraged his family to read at the very least the two books to be found in every Scots house, the

Holy Bible and *The Complete Poetical Works* of Robert Burns, the first edition of whose poems had been published at Kilmarnock on 31 July 1786, when the Brown family were already firmly established at Crathie.

As tenant farmers of the Farquharsons, the Browns were better off than the average crofter of Crathie parish, with their Black-faced (Linton) sheep and small black-horned cattle, scratching a living from niggardly plots, but it is an exaggeration on the part of the Marquis of Huntly to suggest that the family were 'well-to-do'.[28] To augment the family coffers in the early 1840s, John Brown took work as an ostler's assistant and then as stable lad at the coaching inn at Pannanich Wells, which had been redeveloped by Francis Farquharson. Some time later he found work on the Balmoral estate, which at that time was leased on a 38-year agreement by the Hon. Sir Robert Gordon from the trustees of the estate of the late James, Earl of Fife. How John Brown secured the post is not known, but in these days, outside the special hiring fairs usually held quarterly, jobs were obtained by word of mouth. John Brown's duties included the herding of ponies for 13*s* a week.[29] His work being satisfactory, he took up the position of one of the Balmoral gillies and was in this employment when the royal family appeared on Deeside.

By now Balmoral had become the centre of social life in Deeside as guests came and went, hosted by Sir Robert Gordon and his sister Lady Alicia. John Brown and his fellow gillies had a lot of extra duties taking care of the house guests who came with their own liveries, mounds of luggage, guns, rods and dogs. Much to the dismay of John Brown and his fellows, some women took up deerstalking. The gillies stood by, cringing and 'watching their language', as Sir Robert's female guests – ahead of their time – scaled the deer hills. Lady Randolph Churchill remembered the first female deerstalkers:

I cannot say I admire [deerstalking] as an accomplishment. The fact is, I love life so much that the unnecessary curtailing of any creature's existence is more than distasteful to me. Not long ago [at Balmoral] I saw a young and charming woman, who was surely not of a blood-thirsty nature, kill two stags one morning. The first she shot through the heart. With the aid of a powerful pair of field-glasses, I watched her stalk the second. First she crawled on all-fours up a long burn;

emerging hot and panting, not to say wet and dirty, she then continued her scramble up a steep hill, taking advantage of any cover afforded by the ground, or remaining in a petrified attitude if by chance a hind happened to look up. The stag, meanwhile, quite oblivious of the danger lurking at hand, was apparently enjoying himself. Surrounded by his hinds, he trusted to their vigilance, and lay in the bracken in the brilliant sunshine. I could just see his fine antlered head, when suddenly, realising that all was not well, he bounded up, making a magnificent picture as he stood gazing around, his head thrown back in defiance. 'Crash! Bang!' and this glorious animal became a maimed and tortured thing. Shot through both forelegs, he attempted to gallop down the hill, his poor broken limbs tumbling about him, while the affrighted hinds stood riveted to the spot, looking at their lord and master with horror, not unmixed with curiosity. I shall never forget the sight, or that of the dogs set on him, and the final scene, over which I draw a veil. If these things must be done, how can a woman bring herself to do them.[30]

The increasing inclusion of women in such activities soon became the least of John Brown's and his colleagues' worries; the sudden death of Sir Robert Gordon brought to the estate a pall of gloom with much fear of loss of jobs. But soon a rumour started to circulate that Queen Victoria and her family were intent on the tenancy. And so it was that the Fife Trustees successfully negotiated the lease of Balmoral with Prince Albert. The royal family had now grown to six children – Princess Vicky, Albert Edward (b. 1841), the Prince of Wales, Princess Alice (b. 1843), Prince Alfred (b. 1844), Princess Helena (b. 1846) and Princess Louise (b. 1848) – and Queen Victoria planned to include them all in her September 1848 Scots holiday. It was the beginning of a new era for the area around Crathie and the commencement of immortality for John Brown.

One of the greatest changes was the prospect of new employment. The royal family's decision to make Balmoral their Scottish home meant steady work for coachmen, footmen, gardeners, housemaids, launderers and labourers, as well as an increase in groundsmen and gillies. Queen Victoria and Prince Albert took great interest in the lives of the Crathie folk, particularly the families of those who worked at Balmoral.

Throughout her life Queen Victoria made regular visits to the cottages on the estate and to Crathie, and she knew well not only John Brown's immediate family – his uncles, aunts and cousins – but also their lifestyles, too; she sampled their diet of oatmeal and milk, oatcakes and scones, black puddings and potted head (boiled sheep's head in jelly). She admired the women's skills in making blankets, plaids and clothes from local sheeps' wool they spun themselves, and often tailored her gifts to them to supplement their diet and apparel. Just as she enjoyed taking a glass of whisky with her tenants – probably illicitly distilled nearby – she turned a blind eye to the poaching of salmon from her stretch of the Dee or of venison from the hills.

John Brown and the Crathie folk who were to be employed at Balmoral soon realised that their new employers were very enlightened in their views concerning servants. Encouraged by Prince Albert, Queen Victoria was generous in ensuring that the working conditions at Balmoral were conducive to getting the best out of their employees. In later years John Brown and his family would all profit from Queen Victoria's largesse and many estate families benefited from secure tenancy agreements and annuity schemes which were introduced at Balmoral from 1849.

A record of Queen Victoria's attitude to her employees was published by 'One of Her Majesty's Servants' in 1897, in a privately circulated publication entitled *The Private Life of Queen Victoria*. It averred:

Nearly the most charming and womanly phase of the Queen's character is displayed in her relationship to her servants. Of course, all her subjects are her obedient servants, and the greatest grandee of all her large household is bound to render her loyal and faithful service, and indeed does so cheerfully. But I would speak of those humbler beings whom the average man and woman treat as mere menials, but who are, in the eyes of Her Majesty, fellow creatures and friends. There are few people in the world who have received such kindnesses from the Queen as her servants, and few who regard her with more sincere devotion and admiration.

And, indeed the Queen's servants should be faithful to her, for she stands by and protects them to the last. The small lodges at Windsor, Osborne and Claremont [Claremont House, near Esher, Surrey, Queen Victoria's childhood home], and the many cosy cottages at

Balmoral are filled by men and women who have grown grey in the service of the Royal Family. It is the same at Hampton Court, her palaces in London, and houses at Richmond and Kew. Wherever the Queen has any personal jurisdiction and a post or home to give, there may be found old retainers who have served not only her gracious self, but any member of her family. The royal gardens and kitchens, laundries, farms and stables are full of such ancient folk, many of whom remember the Queen as an infant, and whose only talk is of the beneficence of their beloved royal mistress . . .

At the same time it must not be thought that the Queen is a weak mistress. Far from it. The service she exacts is always most responsible, and she desires that it should be performed punctually and well. She is, herself, far too thorough and hardworking a servant of her State and her People not to appreciate and expect the first fruits of everyone's powers. The Queen is a strictly just and honourable woman and expects justice and honour from those about her, from the highest to the lowest.

These character traits of Queen Victoria greatly appealed to John Brown; he believed this was how employers *should* behave, and his respect for her grew as he got to know her better.

When Queen Victoria came to the throne there were two Deans of her Chapel Royal in Scotland, as well as the Dean of the Thistle. These appointees, part of the Royal Household in Scotland, she met but rarely. The Scottish clergy she encountered most frequently were the Presbyterian ministers of Crathie within the united parish of Crathie and Braemar, and the influential Presbytery of Kincardine O'Neil, Synod of Aberdeen. These were not employees of the Balmoral estate but fiercely independent clergy in the spirit of the Disruption of 1843 which had split the Scottish Kirk in matters such as education, poor relief and clergy placements. Thus the clergy were still very influential in Scottish parishes as teachers, counsellors and welfare officers. And as Dr R. Wilson McNair pointed out in his *Doctor's Progress*: 'Everyone sat "under" one or other of them, and it was a point of honour to uphold your choice as the finest preacher in the country.'

By and large the Queen got on well with her Crathie clergy, who were invited to a wide range of royal functions to read prayers, say

blessings and generally socialise. Among long-standing ministers like the
Revd Archibald Alexander Campbell (d. 1907), there were colourful
pastors such as the Revd Archibald Anderson (d. 1866) and the Revd
Dr Norman MacLeod (d. 1872); the latter, famed for his extempore
sermons, introduced the Queen to the works of the poet Robert Burns
by reading them to her, and the Queen turned to him for spiritual
succour after the death of Prince Albert. The Revd Anderson was
deemed a 'character' and many a royal anecdote about him abounded
in the parish and beyond. His church was the one built in 1804 to
replace the old building of St Monire, which had been used until the
end of the eighteenth century. In her volume *Recollections of a Royal
Parish* the late Mrs Patricia Lindsay remembered:

> One member of the congregation in [Queen Victoria's first years at
> Balmoral] used to excite much interest and amusement among
> strangers. This was the Minister's collie, who was a regular attendant
> at church, following Mr Anderson up the pulpit steps and quietly
> lying down at the top. He was always a most decorous, though
> possibly somnolent listener, but he was also an excellent time keeper,
> for if the sermon was a few minutes longer than usual 'Towser' got
> up and stretched himself, yawning audibly.
>
> When the Queen first came, Mr Anderson feared she might object
> to such an unorthodox addition to the congregation, and shut up
> 'Towser' on Sunday. Her Majesty next day sent an equerry to the
> Manse to enquire if anything had happened to the dog, as she had a
> sketch of the church in which he appeared lying beside the pulpit,
> and if he were alive and well, she would like to see him in his old
> place. Greatly to Towser's delight he was thus by royal command
> restored to Church privileges.

Queen Victoria soon began to appreciate the religious fervour of her
new Crathie neighbours who were steeped in the traditions of the
Scottish Reformed Kirk. Ready admonishment was heaped upon
the shepherd, for instance, who went in search of a straying lamb on the
Sabbath, or a youth humming a popular tune on the Lord's Day, or a
girl finishing her sewing – she would be made to unpick each stitch she
had sewn on the holy day. For the Calvinist worshippers, Communion

Sunday in late June was a great gathering when folk flocked to Crathie Kirk by cart and pony, or by a stiff walk over the hills. The sacrament lasted some six hours and although her position as Head of the Church of England precluded her from taking part for some decades until she attended in 1871, the Queen's actions on the day of rest were closely monitored by her neighbours – including actions for admonition. Local tradition has it that Queen Victoria was upbraided to her face by one of the elderly parishioners for doing a good deed on the Sabbath. The Queen pointed out to her: 'Our Lord undertook acts of charity on the seventh day.' 'Ah weel,' replied the relict, 'then I dinna think any more of Him for it.'[31]

One long-term effect of the royal family's appearance on Deeside that the ordinary folk did not expect was the inundation of their village by journalists eager to extract every detail of gossip about the royal family at Balmoral, to satisfy the growing hunger for newspaper coverage of royal events. In due time John Brown became adept at chasing newsmen away from the places where the royal family picnicked.

> *On his service to the Queen*
> 'I wish to take care of my dear good mistress till I die. You'll never have an honester servant.'
> **John Brown**

A special broadsheet carrying only stories of royal visits was published in Aberdeen and people would scan the columns of the *Aberdeen Journal* (Established 1748) at breakfast time to see where the royal family might be that day. Artists set up their easels to capture local colour to run alongside the stories. The newspapers covered royal plans weeks ahead so the burgeoning ranks of royal watchers could gather in towns and villages along the royal route from Aberdeen or Braemar to catch a glimpse of the Queen and her entourage, and the many displays of loyalty and devotion set up along the roads she travelled. And for the first time press stories about royalty in Scotland began to be filed for the London press on a regular basis. Here is what one correspondent reported about Queen Victoria's first visit to Balmoral and Crathie in 1848:

Ballater was reached at half-past 1, where their approach was announced by the booming of cannon on the height of Cairndarroch [*sic*]. An immense assemblage of the inhabitants and summer residents and neighbouring gentry were dressed in full Highland costume. They attracted the attention of the Queen, and Prince Albert beckoned one of the clansmen to the side of the carriage, and questioned him as to the 'sept' he belonged to: several gentlemen had, also, the honour of paying their respects to the Prince.

As soon as the horses were changed, the Royal carriages set off at a rapid pace, crossing the bridge, and taking the south side of the river, and notwithstanding the uneven nature of the ground the journey of nine or ten miles was performed in little more than an hour, bringing Her Majesty to Balmoral about a quarter to three o'clock. At Crathie, about a mile and a half this side of Balmoral, the last public demonstration took place. There was an arch, and in large letters the phrase 'Welcome to your Highland home, Victoria and Albert.'[32]

John Brown was by this time reckoned a competent and diligent, if ascerbic, member of the Balmoral gillies and he played a role in the preparations for the royal family's exploration of their Scottish home. Eight days after their arrival at Balmoral members of the royal party assembled to make their first ascent of Lochnagar, the 3,768ft twin-peaked mountain some 9 miles south-west of Ballater. A tourist guide of the time described it as 'cut by frightful corries; it has on its shoulder a gloomy tarn, overhung by tremendous precipices'. From the north summit, *Cac Carn Beag*, there are spectacular views over the tarn also called Lochnagar ('Loch of the Goats'). Before setting out, Queen Victoria read what Lord Byron had said about the mountain:

> Away ye gay landscapes, ye gardens of roses,
> In you let the minions of luxury rove!
> Restore me the rock where the snowflake reposes,
> If still they are sacred to freedom and love.
> Stern Caledonia, beloved are thy mountains,
> Round their wild summits though elements war,
> Though cataracts foam 'stead of smooth flowing fountains,
> I sigh for the valley of dark Lochnagar!

Oh there my young footsteps in infancy wandered,
My cap was the bonnet, my cloak was the plaid;
On chieftains long perished my memory pondered
As daily I strode through the pine-covered glade.
I sought not my home till the day's dying glory
Gave place to the rays of the bright polar-star;
And fancy was cheered by traditional story
Disclosed by the natives of dark Lochnagar.

Years have rolled on, Lochnagar, since I left you,
Years must elapse, ere I tread thee again:
Nature of verdure and flowers has bereft you,
Yet still are you dearer than Albion's plain.
England, thy beauties are tame and domestic
To one who has roamed o'er the mountains afar!
O for the crags that are wild and majestic,
The steep, frowning glories of dark Lochnagar![33]

Queen Victoria and Prince Albert set off for their jaunt in a postchaise. They drove to the bridge in the deer forest of Ballochbuie some 4 miles south-west of Balmoral. Here had gathered the gillies with the ponies which were to take them up the mountain. The guide for the day was Mr Bowman, a keeper sent by laird Farquharson of Invercauld, and he waited with Prince Albert's appointed gillie Macdonald and Mr Grant, Head Keeper at Balmoral, to supervise the lunch baskets with Batterbury the groom.

Prince Albert went ahead to stalk deer; he was unsuccessful but he shot two ptarmigan before rejoining the main party to ride and climb higher. Four hours after they set out they reached the top of Lochnagar, where they had lunch. The vista, hemmed in by drifting mist, was, said Queen Victoria, 'cold, wet and cheerless'. They began their descent in wind and rain. About a thousand feet from the top the sunshine broke through to reveal splendid views over Invercauld. Back at the carriage which had waited with the grooms below, the royal party were met by the Queen's Physician, Sir James Clark, and Prime Minister John Russell, 1st Earl Russell, who rode back with them to Balmoral.

The Queen rapidly acquired a taste for the countryside around Balmoral and was keen to show off the sights to the seven-year-old Prince of Wales. At Ballochbuie they changed from the postchaise to ponies with the Prince of Wales riding astride the deer saddle of Head Keeper Grant's pony; with a group of gillies from Balmoral, they explored the woods and braes of Craig Daign, and sat for a while in a wooden hurdle 'box' to watch for deer. There Queen Victoria and Prince Albert sketched for a while and the prince broke off from his drawing pad long enough to bag a 'royal'.[34]

During this 1848 holiday Queen Victoria and the royal family attended the Highland Games at Invercauld House. The press reports and the regular attendance of royalty at the future Braemar Gathering added a respectability to the games and guaranteed a popularity which has endured ever since. Although clansmen had gathered on the Braes of Mar since the eleventh century, when King Malcolm III held a competition to select 'his hardiest soldiers and his fleetest messengers', Braemar was not the site of the first modern Highland Games. This honour has been given by historians to the first Highland Society Gathering at Falkirk Tryst in 1781. Although it was mainly a competition for pipers, the gathering developed and by 1826, the year John Brown was born, full-scale games had been established throughout Scotland. Also by 1826, the Braemar Wright's Friendly Society – a charity to aid the sick, the aged, widows and orphans – had become the Braemar Highland Society to promote sport, the Scots language and culture. So here at Invercauld House, Queen Victoria was thoroughly entertained by the panoply of Scots Highland culture, ranging from dancing (once a male-only competition) to the athletic events of pole-vaulting, caber-tossing, hammer-throwing and tug-of-war events. Queen Victoria became the royal patron of the games and a generous contributor to the society's funds. Over the years the games became a royal event at Braemar Castle and Old Mar Lodge, with the Queen herself acting as hostess at Balmoral.

As she travelled to Scotland for the August 1849 holiday aboard the royal yacht *Victoria and Albert*, Queen Victoria called at Cork, Dublin and Belfast on her first visit to Ireland.[35] By 13 August the royal yacht had entered the Clyde and proceeded up Loch Goil into Loch Long to anchor in Roseneath Bay. Prince Albert made several visits ashore around Loch Lomond while the Queen stayed aboard with her senior naval officers.

On 15 August they were at Balmoral after a trip in the *Fairy* to Glasgow to attend presentations by civic dignitaries, and with visits to Glasgow Cathedral, the University and the Exchange. The royal party had proceeded by rail to Perth, with a stopover in the city, and thence by Spittal of Glenshee and Castleton of Braemar to Balmoral. As usual, the royal party were greeted and joined for the last part of their journey by local dignitaries; on this occasion they included General Sir Alexander Duff and Francis Godolphin D'Arcy Osborne, 7th Duke of Leeds, who was staying at nearby Mar Lodge.

A highlight of the 1849 holiday was the royal family's first stay at Altnagiuthasach ('The Hut'), a lodge in Balmoral Forest near Loch Muick, some 9 miles south-east of Balmoral Castle. The royal party set out on 30 August on ponies, and Prince Albert walked the last 2 miles with the gillies. These royal outings were very 'labour intensive', with several attendants needed to supervise the food and equipment. Although the ponies carried the burdens, each one had to be led, as did the ladies' and children's ponies, for the ground was rough. It is certain then, as he was a gillie working with the ponies, that John Brown was involved in royal jaunts from the very first. When the royal family were out picnicking, John Brown usually brewed Queen Victoria's pot of tea. On one such outing early in his royal service in 1851 the Queen remarked it was 'The best cup of tea I ever tasted.'

'Well, it should be, Ma'am,' replied Brown. 'I put a grand nip o'whisky in it.'

It was Prince Albert's custom to fill every moment of his waking life with something practical, so he took a lesson in Gaelic from gillie Macdonald as they walked. Queen Victoria described the scene that met them in a journal entry that would be repeated many times for all their Scottish trips:

We arrived at our little 'bothie' at two o'clock, and were amazed at the transformation [after their first trip to Balmoral they had given orders that the *sheil* be altered]. There are two huts, and to the one in which we live a wooden addition has been made. We have a charming little dining-room, sitting-room, bedroom, and dressing-room, all en-suite; and there is a little room where Caroline Dawson [Maid of Honour] sleeps, one for her maid, and a little pantry. In the other house, which is only a few yards distant, is the kitchen, where the people [ie, her personal attendants] generally sit, a small room where the servants dine, and another, which is a store-room, and a loft above in which the men sleep. Margaret French [the Queen's maid], Caroline's maid, Löhlein [Prince Albert's *Jäger*], a cook, Shackle [a footman], and Macdonald, are the only people with us in the house, old John Gordon and his wife excepted. Our rooms are delightfully papered, the ceilings as well as walls, and very nicely furnished. We lunched as soon as we arrived, and at three walked down (about twenty minutes' walk), to the loch called 'Muich' [sic]; which some say means 'darkness' or 'sorrow'. Here we found a large boat, into which we all got, and Macdonald, Duncan, Grant and Coutts [all gillies] rowed; old John Gordon and two others going in another boat with the net. They rowed up to the head of the loch, to where the Muich runs down out of Dhu Loch, which is on the other side.

The scenery is beautiful here, so wild and grand – real severe Highland scenery, with trees in the hollow. We had various scrambles in and out of the boat and along the shore, and saw three hawks, and caught seventy trout. I wish an artist could have been there to sketch the scene; it was so picturesque – the boat, the net, and the people in their kilts in the water, and on the shore. In going back, Albert rowed and Macdonald steered; and the lights were beautiful.[36]

Queen Victoria was now living in close proximity to her highland retainers and began to know them by name and personality. And soon one name was to stand out: that of John Brown.

CHAPTER TWO

FASCINATING JOHNNY BROWN

Queen Victoria first mentions John Brown in her *Journal* entry for 11 September 1849. She is describing a visit to Dhu Loch with Lady Douro, later the Duchess of Wellington, and lists the gillies in attendance as 'Grant, Macdonald (who led my pony the whole time, and was extremely useful and attentive), Jemmie Coutts (leading Lady Douro's pony), Charlie Coutts, and John Brown going with us: old John Gordon leading the way'. The Queen and Lady Douro rode in a carriage as far as 'Linn of Muich' where the party changed to ponies. Over dreadful tracks in a howling wind they climbed above Dhu Loch to 'some very welcome luncheon' in a sheltered hollow.

On the way down Queen Victoria reported:

The road was rough, but certainly far less soft and disagreeable than the one we came by. I rode 'Lochnagar' at first, but changed him for Colonel Gordon's pony, as I thought he took fright at the bogs; but Colonel Gordon's was broken-winded, and struggled very much in the soft ground, which was very disagreeable.[1]

Part of their return journey was by boat, with John Brown joining the rowers. The Queen concluded:

We were only an hour coming down to the boat. The evening was very fine, but it blew very hard on the lake and the men could not pull, and I got so alarmed that I begged to land, and Lady Douro was of my opinion that it was much better to get out. We accordingly landed, and rode home along a sort of sheep-path on the side of the lake, which took us three-quarters of an hour. It was very rough and very narrow, for the hill rises abruptly from the lake; we had seven hundred feet above us, and I suppose one hundred feet below.

However, we arrived at the hut quite safely at twenty minutes to seven, thankful to have got through our difficulties and adventures, which are always very pleasant to look back upon.[2]

As a matter of course the Queen now included the names of the gillies whenever she wrote about her Scottish jaunts, and the ladies of the court began discreetly eyeing up the handsome Highlanders, from Archibald Fraser Macdonald, whom Prince Albert trained up as his *Jäger*, to Head Keeper John Grant who was dour but striking. The Hon. Eleanor Stanley, one of the Queen's Maids of Honour, noted 'the most fascinating and good-looking young Highlander [is] Johnny Brown'.

Certainly Brown was now playing a more prominent role. Prince Albert observed him as he handled the ponies on their hill walks in his new position as undergroom. Brown seemed the most skilled of the gillies in negotiating the patches of bare granite and dangerously loose scree they encountered on 6 September 1850 as they ascended 3,940ft Ben-na-Bhourd. So Prince Albert decided that John Brown should ride on the box of the Queen's carriage instead of the usual postillion who was unused to the terrain. Prince Albert had grown to like Brown – as one reporter put it: 'The Prince Consort [was] struck by [Brown's] magnificent physique, his transparent honesty and straight-forward, independent-character.'[3]

It was common knowledge in royal circles that the Coburgs 'were cursed with melancholia'.[4] From his marriage to Queen Victoria in 1840 to his death in 1861, Prince Albert was often made 'wretched by the loneliness of exile'[5] as a stranger in a foreign land, and at such times he sought the solace of solitude. Thus he often went off on his own to hunt deer, or to be alone – apart from attendants – at the hut he had built at Feithort. Sometimes the Queen would seek out the prince at Feithort, with Brown leading her pony, but her visits were not encouraged, and she realised that the prince needed time away from his family and his relentless work on efficiency measures for her Household. Now that John Brown was keeping an eye on the Queen when she was out riding, Prince Albert could follow his own agenda of Highland pursuits without feeling guilty. When Albert was away, Queen Victoria and her daughters went on painting picnics, with John

Brown taking them to the best views and the most comfortable locations for their repast. Queen Victoria wrote to Augusta of Prussia, Empress of Germany, that 'I only feel properly *à mon aise* and quite happy when Albert is with me.'⁶ In widowhood it was to be a sentiment she expressed about John Brown. In the meantime, 'Johnny Brown' was in his element.

Victoria's aunt, Princess Adelaide of Saxe-Meiningen, the crowned consort of King William IV, had died in December 1849, and the Queen was still in mourning when her favourite son Prince Arthur, Duke of Connaught, was born in May 1850. Victoria's thoughts had turned to Scotland more and more during her confinement, especially to the plans she had made with Prince Albert for the development of the estate which was now firmly theirs. The purchase of neighbouring Birkhall for eight-year-old Prince Albert Edward, Prince of Wales, meant that he was now the 'first royal landowner on Deeside', and the lease of nearby Abergeldie greatly increased the bedroom space for future royal jaunts. Queen Victoria had already decided that Abergeldie should be made ready for her mother, the Duchess of Kent, so that she could enjoy the healthy benefits of Deeside; more immediately it would help her to get over the death of Queen Adelaide, whom the Duchess regretted offending in life. Albert's memoranda on the plans to improve Birkhall and Abergeldie alongside Balmoral, from developing policies, building cottages and constructing new roads, were constantly fluttering on to Victoria's desk among the state papers from the tiresome Prime Minister Palmerston.

By the time of Prince Arthur's christening on 25 June at Buckingham Palace the Queen was desperate to be away to Balmoral, having heard that the estate staff were busy with alterations. John Brown and the gillies were organising dogs, ponies and country sport facilities for the two new properties. She ached for some fresh air riding 'dear little "Lochnagar"' with Brown at his head.

John Brown was now to be seen close to the royal party, and spectators at the Braemar Gathering on 12 September 1850 particularly noted him as the Queen and her mother, the Duchess of Kent, making her first visit to Scotland, watched 'our gillie [Charles] Duncan' taking part in the lung-bursting race up Craig Cheunnich hill above the Castle of Braemar.

Brown was becoming useful, too, in arranging events. The next day the royal party went to watch salmon '*leistering*' (spearing with a barbed lance), with Brown helping Prince Albert, Colonel Charles Gordon and Lord James Murray to wade out into the Dee. After the 'leistering', John Brown and his companions carried Captain (later Sir) Charles Forbes of Castle Newe and his retainers over the Dee on their shoulders. Prince Albert described the day in a letter to his stepmother, Marie of Württemberg, relating that on arriving on dry land Captain Forbes removed his boot, filled it with whisky and drank a toast to Queen Victoria.[8] The Queen described the actions of all as 'very courteous, and worthy of chivalrous times'.

On 16 September Queen Victoria and a party went on a trip to Loch Muick. The Queen was in a literary mood and reflected:

The moon rose, and was beautifully reflected on the lake, which, with its steep green hills, looked lovely. To add to the beauty, poetry, and wildness of the scene, Coutts played in the boat; [John Brown and] the men, who row very quietly and well now, giving an occasional shout when he played a reel. It reminded me of Sir Walter Scott's lines in *The Lady of the Lake*:

> Ever, as on they bore, more loud
> And louder rung the *pibroch* proud.   [*bagpipe*]
> At first the sound, by distance tame,
> Mellow'd along the waters came,
> And lingering long by cape and bay,
> Wail'd every harsher note away.[9]

Queen Victoria subsequently returned to this 1850 entry in her *Journal* and wrote a footnote to highlight her mention of John Brown in her original text. What she wrote was the first piece of biographical material ever printed about John Brown; it read:

[John Brown] in 1858, became my regular attendant out of doors everywhere in the Highlands; who commenced as gillie in 1848, and was selected by Albert and me to go with my carriage. In 1851 he entered our service permanently, and began in that year leading my pony, and advanced step by step by his good conduct and intelligence. His attention, care, and faithfulness cannot be exceeded; and the state of my health, which of late years has been sorely tried and weakened, renders such qualifications most valuable, and indeed, most needful in a constant attendant upon all occasions. He has since (in December 1865), most deservedly, been promoted to be an upper servant, and my permanent personal attendant. He has all the independence and elevated feelings peculiar to the Highland race, and is singularly straightforward, simple-minded, kind-hearted, and disinterested; always ready to oblige; and of a discretion rarely to be met with. He is now in his fortieth year. His father was a small farmer, who lived at The Bush on the opposite side to Balmoral. He is the second of nine brothers, – three of whom have died – two are in Australia and New Zealand, two are living in the neighbourhood of Balmoral; and the youngest, Archie (Archibald) is valet to our son Leopold, and is an excellent, trustworthy young man.[10]

Queen Victoria's *Journal* shows that several other of her gillies were 'attentive' and deserving of her thanks for good work done, but it is clear by 1850 that John Brown either saw the main chance for his own advancement and perspicaciously played up to the Queen's need for attention, or he was just in the right place at the right time. Brown's attentiveness increasingly allowed him to be familiar with the Queen. For instance, during one outing the Queen and her ladies were making a slippery descent of Craig Nordie. Jane, Lady Churchill, had to be picked up after falling, and Brown remarked: 'Your Ladyship is not as heavy as Her Maa-dj-esty.'

'Am I grown heavier do you think?' enquired the Queen, used to his personal remarks.

'Well, I think you are,' replied Brown as the ladies looked away in some embarrassment.

A highlight of the autumn Scottish holiday of 1852 was the Torch-Light Ball at Corriemulzie, a shooting lodge between Braemar and the Linn of Dee. With John Brown on the box, and accompanied by two ladies-in-waiting, the First Lord of the Treasury, the 14th Earl of Derby, and Colonel Charles Gordon as acting equerry, the Queen and Prince Albert set off in Highland garb for Corriemulzie. The host and hostess,

Mr and Lady Agnes Duff (later the Earl and Countess of Fife), met
them at the door of Corriemulzie. They greatly enjoyed the Ball, and
similar events took place many times at Balmoral when the Queen
herself acted as hostess at the new castle. Queen Victoria remembered
that the location for the Ball was:

> really a beautiful and unusual sight. All the company were assembled
> there. A space about one hundred feet in length and sixty feet in
> width was boarded, and entirely surrounded by Highlanders bearing
> torches, which were placed in sockets, and constantly replenished.
> There were seven pipers playing together, Mackay leading – and they
> received us with the usual salute and three cheers, and 'Nis! nis! nis!'
> (pronounced 'Neesh! neesh! neesh!', the Highland 'Hip! Hip! Hip!')
> and again cheers; after which came a most animated reel. There were
> above sixty people, exclusive of the Highlanders, of whom there
> were also sixty; all the Highland gentlemen, and any who were at all
> Scotch, were in kilts, the ladies in evening dresses. The company and
> the Highlanders danced pretty nearly alternately. There were two or
> three sword dances. We were upon a *haut pas*, over which there was a
> canopy. The whole thing was admirably done, and very well worth
> seeing. Albert was delighted with it. I must not omit to mention a
> reel danced by eight Highlanders holding torches in their hands.[11]

Angus Mackay had been appointed the Royal Piper at Balmoral in
1843, but became involved in a 'royal scandal' soon after the
Corriemulzie Ball. His behaviour became more erratic and he started
to tell people that he and the Queen were married. He was committed
to the care of Dr W. Charles Hood at the Bethlehem Royal Hospital,
Lambeth, in 1854. He was discharged a few months later and drowned
himself in the River Nith in 1855.[12]

Two deaths in the autumn of 1852 were to affect Queen Victoria
significantly. First the eccentric miser John Camden Neild left her the
legacy which enabled Balmoral to be purchased, and then on
16 September, while at Altnagiuthasach, she received a packet from
Colonel (later Sir) Arthur Phipps, Private Secretary to Prince Albert,
enclosing a dispatch recording the death two days earlier of the 83-year-
old Arthur Wellesley, Duke of Wellington, at Walmer Castle, Kent.

Wellington had twice been Tory Prime Minister in her 'Wicked Uncles' time, and had been a trusted adviser. She wrote to her uncle, King Leopold of the Belgians, on 17 September from Balmoral:

We shall soon stand sadly alone; [the Earl of] Aberdeen is almost the only personal friend of that kind we have left. Melbourne, Peel, Liverpool [all former Prime Ministers] – and now the Duke – all *gone!*[13]

The more Queen Victoria felt alone, the more she clung to the familiar. The day she heard the sad news of Wellington, John Brown and the gillies prepared the ponies for a ride to Allt-na-Dearg and the newly built *shiel* of the Glassalt, with a cold lunch served at their destination by Brown. The wet weather reflected the Queen's sadness over the death of Wellington; she remarked: 'Our whole enjoyment was spoilt; a gloom overhung all of us.'[14] All the time John Brown was observing his royal mistress's changes in moods and her need for constant support.[15]

All over the Balmoral estate, and the hills around, are cairns set up by the royal family over the years to remember people and events. One of the first was built on Monday 11 October 1852. The royal family climbed to the summit of Craig Gowan, a 1,437ft wooded hill a mile or so south-east of Balmoral, to watch the building of the cairn, 'which was to commemorate our taking possession of the dear place', wrote the Queen.[16]

John Brown had gone ahead of the royal party to help pull down the existing old cairn, and to prepare the base for the new one. Mackay piped the party to the top and the Queen placed the first stone to be followed by the others in order of rank, until finally all the assembled estate workers and their relatives surged forward to place a stone to make the cairn a lucky place. It took an hour to complete the cairn, while whisky was drunk and reels danced. The Queen had a special treat for 'Monk' – Sir Robert Gordon's old dog that she had acquired with the estate – and Prince Albert climbed to the top of the 8ft tall cairn while the assembled company cheered. It was so *gemütlich*. The 'delightful day' was completed with walks and Prince Albert shot a stag. Alas Princess Victoria, the Princess Royal, upset the happy equilibrium by sitting on a wasps' nest 'and was much stung'.

Almost a year later another significant event took place. On 28 September 1853, in the pouring rain, the royal family set out to the planned site of the new Balmoral Castle to lay the foundation stone. As they gathered at the site the sun came out. Among John Brown's possessions was found a 'Programme of the Ceremony':

The stone being prepared and suspended over that upon which it is to rest, (in which will be a cavity for the bottle containing the parchment and the coins):

The workmen will be placed in a semicircle at a little distance from the stone, and the women and home servants in an inner semicircle.

HM the Queen, and HRH the Prince accompanied by the Royal Children, HRH the Duchess of Kent, and attended by Her Majesty's guests and suite, will proceed from the house.

Her Majesty, the Prince, and the Royal Family, will stand on the South side of the stone, the suite behind and on each side of the Royal party.

The Revd. Mr. Anderson will then pray for a blessing on the work. Her Majesty will affix her signature to the parchment, recording the day upon which the foundation stone was laid. Her Majesty's signature will be followed by that of the Prince and the Royal Children, the Duchess of Kent, and any others that Her Majesty may command, and the parchment will be placed in the bottle.

One of each of the current coins of the present reign will also be placed in the bottle, and the bottle having been sealed up, will be placed in the cavity. The trowel will then be delivered to Her Majesty by Mr. [William] Smith [City Architect] of Aberdeen . . . and the mortar having been spread, the stone will be lowered.

The level and square will then be applied, and their correctness having been ascertained, the mallet will be delivered to Her Majesty by Mr. Stuart (the Clerk of Works), when Her Majesty will strike the stone and declare it to be laid. The cornucopia will be placed upon the stone, and the oil and wine poured out by Her Majesty.

The pipes will play, and Her Majesty, with the Royal Family, will retire.

As soon after as it can be got ready, the workmen will proceed to their dinner. After dinner, the following toasts will be given by Mr. Smith:

'The Queen'.

'The Prince and the Royal Family'.

'Prosperity to the house, happiness to the inmates of Balmoral'.

The workmen will then leave the dinner-room, and amuse themselves upon the green with Highland games till seven o'clock, when a dance will take place in the ballroom.[17]

With the high wind flapping their clothes, the royal party carried out their duties. After observing the workmen at their dinner, Prince Albert went off to slaughter some 'black game', before joining the Queen once more in the evening to watch the evening dancing.

The royal family moved into the new Balmoral Castle on 7 September 1855, two years after the Queen's penultimate child, Prince Leopold, Duke of Albany, was born. The Queen declared of her new Scottish home 'the house is charming, the rooms delightful, the furniture, papers, everything, perfection'.[18] And in Europe another piece of 'perfection' was enacted. Three days after the royal family had taken up residence in their new home the Queen was closeted with the Minister in Attendance, the 2nd Earl of Granville, to discuss the great news. Sebastopol, the Crimean port that had been besieged in October 1854, had at last fallen to the Allies. The Crimean War would not end until April 1856, but on the strength of this news John Brown lit a celebratory bonfire while Grant and Macdonald fired rifles in the air and the new Royal Piper, Ross, blew a selection of suitable *pibroch* tunes.

On 21 September 1855 Prince Albert wrote from Balmoral to the Foreign Secretary, the Earl of Clarendon, concerning a royal 'strict secret' that only one more person, Prime Minister Palmerston, was to be told. Prince Frederick William of Prussia had arrived at Balmoral to seek the hand in marriage of fifteen-year-old Princess Victoria, the Princess Royal, nine years his junior.[19] The princess had no idea why he was visiting, but the German-speaking servants quickly guessed and gossip began to flow to all levels of the Balmoral domestic and estate staff. Such a match was an important part of Prince Albert's 'Coburg Plan', which included *inter alia* the unification of Prussia with the smaller German states under a British-style constitutional monarchy.

Although Queen Victoria indicated her approval of the proposed nuptials, the princess was as yet too young for marriage. Prince Frederick William could return in eighteen months time with a full proposal. In the meantime a betrothal could be contemplated. John Brown accompanied the Queen and the royal party when on the 'engagement day', 29 September, they rode out to Craig-na-Ban, and witnessed the exchange of loving glances and a 'Scottish token'.

Dropping behind the main party, Prince Frederick William and Princess Victoria had dismounted; picking a sprig of white heather, the Prince handed it to the Princess with a kiss and a wish for her to live with him in Prussia. When the royal party regrouped at Glen Girnoch, the Queen knew by the couple's demeanour that Prince Frederick William 'had declared himself'. Thus was set in motion an extraordinary sequence of events. Their marriage would lead to the birth of a son in 1859 who would become Emperor William II of the united Germany Prince Albert wished for — but who, as 'Kaiser Bill', would plunge Europe into disastrous war.

Each year brought several changes and new features at Balmoral. In the year that the Queen's ninth and last child Princess Beatrice was born, on 14 April 1857, a new bridge was opened over the Linn of Dee and the Queen settled down to a regular annual routine of visiting the poor of Crathie parish, an enterprise that John Brown would organise in future years. This year, with her new lady-in-waiting Jane, Lady Churchill, who would serve the Queen constantly until her death in 1900, she bought goods at a local Crathie store to distribute to parish octogenarians.

The year 1858 was a significant one in John Brown's career. On 25 January Princess Victoria married Prince Frederick William at the

---

On John Brown

'[John Brown] was shrewd, a great reader, and was capable of giving a considered opinion on most matters . . . Though Brown had a bluff manner, I never saw him intentionally rude.'

11th Marquis of Huntly,
Captain Gentlemen-at-Arms

Chapel Royal, St James's Palace, and Queen Victoria was left in a depressed and anxious state after surrendering her first-born to an older man. The Queen was shaking so much during the formal wedding picture that she appears blurred on the daguerreotype. The Queen's state had not improved when the royal family arrived at Balmoral that September. Although Queen Victoria was publicly criticised for leaving London while parliament was still in session and the Indian Mutiny was raging, Prince Albert knew that the Queen was approaching one of her 'depressions' and he was determined to get his *Liebes Frauchen* away.

Although it had snowed heavily, the Queen drove round the estate on 18 September with her Commissioner in Scotland Dr Andrew Robertson to view the latest house-building and in the afternoon rode out in her carriage. To get a better view of Prince Albert, off searching for deer, when their carriage stopped at a likely place for hunting, the Queen was carried in a plaid gripping the shoulders of John Brown and Keeper Duncan over the slippery wet grass to a favourite picnic spot by the Corrie Burn. When she returned home she wrote: 'All the Highlanders are so amusing, and really pleasant and instructive to talk to – women as well as men – and the latter so gentlemanlike.'[20]

By this holiday it was clear that Prince Albert's Highland *Jäger* Archibald Fraser Macdonald was not well. He had developed the Victorian curse of consumption (pulmonary tuberculosis) and was no longer able to carry out his duties. Macdonald eventually died at Windsor Castle in May 1860. Who was to take his place? Prince Albert had for some time been observing John Brown, since he was promoted to riding on the box of the Queen's carriage. Yes, Brown had all the qualities necessary; there was no equal in knowledge of the terrain around Balmoral; no one could light a picnic fire with damp wood like Brown; and he was skilled in amusing the Queen while the prince disappeared into the plantations to look for deer. Brown was thus promoted with the Queen's approval. She wrote to Princess Victoria at the *Kronprinzpalais* in Berlin:

Brown has had everything to do for me, indeed had charge of me and all, on all those expeditions, and therefore I settled that he should be specially appointed to attend on me (without any title) and have a full dress suit ... He was so pleased when I told him you had asked for him.[21]

'Fascinating Johnny Brown' was also now privy to royal secrets and the Queen told him Princess Victoria was pregnant. And he was becoming much in demand with other members of the royal family. Prince Arthur requested that Brown go with him and his party on an expedition. '*Unmöglich*' ['not possible'] said the Queen; 'Why, what should I do without him? He is my particular gillie!'[22]

When the snow came Queen Victoria wrote in her *Journal*: 'I wished we might be snowed up, and would be unable to move. How happy I should have been could it have been so!' She had no wish to leave Balmoral and confided in Princess Victoria that to do so was 'more painful' than in past years: 'I know not why,' she added. Her letters to Berlin expressed her need for the Highlands and she took to pondering the verses that the Revd Dr MacLeod had read to her from Robert Burns's poem on the Highlands with the refrain:

> My heart's in the Highlands, my heart is not here
> My heart's in the Highlands, a-chasing the deer
> A-chasing the wild deer, and following the roe –
> My heart's in the Highlands wherever I go.

But was her heart 'a-chasing' some*thing*, or some*one*? Certainly she was in love with the Highlands. But biographer Tom Cullen believed that these outpourings to her eldest daughter were a code: 'My Heart's in the Highlands . . . Yes, that is my feeling, and I must fight and struggle against it.' And the code suggested, opined Cullen, that Queen Victoria had become infatuated with 'Fascinating Johnny Brown', and her 'fight' was her struggle to put such feelings out of her mind.[23]

John Brown settled rapidly into the duties of being the Queen's 'particular gillie', which included taking a prominent place behind her at a variety of royal functions. Important events such as the fête for members of the British Association for the Advancement of Science, on 22 September 1859, became commonplace for him. A few days before, Prince Albert had presided over a meeting of the prestigious British Association at Aberdeen; their work was of great interest to the prince. 'Four weighty omnibuses' filled with 'the scientific men', wrote Queen Victoria in her *Journal*, enjoyed an afternoon of Highland games; and the Queen particularly noted that 'Brown's father and brothers' mingled with the official guests.

Each of her *Journal* entries for royal jaunts in Scotland now seems to include some mention of John Brown for a while. The first to take place after the fête was on Friday 7 October, when the royal family made an ascent of 4,296ft Ben Macdhui, one of the Cairngorms, 19 miles west-north-west of Castleton of Braemar. They proceeded by 'sociable'[24] changing to post-horses at Braemar. At Shiel of the Derry their ponies were waiting for the ascent. Brown led the Queen on a pony called 'Victoria' up the stony track and into heavy mist on the top of Ben Macdhui. There the Queen, the Prince of Wales and Princess Alice took lunch in 'a piercing cold wind', which dispersed the mist to open up grand views of stupendous scenery. Whisky and water refreshed the Queen – Brown said 'pure water would be too chilling' – who partook of tea once they had descended back to Shiel of the Derry.

This jaunt was a dress-rehearsal for four important 'expeditions' that the Queen and Prince Albert made to various parts of Scotland; they were dubbed the 'Great Expeditions' by Queen Victoria. The First Great Expedition was to Glen Fishie and Grantown-on-Spey. With John Brown and Keeper Grant on the box, Queen Victoria set off from Balmoral attended by General the Hon. Charles Grey, then Prince Albert's Private Secretary, and Jane, Lady Churchill.

Writing in her *Journal* at 'Hotel Grantown' – really a coaching inn – on Tuesday 4 September 1860, Queen Victoria traced their route in the 'sociable' via Linn of Dee, where they changed ponies for an exploration of the banks of the Geldie Burn as it enters the Dee, and thence on to the Fishie Burn and lunch. By this time John Brown was observing Queen Victoria's dietary preferences and began to make sure that all the items she enjoyed were packed in the picnic hampers or were available at Balmoral whenever possible. He became an expert, for instance, in hunting down the Queen's favourite pralines.[25]

Chatting to Lord and Lady Alexander Ramsay, met along the way, the Queen's party rode on to the ferry of the Spey and a fine view of Kinrara, some 3 miles south-west of Aviemore station, with the adjacent hill of Tor of Alvie then crowned only by the last Duke of Gordon's monument. Grant and Brown helped negotiate the ferry across the Spey to where carriages waited. As was her wont, Queen Victoria had insisted that the party went on their expedition incognito. As she explained:

We had decided to call ourselves 'Lord and Lady Churchill and party', Lady Churchill passing as 'Miss Spencer', and General Grey as 'Dr. Grey'! Brown once forgot this, and called me 'Your Majesty' as I was getting into the carriage; and Grant on the box once called Albert 'Your Royal Highness'; which set us off laughing, but no one observed it.[26]

During their overnight stay at the coaching inn at Grantown, the Queen noted: 'Grant and Brown were to have waited on us [at table], but were bashful [ie, drunk] and did not'. The *Journal* entry included a description of the 'very fair' dinner of Highland cuisine that was served:

soup, 'hodge-podge' [a pudding of indeterminate contents], mutton-broth with vegetables, which I did not much relish, fowl with white sauce, good roast lamb, very good potatoes, besides one or two other dishes, which I did not taste, ending with a good tart of cranberries.[27]

The next day, Wednesday 5 September, Queen Victoria's maid reported to her that Grant and Brown, along with the other attendants, had spent a 'very merry' night in the commercial travellers' accommodation. Throughout their stay the proprietress of the inn was fooled by the various aliases of the party and did not recognise her monarch. The party moved on to Castle Grant, Morayshire, the home of the wealthy Earl of Seafield, just over a mile from Grantown, which the Queen described as looking like a 'factory'. When they passed through Grantown on their return, the royal party had been unmasked and the town was thronged with waving, cheering people, their erstwhile hostess still in her paper curlers waving a flag from the window of her hostelry.

Travelling in her carriage with the leather cover drawn up – because of the midges – Queen Victoria and her party made a slow pace, because of tired horses, to Tomintoul in Banffshire, noted as the highest village in the Highlands at 1,160ft above sea level and much patronised for its angling. Queen Victoria was not impressed by its ambience; she wrote:

Tomintoul is the most tumble-down, poor-looking place I ever saw – a long street with three inns, miserable dirty-looking houses and people, and a sad look of wretchedness about it. Grant told me that it was the dirtiest, poorest village in the whole of the Highlands.[28]

This was an uncharacteristically negative entry for the Queen to write of her beloved Highlands, but she may have been irritated by the inn incident. She went on:

> While Brown was unpacking [their picnic lunch] and arranging our things, I spoke to him and to Grant, who was helping, about not having waited on us, as they ought to have done, at dinner last night and at breakfast, as we had wished; and Brown answered, he was afraid he should not do it rightly; I replied we did not wish to have a stranger in the room, and they must do so another time.[29]

In the future Brown would regularly be inebriated while on duty, yet he learned the lesson about the Queen not liking strangers around her and became protective. After lunch, the party travelled along the banks of the River Avon in southern Banffshire. Time was getting late so the party sped up, and the Queen was astonished at the rate John Brown could stride out as he led a trotting 'Fyvie'. Later that day the Queen wrote in her *Journal* how her Highland servants'

> willingness, readiness, cheerfulness, indefatigableness, are very admirable, and make them most delightful servants. As for Grant and Brown they are perfect – discreet, careful, intelligent, attentive, ever ready to do what is wanted; and [Brown], particularly, is handy and willing to do everything and anything, and to overcome every difficulty, which makes him one of my best servants anywhere.[30]

Brown's interpretation of the Queen's 'wants' often raised eyebrows among her courtiers. For instance, John Brown was once asked by one of the Queen's Maids-of-Honour if he had tea in the picnic basket. He replied: 'Well no, Her Maa-jd-esty, don't much like tea. We tak oot biscuits and speerits [whisky].'

Safely back at Balmoral the Queen declared that her 'First Great Expedition' had been 'delightful' and 'successful'.

Invigorated as she usually was at Balmoral, Queen Victoria returned to Windsor unprepared for the cruel blows of fate that lay in the immediate future. On 9 March 1861 the royal physicians decided to operate on a growth on the Duchess of Kent's arm. At seventy-four she seemed to make a good recovery, but a turn for the worse brought the Queen hurrying to her mother's bedside at Frogmore Lodge, Windsor. There she kept vigil until the Duchess died on the morning of 16 March. Immediately Queen Victoria went into a 'nervous decline'. She had only recently been reconciled to her mother after years of rancour, the Duchess having bitterly resented her daughter's decision to rule without her mother's interference.

On Deeside the Duchess would be remembered for years as a plump but attractive old lady, readily recognised, as she drove out of Abergeldie Castle in her carriage, since she insisted on wearing her hair in bunches of ribboned ringlets on either side of her face. In her grief the Queen recalled that when they had left Balmoral the last time, John Brown had been almost reluctant for them to go. He had declared to her his hope that they would have no illness during the winter and return safely to Balmoral. Above all, he had emphasised, that there be no deaths in the family. It had been a strange *vorbedeutung* (prophecy), mused the Queen, of what was to come. First the Duchess's old Comptroller, Sir George Couper, had died, then a few days later 'dearest mama'. When would it end?

George William Frederick Villiers, 4th Earl of Clarendon and erstwhile Foreign Secretary, was among those courtiers exasperated by what he saw as the Queen's self-indulgence in being 'determined to cherish her grief'. He commented to Louise, Duchess of Manchester: 'I hope this state of things won't last, or [the Queen] may fall into the morbid melancholy to which her mind has often tended and which is a constant cause of anxiety to Prince Albert.'[31] Following the interment of the Duchess of Kent at the royal mausoleum at Frogmore, Prince Albert took the Queen, still in deep mourning, off to Balmoral to try to stimulate once more her will to survive and to encourage her to 'take things as God intended them'.

On Friday 20 September 1861 the royal family set off for the 'Second Great Expedition' to Invermark and Fettercairn. With Grant and Brown in their usual positions on the 'sociables', and accompanied by

Princess Alice and her new fiancé, Prince Louis of Hesse-Darmstadt, the royal party set off for Bridge of Muick where they transferred to ponies. By peat-road and glen they rode to Corrie Vruach where they encountered the 11th Earl of Dalhousie, a two-term Secretary at War, who welcomed them to his Scottish 'March' and joined them for lunch at Invermark, Angus, where John Brown unpacked the Queen's sketching materials.

Later, her easel folded away, the party rode on past ruined Invermark Castle and on to Lord Dalhousie's shooting lodge for a rest and then on to the village of Fettercairn in south-east Kincardineshire. They stayed at the Ramsay Arms, with their courtiers lodging at the Temperance Hotel opposite. This time Grant and Brown controlled their drinking in order to wait at table sensibly, for fear of being banished to the Temperance establishment. The Queen remarked that they 'were rather nervous, but General Grey and Lady Churchill carved, and they had only to change the plates, which Brown soon got into the way of doing'.[32]

A moonlit walk took them to the Town Cross. This was the stump of the medieval cross of Kincardine which still bore ancient marks indicating the length of the old Scottish 'ell', a measurement of cloth. Prince Louis paused at this relic, which had once enjoyed pride of place in the now-vanished ancient county town, in the shadow of the royal residence of Kincardine Castle, and read out the weathered proclamation on charities.

Again the party was travelling incognito and Brown and Grant managed to keep other guests away from the rooms being used by the Queen. 'What's the matter here?', one had asked, only to be informed that the royal group was 'a wedding party from Aberdeen'. The enquirer was entertained to breakfast by Brown and Grant. Queen Victoria noted that Brown 'acted as my servant, brushing my skirt and boots and taking any messages'.[33]

The journey continued past Fasque, the home of Sir Thomas Gladstone, the estranged brother of the Chancellor of the Exchequer, W.E. Gladstone, and on to the magnificent views of Cairn o'Mounth. Dog-carts succeeded ponies and carriages in carrying the royal party on their way through the open country with its fine vistas towards Aberdeen. In order to rest the horses, wrote Queen Victoria, 'Alice,

Lady Churchill, and I, went into the house of a tailor, which was very tidy, and the woman in it most friendly, asking us to rest there; but not dreaming who we were'.[34]

Through Glen Tanar the royal party made their way back to Balmoral. At Ballater the former Duchess of Kent's carriage waited to take them on the last lap of their journey. The Queen admitted to feeling sad at the sight of her mother's carriage but declared that the scenery had done her good.

The 'Third Great Expedition', this time to Glen Fishie, Dalwhinnie and Blair Atholl, began on Tuesday 8 October. By Braemar and the Linn of Dee to the Geldie Water they rode in carriages to be met by the royal ponies which had gone on ahead with General Grant, the main organiser of this jaunt. With the Queen safely mounted on 'Inchrory', and led by John Brown, they forded the river and went through beating rain and wind into Glen Fishie. Brown waded her horse through Etchart Water while the Queen watched in dismay as a gillie dropped their bundle of dry cloaks into the water.

After a hurried lunch they made their way over rough ground, through myriad burns, and past the ruins of crofters' cottages, their inhabitants long gone as a consequence of the Highland Clearances. Meeting up with the carriages, which had come by the road route, they drove on to Kingussie where Brown and Grant kept a crowd away as they paused for refreshment. They drove on through Newtonmore to the inn at Dalwhinnie. Travelling incognito meant roughing it in these sparsely populated areas and the Queen recorded that they had a frugal supper of 'two miserable, starved chickens, without any potatoes' or pudding. The main task of the evening was taken up with drying clothes for the morning and John Brown and the rest of the servants picked at what remained of the scraggy chickens for their even more meagre supper.

On 9 October the party awoke to find Highlander Cluny Macpherson, through whose lands they were passing, with a piper and Volunteers drawn up at the inn to salute them. He had been apprised of their coming. Then it was off through Drumochter Pass from Inverness-shire into Perthshire. Near Dalnacardoch they were met by George Augustus Frederick John Murray, 6th Duke of Atholl, who rode with them into the heart of his estates and his home at Blair Castle which the Queen had visited some seventeen years earlier.

The royal party were met at the door of Blair Castle by the Queen's old friend Anne, Duchess of Atholl, along with Miss McGregor, who was to help the Queen in the future with her controversial writings about her life in Scotland, which included comments on John Brown. After coffee with the Duchess, the royal party climbed into carriages, with the Queen in a curiously shaped four-wheeled 'boat carriage', and drove off to Glen Tilt, a narrow glen extending from Blair Atholl, with its guardian summit of Ben-y-Gloe. The royal ponies had been taken to the Earl of Fife's shooting lodge at Beynoch, where the Duchess of Atholl left the party as it went on its way, guided by the Duke and escorted by a dozen of his 'private army', the Atholl Highlanders, preceded by two pipers. On rough ground the duke offered to lead the Queen's pony, but she demurred as John Brown took the reins. Laughingly she said to the Duke: 'Oh no, only I like best being led by the person I am accustomed to.'[35]

While Brown and the others unpacked lunch at Dalcronarchie the Queen sketched, then they were off again to ford the rain-swollen River Tarff. Again the Duke offered to lead the Queen's pony across, but she insisted that John Brown – 'whom I have far the most confidence in' – should take her across. The soaked party followed the precipitous road with John Brown struggling to help the Queen's pony keep its footing on the slippery terrain. At the border between Perthshire and Aberdeenshire the party stopped. The Duke called on all present to toast the Queen and Prince Albert with the Gaelic toast: '*Nis!-nis!-nis! Sit air a-nis! A-ris – a-ris – a-ris!* (Now, now, now! That to him, now! Again, again, again!') On behalf of the Queen, Keeper Grant proposed three cheers for the Duke of Atholl, and the Queen's pony became restless at 'the vehemence of Brown's cheering'.

The party was met at Beynoch shooting lodge by the Countess of Fife who gave them tea. Saying farewell to the Duke of Atholl the royal party returned to Balmoral, having covered 129 miles in two days. The Queen reflected in her *Journal*:

This was the pleasantest and most enjoyable expedition I *ever* made; and the recollection of it will always be most agreeable to me, and increase my wish to make more! Was so glad dear Louis [Prince Louis of Hesse-Darmstadt] (who is a charming companion) was with us.

Have enjoyed nothing as much, or indeed felt so much cheered by anything, since my great sorrow [the death of the Duchess of Kent].[36]

The 'Fourth Great Expedition' began on Wednesday 16 October 1861. Their route this time took them from Balmoral to Loch Callater and thence Ca-Ness, and home by Cairn Lochan and Shean Spittal Bridge. The Queen rode 'Fyvie' and the party included Princess Helena, then fifteen, who had never been on a 'Great Expedition' before. The Queen was delighted with the scenery which, she said, 'gave me such a longing for further Highland expeditions!'[37] Sadly, there were to be no more with Prince Albert at her side.

At the end of their holiday, and just before she left for Windsor Castle, the Queen wrote to her uncle, King Leopold of the Belgians, expressing her first written appreciation of John Brown:

We have had a most beautiful week, which we have thoroughly enjoyed – I going out every day about twelve or half-past, taking luncheon with us, carried in a basket on the back of a Highlander, and served by an *invaluable* Highland servant I have, who is *my factotum here*, and takes the most wonderful care of me, combining the offices of groom, footman, page, and *maid*, I might almost say, as he is *so* handy about cloaks and shawls, etc. He always leads my pony, and always attends me out of doors, and *such* a good, handy, *faithful*, attached servant I have nowhere; it is quite a sorrow for me to leave him behind.[38]

While leading Queen Victoria's pony John Brown would pass on any gossip he had heard around the court to the Queen, and tell her any new jokes he had gathered. One which amused the Queen – who had a keen sense of humour – concerned a coach service. In Victorian times horse-drawn public service vehicles linked the main towns of Scotland. The carriage which ran between the Perthshire towns of Blairgowrie and Dunkeld was called the 'Duchess of Atholl' and was based at the 'Duke of Atholl's Arms' in Dunkeld. John Brown told the Queen that at the terminus was the notice: 'The Duchess of Atholl leaves the Duke's Arms every lawful morning at six o'clock.'

As they settled back into their usual routines at Balmoral, following the departure of the royal family, back at Windsor Castle Prince Albert descended into a state of gloom. For him 1861 was an *annus horribilis*. His hopes for a new democratic era developing from the 'Coburg Plan' for Prussia had faded. That country's new monarch, William I, who would become Emperor of Germany in 1871, father-in-law of his beloved daughter Princess Vicky, had promoted a militaristic policy and had crowned himself with Teutonic splendour at Königsberg as the royal family had holidayed at Balmoral. Poor Vicky's role in Prussia as Crown Princess was being sadly undermined as the British press attacked everything German. The Prince had suffered much private grief over the death of his mother-in-law and more was to come when his cousin Prince Ferdinand of Coburg's son, King Peter V of Portugal, died of typhoid, along with two brothers. Albert's aspirations for a Coburg-Braganza dynasty to democratise Portugal were thus dashed.

At home Prince Albert Edward, Prince of Wales, had returned in shame from the Curragh Camp, Dublin, where he had been serving with the 1st Battalion Grenadier Guards. The errant Prince of Wales had had a sexual fling with the loquacious Burlington Arcade tart-cum-'actress' Nellie Clifden. News of the affair could easily scuttle plans for the Prince's engagement to Princess Alexandra of Denmark. Prince Albert's interview with the Prince of Wales, who had returned to Cambridge, on 25 November, had been unpleasant for both despite the Prince of Wales's contrite attitude. Added to this the outbreak of the American Civil War had caused the Union Navy to intercept the British vessel SS *Trent* and the arrest on board of two Confederate States envoys threatened to cause a diplomatic row. Prince Albert had worked hard through the night to water down the peremptory communiqué from the Liberal government of Lord Palmerston, which demanded reparation from President Abraham Lincoln's administration. Prince Albert's conciliatory phrases allowed Lincoln to save face and war with the Union States was averted.

Prince Albert was exhausted, depressed and ill. As Christmas approached he became weaker and weaker in body and spirit. Although he insisted that he was not ill, his physicians, the doddering Sir James Clark and the obsequiously compliant Dr William Jenner, realised that typhoid had him in its grip. Nevertheless they advised the Queen that there was no cause for alarm and Prince Albert remained untreated.

Lying in the Blue Room of Windsor Castle, Prince Albert began to drift in and out of consciousness; he was delirious, but in a moment of clarity he asked that Princess Alice play his favourite Lutheran hymn *Ein feste Burg ist unser Gott*. All who gathered in the anterooms to the Blue Room, which only Queen Victoria and Princess Alice were allowed to enter, could now hear the Prince's tortured, laboured breathing. As the Prince sank into his final unconsciousness he lapsed into German. *Wer ist da?* he said to an unrecognised Queen Victoria. *Es ist das kleine Frauchen*, she whispered. He responded: *Gutes, kleines Frauchen*. His clutching hand, which Queen Victoria was holding, went limp, and Prince Albert died at around 10.45pm on Saturday 14 December 1861.

Only in later years was Queen Victoria able to write about the final scene:

> Two or three long but perfectly gentle breaths were drawn, the hand clasping mine and . . . *all, all* was over . . . I stood up, kissed his dear heavenly forehead & called out in a bitter and agonising cry 'Oh! my dear Darling!' and then dropped on my knees in mute, distracted despair, unable to utter a word or shed a tear. Ernest Leiningen & Sir C. Phipps lifted me up, and Ernest led me out . . .[39]

On 23 December, the day of Prince Albert's funeral at St George's Chapel, Windsor, London was described as being like 'a city struck by the Plague'.[40] Sir William Hardman reflected: 'all shops shut or partially so, and all private houses as much closed as if each owner had lost a near relative'.[41] Stunned as they were at Balmoral, the nation was doubly shocked since no official medical bulletins had been issued concerning Prince Albert until a few days before his death. Queen Victoria had retired to Osborne on 19 December and was unable to face attending the funeral service. Instead she buried herself in her grief amid the relics she had gathered of Prince Albert's life. His memory was to be her future cult; her grief a prison for members of her Household.

At Balmoral John Brown and the other retainers laid out the decorations of mourning. They were all conscious of the passing of an era. For John Brown it was the beginning of a new stage in the enhancement of his career.

CHAPTER THREE

To Serve Her All His Days

During the spring of 1862, Queen Victoria made her first visit to Balmoral after the death of Prince Albert. Her grief was still raw on that rainy day as she was greeted at the door of the castle by Commissioner Dr Andrew Robertson and Head Keeper John Grant. She wrote of her feelings to her eldest daughter Princess Victoria in Prussia:

> Oh! darling child, the agonising sobs as I crawled up with Alice and Affie! [Prince Alfred, Duke of Edinburgh and Saxe-Coburg] The stag heads – the rooms – blessed, darling Papa's room – then his coats – his caps – kilts – all, all convulsed my poor shattered frame![1]

The Queen felt suicidal. She felt a surge of her feared Hanoverian madness; she wrote her will.

There was no spot in Queen Victoria's kingdom that was as well preserved in Prince Albert's organisational aspic as Balmoral. A new strict disciplinary directive was issued from whichever room the Queen happened to be in. Every hour footmen, ladies-in-waiting and maids were dispatched with notes, memos and letters conveying the royal instructions on how Balmoral and its occupants were to function. The message-carrying entered the realms of farce: the Queen was known to pen notes to Sir Henry Ponsonby, her secretary, who might be only yards away.

From 1862 a new Balmoral practice – dubbed 'Balmorality' by those who felt its sting – came into use. The list of rules was endless. The Queen's ladies were not to leave the castle unchaperoned, and certainly not alone on unsupervised picnics with gentlemen of the court. Again no one was to quit Balmoral until the Queen had gone out – lest she need them. The long-suffering princesses – daughters and grand-daughters – were not to hobnob with gentlemen of the Household, and there were to be no unchaperoned walks in the grounds for them either.

John Brown was to play a prominent part – not always decorously – every 26 August from 1862, the anniversary of Prince Albert's birth. The gillies, the estate tenants in their best clothes and the entire Household in morning dress were expected to assemble at the obelisk presented to the Queen by the estate workers to the memory of Prince Albert.[2] Here they would toast the departed Prince in whisky. Queen Victoria only stayed long enough to hear a short prayer of thanksgiving and quietly returned to the castle in her carriage, perhaps because she knew what would happen next. John Brown and the other gillies set up a trestle table by the wood and generous libations were handed out. Queen Victoria turned a blind eye to the state of her gentlemen as they slowly returned to the castle, while John Brown was known to sleep off his indulgence in the woods, sometimes lying alongside courtiers in frock coats and top hats. Although abstemious herself, and critical of those who over-indulged, Queen Victoria was to retain a curious myopia about her gillies and their drunkenness. Her laxity was to cause her further grief.

When it came to choosing new 'below-stairs' staff at Balmoral, the Queen often asked John Brown's advice; his candidates tended to be in his own image. Once he was approached by a man wishing to obtain a position for his son in the Royal Household. 'He's a good lad who does na' swear, drink or play cards,' said the father proudly of his twenty-year-old son.

'Weel,' replied Brown. 'I'm verra sorry, but he sounds too guid tae live lang – and the Queen disna like the quick-deeing [dying] kind.'

On another occasion, a young footman cackhandedly dropped a silver salver, rattling the Queen's nerves. She ordered that he be demoted to the kitchens. Brown, who had an eye on the young man and thought that he had potential as a royal servant, brought up the subject with the Queen: 'What are ye daein' tae that puir laddie? Hiv' ye never drappit onything yersel?' Next day the young servant's livery was restored.

One incident stands out in the story of John Brown. During the evening of Wednesday 7 October 1863, around 7pm, Queen Victoria was travelling in a two-horse 'sociable' landau. The hoods of the carriage were down to enable the Queen and her daughters, the Princesses Alice and Helena, to enjoy the mountain road scenery as they sped from Loch Muick to Balmoral. On the two-seater box sat John Brown and the coachman William Smith, and behind the royal ladies sat Princess Alice's blackamoor servant Wilhelm, from the household at Darmstadt. As John Brown had handed them into the carriage, Queen Victoria noticed that William Smith was 'confused' – one of her idiosyncratic definitions of drunk.

From time to time Smith swerved the carriage off the road on to the rough verges. This so alarmed Princess Alice that for a while John Brown led the horses. As this made progress too slow, he remounted and held a lantern aloft to assist Smith's vision of the road. Some 2 miles from Altnaguithasach another swerve caused the 'sociable' to tip over, throwing its occupants on to the verge. The princesses escaped unhurt, but Queen Victoria sustained minor facial injuries and a staved thumb. Brown hurt his knee as he jumped clear. Quickly recovering himself Brown assisted the Queen to her feet with a characteristic: 'The Lord Almighty have mercy on us! Who did ever see the likes of this before? I thocht ye were all kilt!'[3]

At last they reached Balmoral at about 10pm, where they were tended by Dr Jenner. In her *Journal* the Queen lamented that she had no Prince Albert to tell of the adventure; but she was sure, she told her daughter Alice, that the Prince knew of the mishap and 'I am sure he watched over us.'[4] She also noted: 'We are agreed that Smith was quite unfit to drive me again in the dark', and the coachman was pensioned off in 1864. Later she was admonished by W.E. Gladstone, then Chancellor of the Exchequer and Minister in Attendance at Balmoral, for taking drives along the darkened roads. She closed her ears to his lecture, but was later furious that Gladstone recounted the accident to Prime Minister Palmerston.

But that was all in the future. During September 1862 Queen Victoria visited Prince Albert's childhood haunts at Coburg, a few months after the Second Great Industrial Exhibition to honour the Prince Consort, who had been the 'titular father' of the Great Exhibition of the Works of Industry of All Nations at the Crystal Palace in May 1851.[5] John Brown travelled down with other gillies to view the vast range of artefacts exhibited. Meanwhile at Windsor Queen Victoria's mood was darkening.

'Oh! to think of my beginning another year alone,' wrote the Queen in her *Journal* on 14 December 1862.[6] It was the first anniversary of Prince Albert's death and she attended a service conducted by the Very Revd Dr Arthur Penrhyn Stanley, Dean of Westminster, in the Blue Room at Windsor Castle where the Prince had died. Queen Victoria's reaction to Prince Albert's death was to promote a caricature of royal mourning. For her Household and family court mourning lasted a year; for the Queen it endured the whole of her remaining years. She even had the Blue Room photographed so that every item was logged, never to be moved. Above her bed was always hung a photograph of Prince Albert on his deathbed, and on her bedside table rested a plaster cast of his right hand. For years she slept clutching Albert's nightclothes.

On 18 December 1862 Prince Albert's remains were transferred from St George's Chapel at Windsor to the royal mausoleum that Queen Victoria had commissioned at Frogmore, to be entombed in the presence of the royal family while the Dean of Windsor, the Very Revd & Hon. Dr Gerald Wellesley, intoned prayers. The royal mausoleum, with its white marble effigy of Prince Albert by Baron Carlo Marochetti, was to be a place of sanctuary for Queen Victoria, who kept the keys to the sepulchre always with her.

Queen Victoria's sense of loneliness increased, particularly after the weddings of two of her children. On 1 July 1862 her second daughter Princess Alice married Grand Duke Louis of Hesse-Darmstadt, and on 10 March 1863 the Prince of Wales married Princess Alexandra ('Alix') of Denmark, in St George's Chapel, Windsor. The Queen, dressed entirely in black except for the blue ribbon of the Order of the Garter, watched the proceedings from Catherine of Aragon's closet. On their wedding day Queen Victoria wrote in her *Journal*: 'Here I sit lonely and desolate, who so need love and tenderness . . .'[7] Queen Victoria craved the presence of a loving, caring man to alleviate her bitter sense of loss of Prince Albert, and her depression brought on a further bout of fear that she was losing her mind. But just such a man as she needed was about to step on to the royal stage, to form with her an enduring relationship of mystery and scandal.

On the way to her autumn 1863 holiday at Balmoral, the Queen decided to break her journey at Perth to visit her old friend Anne,

Duchess of Atholl, who had been Mistress of the Robes from 1852, then one of the Ladies of the Bedchamber since 1853. The Queen had heard that Anne's husband, the 6th Duke, was gravely ill. The Duchess had been at Windsor when Prince Albert died and the Queen was anxious to comfort her friend in her trial. On 15 September the Queen travelled with General Grey, Princess Helena and Lady Augusta Bruce from Perth to Blair Atholl by special train on the newly opened Perth & Inverness Railway Company line. Although desperately ill, the Duke managed to accompany the Queen and party to Blair Atholl station on their departure. The Duke died on 16 January 1864.

The Blair Atholl trip plunged the Queen once more into gloom, but with John Brown to fuss over her she soon began to brighten up. The growing influence of John Brown at Balmoral was largely due to the fact that the castle and estate were run in entirely different ways from Queen Victoria's other homes. Because it was not regulated by the rigid and ancient protocol of, say Windsor or Buckingham Palace, Queen Victoria presided over a kind of 'Scullery Court' at Balmoral, which allowed her to fret over the details and trivia of its daily life. In all this John Brown encouraged the Queen to be involved. When the Queen visited the stables John Brown was always there to answer questions and involve her in sentimental fuss over her 'dear little Highland ponies'. He gave advice as to which beast should be given to which rider, and together they worked out a system of five categories of pony, based on mettle and stamina, linked to guests' and Household members' riding skills. This led to many quarrels between John Brown and the keepers and fishing beat organisers, for John Brown offered his advice freely on matters beyond his basic duties. The sound of Head Keeper John Grant and John Brown arguing – usually about Brown's outspoken opinions about how the gun room and fishing rights on the Dee should be organised – became a regular occurrence.

During the summer of 1864 Princess Alice, who had not yet been replaced by her youngest sister Princess Beatrice as her mother's close companion, was concerned at the Queen's brooding and lack of animation outside her state papers and domestic activities. She discussed the situation with Dr Jenner and Sir Charles Phipps, the Keeper of the

Privy Purse. Jenner averred that the Queen needed more exercise and fresh air. The Queen, opined Princess Alice, had always enjoyed the pony cart rides at Balmoral; perhaps these could be introduced at Windsor and Osborne as a regular feature of the daily routine. The two courtiers agreed that the suggestion had some merit. Was not the pony cart led by that handsome Johnny Brown?, recalled the Princess. She further pointed out that since her mother hated change or the appearance of unfamiliar faces around her, why not bring down Johnny Brown from Balmoral to organise the pony rides. It was agreed to make the suggestion to the Queen, who gave her permission and John Brown was summoned to Osborne House in December 1864.

Back in 1843 Queen Victoria and Prince Albert had talked about securing for themselves a retreat which would give them privacy and freedom to relax. On hearing that the Osborne estate, near East Cowes on the Isle of Wight, was up for sale they decided to investigate further. The Queen knew and liked the Isle of Wight; she had been taken there by her mother in 1831 and 1833, and had already ridden in her carriage through the estate and inspected the three-storey eighteenth-century old Osborne House, with its splendid views of Southampton Water, Cowes Roads and the Royal Navy anchorage at Spithead. The asking price was £28,000, and on Prince Albert's prompting they decided to rent the place for a year, at £1,000 p.a., to see if it was suitable; this they did on 1 May 1844.

The royal couple made their first visit to Osborne in October, sailing across the Solent in blustery showers, and were immediately struck by the property's potential for privacy. Osborne was seen to be ideal in every way and negotiations to purchase were begun with the vendor, the unpredictable Lady Isabella Blachford. By the end of December 1845, despite Lady Blachford's mercenary nitpicking, the 342 acre Osborne estate was secured, along with the house, its furniture and contents and various neighbouring farms and properties to make up a new estate of 1,727 acres, all for £67,000.[8]

Prince Albert now set about creating a new home for his family, to designs supervised by the famous builder Thomas Cubitt, whose fine town-houses in London's Belgrave Square and Eaton Square were the prestigious homes of the well-to-do. The foundation stone for the new house was laid on 23 June 1845. The family lived in the Italianate tower-dominated wing known as the Pavilion, of which they took possession on the evening of the 14 September 1846; the Household Wing was ready in 1847; and Old Osborne House was demolished to make way for a new Main Wing.

The royal family established a routine of visiting Osborne around four times a year, in the spring, on Queen Victoria's birthday (24 May), in July and just before Christmas. After Prince Albert's death in 1861 his room at Osborne was preserved exactly as if he had just left it for a moment and would return. Queen Victoria now always spent her wedding anniversary (10 February) at 'Dear Desolate Osborne', which was to be the main setting for her slow recovery from her 'morbid melancholy'.

With John Brown at her pony's head, Queen Victoria soon settled into a pattern of daily rides. The Queen's favourite pony, 'Lochnagar', had been brought from Balmoral with John Brown. She wrote:

I find this quiet riding, in these dear grounds, woods and fields by the sea, very pleasant, and the motion of the pony's gentle walk, soothing. But it is a sad alternative for the delightful long walks with my beloved one.[9]

A few months after his appointment John Brown accompanied his royal mistress and her suite on a visit to Princess Alice at Darmstadt, where she unveiled a statue to Prince Albert. This trip was followed by a visit to the 10th Earl of Dalhousie's shooting lodge at Invermark. Here Queen Victoria realised that John Brown had a fine sense of direction and was able to assess his surroundings with great accuracy. Hating the unfamiliar, she began to rely on Brown to explain the layout of houses called on and places visited. After the Invermark visit, Queen Victoria spent a few days in September 1865 at Dunkeld to comfort the newly widowed Anne, Duchess of Atholl. Brown and Grant were in attendance, and for once Brown's sense of direction failed him.

The royal party was returning to Dunkeld from Loch Ordie Lodge in the sheeting rain when coachman Smith took a wrong turning and took them into the heart of a wooded area with rough tracks. They soon became lost. Grant jumped down to walk ahead with a lantern and John Brown led the horses. Queen Victoria became agitated but was 'reassured' by Brown's presence. General Grey politely asked the

Duchess where they were and Brown rudely interrupted: 'The duchess don't know at all where we are!'

It was after this trip that the Queen wrote:

Was much distressed at breakfast to find that poor Brown's legs had been dreadfully cut by the edge of his wet kilt on Monday, just at the back of the knee . . . Today one became so inflamed and swelled so much, that he could hardly move.[10]

Despite being in pain John Brown refused to abandon his duties and continued to accompany the Queen on her jaunts.

Queen Victoria's daily habits became enshrined in a formula. One courtier set it down:

THE QUEEN'S DAILY ROUTINE

FOR OSBORNE: As soon as the weather permits the Queen breakfasts outside in an open marquee. In Summer this is at 10am.

Then Brown brings her private letters, which have been sorted by a lady-in-waiting.

Brown reads the newspapers to her, and discusses current affairs.

A morning ride around Osborne with Brown.

11am. A footman arrives with dispatch boxes of State papers.

The Queen works on them until 1pm.

Afternoon rest.

The afternoon estate ride, or beyond.

The rest of the day occupied by State affairs, meals, receptions.

FOR BALMORAL: The Queen rises early.

Morning walk in the gardens before breakfast, which, if fine, is taken outside the garden cottage.

Brown brings letters.

Queen writes private letters; Brown folds them and seals them in envelopes. Prepares them for postal courier.

Very little State work done at Balmoral. Matters dealt with *ad hoc* through the Minister in Attendance.

Morning and afternoon rides if weather suits.

FOR WINDSOR: Royal Headquarters. Much State Work.
Few allowed into private sitting room where the Queen works at a broad desk. Brown stands guard in corridor outside fending off even the highest in the land.[11]

John Brown was always prompt in his appearance for the daily drives. As E.E.P. Tisdall remarked:

He came to take her for daily drives, morning and afternoon. He pushed aside bowing lackeys in gaudy finery. He was brusque with the ladies who fluttered like frightened chickens in his way. The carriage was his preserve. It was his task to see that the Queen was settled among her cushions, his horny fingers which must ensure that her jacket was buttoned against the wind, his hands which must spread the shawl about her shoulders. Others had tended her as their Queen and mistress. John Brown protected her as she was, a poor, broken-hearted bairn who wanted looking after and taking out of herself.[12]

John Brown quickly settled down to his new pattern of life, first at Osborne, then at the other royal residences. For the rest of his years in royal service he took his daily orders directly from the Queen. Wherever the Queen happened to be John Brown reported to her after breakfast and lunch for his instructions. She found him to be attentive and meticulous in carrying out her commands. She wrote to her uncle, King Leopold of the Belgians: 'It is a real comfort for [Brown] is devoted to me – so simple, so intelligent, so unlike an ordinary servant.'[13]

She was able to confirm her delight to Princess Victoria: '[Brown] is so quiet, has such an excellent head & memory . . . It is an excellent arrangement [having him at Osborne], & I feel I have here always in the House a good, devoted Soul (like your Grant) – whose only object & interest is my service, & God knows how much I want to be taken care of.'[14] This last phrase spells out a vital clue to the developing relationship between Queen Victoria and John Brown, and its future interpretation. Queen Victoria longed to be over-indulged, and fussed over by a man, with the underlying desire to acquiesce to a strong masculinity.

When at Balmoral, Brown also was to be the conduit of any instructions she had for the gillies as she was nervous that some members of her Household – particularly those with military backgrounds – would offend what she took to be Highland sensibilities; she once said to Prince Arthur's governor, Major-General Sir Howard Elphinstone: 'It will never do to speak harshly or dictatorially to Highlanders; their independence and self-respect and proper spirit . . . make them resent that far more than an ordinary . . . English servant.'[15]

Alas, the Highlanders' 'sensibilities' were not a two-way understanding; daily Queen Victoria used John Brown to convey messages to her Household, little realising – or, if she did, ignoring the fact – that John Brown's manner grew gradually more tactless and acerbic. On one occasion Sir Charles Grey, erstwhile secretary to Prince Albert and now on the Queen's own secretariat, was sent a message via John Brown which he delivered in a rude manner. Sir Charles's daughter Louisa, Countess of Antrim, who was in the Queen's service as a Lady-in-Waiting from 1891, recalled: 'My father refused to accept the message in this [rude] form'. Thereafter, the Countess averred, the two men bore each other a grudge.[16]

In relaying the Queen's instructions John Brown would often act without diplomacy or grace. On one occasion he was sent to the billiard-room at Windsor to convey a dinner invitation to the Lords-in-Waiting. Brown pushed open the door, surveyed the company of aristocrats and bawled: 'All what's here dines with the Queen.' The Mayor of Portsmouth once visited Osborne to convey an invitation to the Queen to inspect a force of Volunteers. She did not feel able to do so and sent Brown with her apologies to where the Mayor was waiting in the equerries' room with Sir Henry Ponsonby. Brown, however, in his usual brusque way, informed the startled Mayor: 'The Queen says saretenly not.'

Quite often John Brown's construing of Queen Victoria's orders was idiosyncratic, with the Queen invariably accepting Brown's interpretation when complaints arose among those whom the orders concerned. Her attitude also extended to Brown's brothers on the royal staff, one of whom, Archie, was to cause a major furore.

Prince Leopold George Duncan Albert, Duke of Albany, Queen Victoria's eighth child and fourth son, was born at Buckingham Palace on 7 April 1853. He first met John Brown in 1860, when the gillie took the little Prince for a ride on 'Topsy', with Brown holding the pony's head.[17] In July 1865 John Brown's brother Archie was appointed 'Brusher' – a junior valet – to Prince Leopold; he was chosen for the task by Victoria as Archie was strong enough to carry her haemophiliac son to safety should he get into scrapes.

In April 1865 a quarrel broke out between Archie and Lieutenant Walter George Stirling, a cavalry officer in the Royal Horse Artillery and Prince Leopold's new governor. Exactly what the quarrel was about has long been forgotten, but Stirling's military bearing was considered 'harsh and arrogant' and it is clear that he did not understand the special kid-glove deference that Queen Victoria expected for John Brown and his kin. Stung by Stirling's attitude, the rather dim-witted Archie – who was no match for his elder brother's percipience – complained to John Brown; somewhat disappointed by the tardiness of Archie's promotion to valet, John Brown complained to the Queen.

Stirling would have to go. Leopold's former governor, Major-General Sir Howard Elphinstone, spoke up on Stirling's behalf; could he perhaps be transferred to Prince Arthur's Household? No, the Queen was adamant. Stirling was dismissed with a generous leaving present from the Queen, and a veiled warning that he should not tittle-tattle about the Browns nor comment publicly on the reason for his dismissal. Queen Victoria was already aware of the growing gossip about her and John Brown, and she wanted no fuel to be added to the fire of scandal. Prince Leopold was disappointed and angry at Stirling's dismissal but kept in touch with the officer mostly by letter until the Prince's death at Villa Nevada in 1884.[18] From that day Prince Leopold formed a hatred for John Brown and his family. In a letter to Stirling of 3 September 1868 Leopold wrote of his growing distaste for the Browns:

I am rather in the grumps just now about everything, the way in which I am treated is sometimes too bad (not Mr Duckworth, of course not, he is only too kind to me) but other people. Besides that 'J.B.' is fearfully insolent to me, so is his brother [Archie]; hitting me on the face with spoons for fun, etc – you may laugh at me for all this; but you know I am so sensitive, I know you will feel for me – their impudence increases daily towards everyone.[19]

The Revd Robinson Duckworth, by the by, was tutor to Prince Leopold and was himself later to fall foul of Brown interference. The whole Stirling episode was to add momentum to the growing anti-Brown feeling below stairs. The Household interpreted the removal of Stirling as Queen Victoria supporting an insubordinate servant against a superior; it contributed to falling staff morale.

There were also problems with another of John Brown's brothers. The Queen became annoyed at Donald Brown's truculent attitude and his negligence of his duties. Things were made worse as Donald Brown had regular altercations with his neighbours first at Windsor then Osborne. The Queen commented thus to her physician Dr James Reid:

I am greatly disappointed and shocked to hear of Donald Brown's most extraordinary and improper conduct. He wished to leave Osborne as he could not agree with anyone there when everything had been done to suit his wishes. He has been at the principal gate at Windsor Castle, where the duties are very slight, and where his predecessors have always lived, contented and satisfied. But he does nothing but complain, and to my astonishment and great displeasure I hear that he disobeys orders, interferes with the guard, and refuses to open the gates on the terrace, which all other porters at that gate, where he is, have done. He should feel that it was *entirely out of regard* to his *excellent* eldest [*sic*] brother John that he got the place of Extra Porter, and then, after some years, of Regular Porter. He has been more indulged, and more has been done for him than for any other person in his position, and yet he is never satisfied. This is extremely ungrateful, and besides sets a very bad example to the other servants in a similar position. He must be told *plainly* and *decidedly* that if he does not obey orders which are now conveyed by Lord Edward Clinton, Master of the Household, I shall be obliged to pension him which, for the sake of his brother, I should regret, but he must promise in writing to do what are *his duties*: if he refuses to do so he *must be pensioned.*[20]

It seems that Donald Brown listened to the reasonable fellow-Scot Dr Reid and complied; the Queen chose Reid for this task as the unbending Lord Edward Pelham-Clinton did not understand the perceived royal 'sensibilities' towards Highlanders.

In February 1865 Queen Victoria wrote again to her uncle, King Leopold of the Belgians, telling him that she had firmly decided to keep her 'excellent' Highland servant John Brown to hand 'to attend me always'. Thus John Brown was given the title 'The Queen's Highland Servant', with a salary from the Privy Purse of £120 per annum.[21] A new employment pattern was set out for him in a memorandum dated 4 February 1865. In essence it confirmed that Brown would take his orders directly from the Queen, and none but her; he would be in attendance both outdoors and in. 'He is to continue as before cleaning her boots, skirts and cloaks unless this proves too much.'[22] Ten months later it seems to have proved 'too much' as we find John Brown with someone to clean his boots, and to dry the Queen's dogs when they came in sodden.

The Prince of Wales and Princess Victoria were very much against Brown's appointment as Highland Servant and the memorandum horrified them. They feared that Brown would have too much influence over the Queen, as had her governess and Lady-in-Attendance to 1842, Baroness Louise Lehzen.

The memorandum established a 'status' and 'salary' structure for John Brown that no other servant was to achieve. He was to have holidays if he wished; this meant that he could remain at Balmoral for a few days after the Queen left. In the event he took little time off throughout his royal service. Writing to Princess Victoria from Balmoral on 5 June 1865 Queen Victoria noted: 'As for Brown I never saw such an unselfish servant; he won't take any leave (which I have never seen before in any one male or female, high or low) and my comfort – my service are really his only objects.'[23]

Brown was to have a cottage at Balmoral should he marry. Although he never did marry, Queen Victoria still gave him a cottage 'for retirement';[24] it is called in Gaelic *Baile-na-Coile* ('Town-of-the-Woods') and is situated near Craig Gowan. Although it was furnished with gifts that John Brown accumulated while in royal service he never lived there, yet after his death his coffin rested at the house the night before he was buried at old Crathie churchyard.

By the end of 1866 John Brown's salary was raised to £150, and to £230 in 1869, with an allowance of £70 for clothes; the basic salary was later raised to £310. In 1872, the year John Brown was officially designated 'Esquire', his salary was raised to equal the Household rank of Page of the Backstairs at £400.[25] All this was in accordance with Queen Victoria's growing affection for John Brown: 'You will see', she wrote to him in 1872, 'in this the great anxiety to show more & more what you are to me & as time goes on this will be more & more seen & known. Every one hears me say you are my friend & most confidential attendant.'[26]

While all this was solid advancement for John Brown, it must be remembered that he was always considered by Queen Victoria to be of lesser rank as a servant than Rudolph Löhlein.[27] Because he closely resembled Prince Albert in figure and face, courtiers believed the gossip from Coburg that Löhlein was the Prince's half-brother, the illegitimate offspring of Prince Albert's father Ernest I, Duke of Saxe-Coburg-Gotha. Löhlein had been brought up by a forester on the family estate of Fullbach, near Coburg, and came to Queen Victoria's court in 1847 as Prince Albert's *Jäger*, being promoted to valet in 1860.[28] After Prince Albert's death Queen Victoria made Löhlein her 'Extra Personal Attendant', a post he held until he retired in 1884; he died in 1886. Brown's title, 'The Queen's Highland Servant', did not entirely die with him; on his death it was assumed by his cousin Francis Clark and Brown's brother Hugh became 'Extra Highland Attendant' to assist Clark; on the latter's death the post passed to William Brown.

Brown was a walking encyclopedia of Queen Victoria's likes and dislikes, the latter greatly outweighing the former. What is more, he understood what made the Queen feel *gemütlich*, a word she often used. It has been long rumoured that John Brown kept a 'secret diary' of his life in royal circles.[29] If he did, it has never been publicly identified. Certainly he very soon realised that Queen Victoria was a complex character, her personality shaped in her youth when she was subject to the manipulations of royal factions at her Court, particularly the machinations of her mother's Comptroller Sir John Conroy.

Brown came to understand the Queen's many contradictions of character. She was a fundamentally courageous woman, but Brown found her nervous of a whole range of things, from meeting people she did not know when she was out driving, to simply being alone. In a single morning Brown might observe her being selfless and thoughtless, diplomatic and insensitive, understanding and unloving, forebearing and mean, serene and convulsive. Though clingy, she was every inch a Queen, and an English one at that, though she admitted feeling 'Scotch' at Balmoral. Yet Brown had been surprised, as many others were, that she spoke and wrote flawless German and her Court had many Teutonic aspects.[30]

Brown knew that the Queen disliked bishops, but she had particular respect for John Coleridge Patterson, the first missionary Bishop of Melanesia. To Brown she once said: 'I am sure that the dear Bishop will go straight to Heaven when he dies.' 'Weel, God help him when he meets John Knox,' replied Brown. Victoria's dislikes also included babies and bright lights, the latter providing her main reason for being an unenthusiastic supporter of electricity. Yet she liked sermons, religious services and the activities of her grandchildren. She cared not for people with loud voices, hot rooms, coal fires, motor cars and telephones, although during the latter years of her life she found telephoning more efficacious than her famous written memos – usually of complaint – to Household staff. Of all the personalities at court, the Queen particularly disliked Prime Minister William Ewart Gladstone. Brown was aware of the fact that the Queen disliked Gladstone and had complained that the Prime Minister addressed her as if she were a public meeting. So at one audience when Gladstone was droning on longer than usual, Brown made an attempt to rescue the Queen by blurting out: 'Ye've said enuff.'

The Queen did not approve of the education or indulgence of the working classes, averring that education made them unfit for domestic service or industrial work. Education of women was anathema to her, as was female suffrage, and she was censorious of female fashion that did not please her. Although she never tired of telling people that she was the daughter of a soldier, she disliked anyone who brought what she construed as 'military ways' to her Household. Her interest was always of the keenest when discussing military matters; her involvement included personal approval of promotions of officers above the rank of colonel to changes of uniform; and she was well versed in the history of regiments. She took particular delight at military reviews, with John

Brown sitting on the box of her carriage, in having a running conversation with him on what was happening.

Death duties and income tax were of particular repugnance to the Queen, yet she 'willingly' paid the latter when it was introduced by Prime Minister Robert Peel in 1842. Under the influence of John Brown she became more ambivalent in her extreme disgust of tobacco, making courtiers and honoured guests alike go into the garden to smoke. John Brown arranged for a little ante-room at Balmoral to be used by smokers, and there could be found a group of courtiers in all their finery kneeling in a semi-circle around the fireplace blowing the fumes of their 'filthy habit' up the chimney.[31] One man defied the Queen's 'No Smoking' notices dotted around her homes. Albert, King of Saxony, was a heavy smoker and averred that he could not be without a cigar for long; pulling rank as a king he walked boldly down corridors and staircases puffing confidently, the Household cringing at the thought of the Queen's wrath.[32] Nevertheless, John Brown told the Queen that smoking was a 'good thing' when out in the hills to keep midges away, and at picnics the Queen and Princess Beatrice were seen puffing away at his direction for this purpose.[33]

At Balmoral another of Queen Victoria's dislikes, shooting, was indulged with fervour. Because Prince Albert had been fond of the pastime, it was indulged; because Brown said it was a vital part of Balmoral life for guests and courtiers alike it was humoured. When Princess Helena's husband, Prince Christian of Schleswig-Holstein, lost an eye while shooting alongside the cack-handed Prince Arthur, the Queen was greatly upset and bought her son-in-law a boxed set of glass eyes; one of them was 'bloodshot' for when he had a cold or had indulged too enthusiastically the night before.

From his first days at Osborne then, John Brown began a close study of his royal mistress and in this was to be found the fundamental key to any mystery about his rise to prominence. Queen Victoria craved friendship, and the best kind of all was defined as a knowledge and indulgence of herself; John Brown provided that.

When conducting guests around royal properties like Windsor Castle, Brown would point out portraits and artefacts relevant to the Queen's life, adding snippets of her biography. Pausing before pictures of her babyhood, coronation and marriage he would boom: 'Her Maa–dj-esty was born on 24 May 1819 at Kensington Palace, she's seven years older than me. She ascended the throne on 20 June 1837 on the death of her uncle, a silly buddy by all accounts, and was crowned at Westminster Abbey on 23 June 1838. She married Prince Albert at the Crown room, St James's Palace, on 10 February 1840; the Queen and me remembers all these anniversaries.'[34]

Queen Victoria began to be more aware and more indulgent of John Brown's 'Highland sensibilities'. Curiously, she started to plot her foreign excursions to avoid places where he was not accepted or welcomed. For instance, after King Leopold of the Belgians died in 1865, she began to re-route her entourage on its way to the German Court, usually via Brussels, to Paris and Cherbourg instead. Why? John Brown's true worth and position had not been recognised by the Belgian Court, which had not arranged for Brown to have his own suite of rooms near her own.

John Brown disliked foreigners, their tongue, their scenery, their food and their effluvia. His distaste prevented the Queen from enjoying to the full the pleasures of her jaunts abroad, or from being adventurous, as he transplanted her routines of Balmoral to such locations as Baveno. The heat made him feel ill, and fearing the assassination of his royal mistress he discouraged the stopping of her carriage for her to enjoy vistas.

Paris was quite different. The French, considering all *rosbifs* to be completely mad, understood what they took to be British royal eccentricity and treated Brown with dignity. In due time President François Paul Jules Grévy accorded John Brown a special bow of recognition. Brown was particularly taken with the English-educated Anglo-French National Assembly Member William Henry Waddington, who once called on the Queen at the British Embassy in Paris. Waddington's wife recalled that Brown and Waddington 'shook hands, and Brown begged him to come to Scotland, where he would receive a hearty welcome'.[35]

From time to time John Brown would give the Queen little gifts. On one occasion he produced 'a dozen cheap egg-cups of gay and florid design'.[36] To the complete surprise of her ladies, the Queen accepted the garish utensils with the delight that she had usually reserved for

Prince Albert's little *Geschenk* (gifts) which he usually inscribed *Meiner theuren Victoria von Ihrem treuen Albert* (To My dear Victoria from her faithful Albert). The egg-cups were used every Sunday on the Queen's breakfast table, until they were finally all broken years after John Brown's death.

The year 1866 was to bring Queen Victoria many changes, which she had always hated. Yet it was also a turning-point in her widowhood. To a certain extent her grief for Albert was abating, but still she remained reclusive by temperament. It was her paramount wish, she informed her dearest friends, to 'throw everything up and retire into private life', with the intent of working for the 'poor and sick'.[37] She told her old friend Augusta of Saxe-Weimar, Queen-Empress of Prussia: 'My political and queenly tasks are the hardest for me . . . Only a sense of duty and the knowledge that my Angel [Prince Albert] wishes it and that I must answer to him, force me to carry this out.'[38]

The Queen's sense of duty was strengthened by her disappointment in what she saw as the fatuous and immoral nature of her eldest son, the Prince of Wales; daily he convinced her of his unfitness to rule. Yet John Brown's influence encouraged the Queen to see that her grief from the past could be a shrine to which she might return from time to time, but need not be a jail in which she permanently lived.

Domestically the Queen now had to face important changes in her Household. Prince Albert's former private secretary Sir Charles Phipps became a private secretary to her in parallel, but not very harmoniously, with General Charles Grey. Sir Thomas Biddulph, Master of the Household, was appointed joint Keeper of the Privy Purse with General Grey, with Biddulph concentrating on the financial aspects of the role, while Sir John Cowell took up the post of Master of the Household. All were to cross swords from week to week with John Brown, who remained well and truly secure from change as the Queen's most trusted servant. Brown appeared wherever she did in public, stood by her chair as she worked to keep her free from interruption, and to her other servants' great amusement walked behind her with a plaid over his arm to which were pinned the Queen's memos, messages and missives.[39]

On 6 February 1866, in a state of nervous agitation, Queen Victoria went in procession to the opening of Parliament; this was the first time she had done so since Albert's death. In March she attended a military review, again for the first time since the Prince died. She had once enthusiastically enjoyed these reviews, dressed in a scarlet tunic with a general's sash and hat plume, and riding her bay 'Alma', a scene immortalised by the painter George Housman Thomas. This time she attended in her carriage, with John Brown on the rumble seat. One paper recorded: 'Gillie Brown seems by degrees to have fallen into the position in the household of the Queen such as was occupied by Roustaen, the Mameluke, near the person of Napoleon the Great.'[40]

More nervous agitation was to assail the Queen on Thursday 5 July, the wedding day of Princess Helena to Prince Christian of Schleswig-Holstein, fifteen years her senior, at the private chapel at Windsor Castle. In the crowd massed in the corridor outside the Queen's bedroom, where Princess Helena was dressing, stood John Brown in Highland dress. Queen Victoria was 'firmer' in her confidence when she travelled by royal train to Wolverhampton to unveil Thomas Thornycroft's equestrian statue of Prince Albert on 30 November. Among the postilions in Ascot livery stood John Brown in Highland dress, this time wearing the black crape ribbon with its purple silk band bearing the legend 'In Memory of Prince Albert'.

In this year of 1866 the railway line to Ballater was opened, but for a long time the Queen would never use it, because Prince Albert had never been associated with it.[41] The Queen did not have her own waiting room at Ballater until 1889. Throughout her life the Queen remained afraid of railway accidents, and commanded that the royal train should go no faster than 50 miles per hour. Once the Queen sent John Brown down the platform, when the royal train had stopped at Wigan, with a message for the driver to slow down; to this message Brown added: 'Her Maa-dj-esty says the carriage was shaking like the Devil.'

On 26 June 1866 the Liberal government led by John, 1st Earl Russell, fell over the defeat of the Reform Bill. The Queen put pressure on Russell to remain in his post; after all, Prussia had just declared war on Austria and the monarch insisted that her ministers 'should not abandon their posts' at this crucial time. Yet, even as the Tory Edward Stanley, 14th Earl of Derby, was forming a new government on 28 June the Queen departed for Balmoral. The establishment was appalled at what they regarded as the monarch's hypocrisy and dereliction of duty; on every hand the Queen was criticised: 'If she will not work, she should abdicate', said many in high places. And placards bearing the words 'What do we pay her for?' appeared on London's thoroughfares.

'John Brown will not let her [leave Balmoral]', the just-resigned Prime Minister's daughter-in-law Lady Russell wrote in her diary, echoing the growing awareness that the Highland servant was exerting power over the Queen. One who knew this to be untrue was Lord Derby's Leader in the House of Commons and Chancellor of the Exchequer, the flamboyant 62-year-old Jew-turned-Christian Benjamin Disraeli, whom Queen Victoria elevated to the earldom of Beaconsfield in 1876.

Disraeli was to become a prominent figure in the John Brown story; he knew how to handle Brown, as he did the Queen. Flattery was his main weapon. Queen Victoria's grand-daughter Princess Marie Louise, daughter of Princess Christian of Schleswig-Holstein, remembered a young woman being 'taken in to dinner one night by Gladstone and, the following night, by Disraeli. She was asked what impression these two celebrated men had on her. She replied thoughtfully, 'When I left the dining-room after sitting next to Mr. Gladstone I thought he was the cleverest man in England. But after sitting next to Mr Disraeli I thought I was the cleverest woman in England!'[43] Whenever they met, Disraeli, who succeeded Derby as Prime Minister in 1868, was more than polite to Brown, who was an ardent Tory and actually sent Disraeli salmon he had caught himself in the Dee. Disraeli and John Brown had one thing in common in their handling of the Queen: both treated her as a woman, they fussed over and cajoled her, and fed her titbits of gossip. And like her two 'in-laws', Princess Helena of Waldeck-Pyrmont, wife of Prince Leopold, and Prince Henry of Battenberg, husband of Princess Beatrice, they were not 'overawed' by her.

As journalists looked round for stories to cater for the developing interest in royal activities, John Brown began to be talked about more and more. In July 1866 genuine stories were a little thin on the ground and the editors of the well-established weekly satirical magazine *Punch; or the London Charivari*, which had first appeared on Saturday 17 July 1841, thought they would pull the collective leg of the public with a spoof 'Court Circular'. On 7 July they published this 'royal bulletin':

Balmoral, Tuesday.
Mr John Brown walked on the slopes.
He subsequently partook of haggis.
In the evening Mr John Brown was pleased to listen to a bagpipe.
Mr John Brown retired early.

Thus *Punch* was the first publication to sneer at John Brown. But the flames of gossip were to be further fanned as the crowds flocked to the 99th Royal Academy Spring Exhibition on 6 May 1867. Many people, who had never been to such an exhibition before, were perplexed by a large painting by Sir Edwin Landseer entitled 'Her Majesty at Osborne in 1866'.[44] For the first time that anyone could remember the Queen's picture provoked sniggers and outright laughter as visitors stood before it. One critic wrote: 'If anyone will stand by this picture for a quarter of an hour and listen to the comments of visitors he will learn how great an imprudence has been committed.'[45]

The picture showed the Queen, dressed in severe mourning, facing right and reading a letter while mounted on her pony 'Flora'. Behind, the viewer's eye is directed up the path to the terrace at Osborne, where on the tower the clock stands at a minute or two after 3pm. The Queen's gloves, letters and red state papers box lie on the ground and nearby are her Border collie 'Sharp' and her Skye terrier 'Prince'. On a seat on the grass, behind, sit the Princesses Louise and Helena. But what people flocked to see was the black-kilted figure of John Brown holding the horse's head.

The gossip machine engaged a higher gear. So all the rumours were true? The secret was out; this was how Her Majesty spent her spare time, with the hired help! The critics were unanimous: 'We trust it will be deemed no disloyalty either to the sovereign or to the reputation of the painter to say . . . there is not one of Her Majesty's subjects will see this lugubrious picture without regret.'[46] In contrast, the Queen was delighted with the picture and ordered that an engraving be made of it for immediate reproduction; for this John Brown's beard was trimmed to suit his current shaving fashion! By the time the genre painter George Housman Thomas painted 'The Visit to the Mausoleum' in 1869, again showing Queen Victoria in mourning and riding on 'Flora' alongside Princesses Helena and Louise, with John Brown at the pony's head, the public were becoming used to a more public persona for John Brown.[47]

These were two of a series of 'John Brown royal portraits'. In 1875 the Hungarian-born painter Heinrich von Angeli was commissioned by Queen Victoria to paint a head and shoulders portrait of John Brown; the likeness had to be taken from a photograph as Brown refused to sit. There were also several pictures of John Brown painted posthumously: 'John Brown at Frogmore' was produced in 1883 by the German portrait painter Carl Rudolph Sohn, while animal painter Charles Burton Baxter painted two versions of 'John Brown with Dogs at Osborne', again in 1883.[48]

John Brown paid no attention to the increased gossip engendered by his portrait and got on with his royal duties, which included a self-appointed position as Queen's entertainer when he felt she needed to be lifted out of depression. Brown was instrumental in introducing Queen Victoria to the subtleties of Scottish customs, many of them with distinct Highland variations. The Queen was to remember particularly the Hallowe'ens of 1866 and 1867. From the Revd Dr Norman MacLeod, the Queen was to learn that the early Christian Church in Scotland had grafted a Christian festival on to a pagan one. So the Scots Hallowe'en – the Feast of All Hallows' (or All Saints') Eve was grafted on to the ancient Celtic festival of *Samhuinn*, which marked the beginning of the Celtic year and the return of cattle to the fold from their winter grazing. It was a time in Scotland's folklore year when ghosts, witches and fairies were deemed to be abroad. Underlining the eeriness of Hallowe'en John Brown read to the Queen Sir Walter Scott's lines:

On Hallowmass Eve, ere ye boune to rest,
Ever beware that your couch be blest;
Sign it with cross and sain it with bead,
Sing the Ave and say the Creed.

For on Hallowmass Eve the Nighthag shall ride,
And all her nine-fold sweeping on by her side,
Whether the wind sing lowly or loud,
Stealing through moonshine or swathed in a cloud.

He that dare sit in St Swithin's Chair
When the Nighthag wings the troubled air,
Questions three, when he speaks the spell,
He may ask and she must tell.

As a true Calvinist John Brown had no truck with such 'popish practices' but he told the Queen that he remembered the Highland mothers singing this ditty in Gaelic at Hallowe'en:

Hallowe'en will come, will come;
Witchcraft will be set a-going;
Fairies will be at full speed,
Running in every pass.
Avoid the road, children, children![49]

During a visit to Head Keeper John Grant's mother on 31 October 1866, Queen Victoria noted how the local children paraded for her with burning torches and how Hallowe'en bonfires were lit across the Dee from Balmoral which 'had a very pretty effect'. Next year the Queen, Jane, Lady Ely, Princess Louise and Prince Leopold, with the keepers and their wives and children, all led by John Brown, and carrying torches, processed around Balmoral Castle while Piper Ross played his bagpipes. It was Brown, too, who encouraged the Queen to keep up the age-old practice of 'Burning the Witch' at Balmoral. Quoting an old text, the folklorist Florence Marian McNeill recorded the event:

A huge bonfire was kindled in front of the castle, opposite the main doorway. The clansmen were mustered, arrayed in Highland garb. At a signal, headed by a band, they marched towards the palace. The bonfire was kindled so as to be in full blaze when the procession reached it. The interest of the promenade was centred on a trolley on

which there sat the effigy of a hideous old woman or witch called the
Shandy Dann. Beside her crouched one of the party holding her
erect while the march went forward to the bagpipes' strain. As the
building came in sight, the pace was quickened to a run, then a
sudden halt was made a dozen yards or so from the blaze. Here, amid
breathless silence, an indictment is made why this witch should be
burned to ashes, and with no one to appear on her behalf – only this
advocatus diaboli, paper in hand – she is condemned to the flames.
With a rush and a shout and the skirling of bagpipes, the sledge, and
its occupants are hurled topsy-turvy into the fire, whilst the
mountaineer springs from the car at the latest safe instant. There
follow cheers and hoots of derisive laughter, as the inflammable
wrappings of the Shandy Dann crackle and splutter out.

All the while the residents of the Castle stand enjoying this curious
rite, and no one there entered more heartily into it than the Head of
the Empire herself.[50]

By 1867 resentment towards John Brown was growing both at court
and in political circles. Most of the Queen's immediate family disliked
John Brown and his brothers, with the Prince of Wales and Prince
Leopold being his chief opponents. Princess Louise, the Queen's fourth
daughter and sixth child, also had a grumbling resentment of the
Highland Servant. This was to come to a head around the time that the
Queen summoned Edgar Boehm to Balmoral to prepare a bust of John
Brown. Boehm was there for three months and formed a distinct and
negative opinion of Brown.[51] At this time Princess Louise was
unmarried, in her twenties and delighted in flirting. She formed a
certain passion for Boehm while he gave her 'modelling lessons' and
'they became intimate, through not to the extent of actual love-
making'.[52]

It seems that on one occasion Queen Victoria joined John Brown to
witness Boehm at work on the servant's bust, and they walked in on the
sculptor and the Princess embracing. The Queen was furious and
upbraided her daughter. Princess Louise, in her anger, accused John
Brown of spying on her and running to the Queen with tittle-tattle.
The Princess added that she would not put up with Brown's insolence.
John Brown's supposedly impertinent remarks were the subject of

regular complaints brought to the Queen by her children.

This incident added some urgency to Queen Victoria's determination to get the highly sexed Princess Louise safely married. Her choice of husband, however, was a disastrous one for the Princess. John Ian Campbell, Marquis of Lorne (1845–1914), eldest son of George, 8th Duke of Argyll and his Duchess Elizabeth, was widely accepted as a homosexual. Life together after their marriage at St George's Chapel, Windsor, on 21 March 1871 was a long trail of misery. To their wedding present from the royal domestic servants John Brown contributed a hefty 30 guineas, whereas Sir Henry Ponsonby only added 10 guineas.

> *On Politics*
> As a staunch Highland Tory, John Brown had little time for Liberal Prime Minister Gladstone. He was particularly incensed by government policy in 1872 and during a discussion with Sir Henry Ponsonby on the subject remarked in reply to Sir Henry's observation that Brown wanted the Liberals out: 'A good thing too, the sooner they go the better. That Gladstone's half a Roman [Catholic] and the others had better be gone. We canna have a worse lot.'

Should Brown's generosity have been intended to impress the Princess, it failed, and the reverse was the result. Pointedly she commented: 'I don't want an absurd man in a kilt following me everywhere.'[53] Princess Louise was to remain childless and in 1900 Lorne became the 9th Duke of Argyll.

Although she was probably entirely innocent of adultery, or even of fornication before marriage, the hot-house atmosphere of Queen Victoria's court gossip, wherein John Brown was a leading contributor, linked Princess Louise with a series of men as well as Boehm. There was Colonel (later General Sir) John McNeill, one of their suite when her husband became Governor-General of Canada, architect Sir Edwin Lutyens, and Colonel William Probert, her equerry. There was also another man who would regularly cross swords with Brown and later became a principal Brown detractor. This was Colonel (later Sir) Arthur Bigge, whom Queen Victoria had appointed as groom-in-waiting.[54] Bigge's duties at Balmoral, in particular, were undemanding and were an easy billet after his career in the Royal Artillery. On one occasion Bigge was relaxing in a Balmoral ante-room when John Brown entered and smugly announced: 'Waal, ye'll not be going fishing today,' adding, 'Her Maa–dj–esty thinks it's about time ye did some work.'[55] From that day Bigge bore Brown a grudge.

Sir Frederick Ponsonby, Treasurer to King George V and Keeper of the Privy Purse to King George VI, recalled a 'JB incident' concerning Princess Louise's supposed lover Colonel McNeill. John Brown entered the equerries' room at Osborne House one day with a message from the Queen concerning a set of carriages that she wanted made ready. Brown hovered, waiting for a reply after delivering the message, and was told by the brusque McNeill to wait outside while he prepared the order for the coaches.

Brown complained to the Queen that McNeill had been 'over-bearing in his manner' and 'had shouted at him as if he was a common soldier'. A few hours later McNeill received a memo from Queen Victoria enquiring if he wished for a posting to India. She suggested that such a position was a definite demotion. Puzzled by the Queen's memo, he took it to his father, Sir John Carstairs McNeill, an old Indian campaigner. Sir John worked out the Queen's intent and advised his son to reply to the Queen accepting the post. He should add that as colleagues and friends would enquire why he was leaving royal service, could the Queen supply him with the reason for his being offered India. The Queen made no response and Colonel McNeill remained at his post. For a number of years thereafter the Queen did not speak to him and made sure that his duties never brought him to Balmoral or Osborne where she would have to meet him.[56]

There were to be more serious examples of opposition to Brown. One such became notorious in political circles. Queen Victoria intended to have John Brown ride on the box of her carriage at the Review of the Troops in Hyde Park on 5 July 1867. The Prime Minister, the 14th Earl of Derby, with some trepidation suggested to the Queen that the growing dislike for Brown might cause scenes of an 'unpleasant nature' if he took such a prominent place at the Review. Queen Victoria was immediately annoyed at the suggestion. She wrote of her irritation to her equerry Lord Charles Fitzroy: 'The Queen [she usually wrote of herself in the third person] is much astonished and shocked at an attempt being made by some people to prevent her faithful servant going with her to the Review in Hyde Park, thereby making the poor, nervous shaken Queen, who is so accustomed to his watchful care and intelligence, terribly nervous and uncomfortable . . . what it all means she does not know . . .'[57]

Lord Derby wrote to General Sir Charles Grey that he had been informed by the erstwhile Liberal MP, Lord Edward Berkley Portman, that a hostile reception for Brown was being planned by the lawyer and political agitator Edmund Beales and his 'roughs' of the Reform League. How was such an embarrassment to be headed off, asked Derby? Could Brown have 'some slight ailment' which would necessitate his falling out of the duty? Should Brown be approached in such a way, Grey knew he would immediately complain to the Queen. Grey bit the bullet and told the Queen of the intent to hold anti-Brown demonstrations. 'The Queen will not be dictated to', she replied, using one of her favourite phrases of late. She did, however, withdraw her objections to Brown not being there. The problem resolved itself: Derby cancelled the Review as the Queen went into deep mourning following the assassination of her Hapsburg kinsman Ferdinand-Joseph Maximilian, Emperor of Mexico, at Queretaro in Mexico on 19 July, by republican leader Benito Pablo Juárez.

Despite all this aggravation, the comforting presence of John Brown was always appreciated on Queen Victoria's more poignant occasions. One such occurred on Tuesday 15 October 1867, the twenty-eighth anniversary of her 'blessed engagement day' to Prince Albert in 1839. On that rainy morning Queen Victoria was to unveil a statue of Prince Albert at Balmoral, just above Middleton's Lodge. The statue was a gift from the Queen to the Balmoral tenantry. As Queen Victoria and Jane Ely, her Lady of the Bedchamber, sat in the royal carriage soaked by the deluging rain, with the 93rd Highlanders drawn up alongside the crowd of servants and tenants, John Brown's stentorian voice rose above the others in a verse of the 100th Psalm. A bedraggled Revd Dr Taylor said a short prayer and the statue was unveiled after some snagging of the cover. After the soldiers had presented arms, the pipers played, and the Queen gazed sadly at 'the dear noble figure of my beloved one, who used to be with us here in the prime of beauty, goodness, and strength'; the Balmoral Commissioner Dr Robertson then made a speech on behalf of the servants and tenants. As the gunsmoke of a *feu de joie* spread over the crowd, John Brown sprang on to the box and the royal party drove away to the sound of God Save the Queen, 'sung extremely well' noted the Queen.[58]

Anyone describing Queen Victoria's life in 1868 would probably have settled on the word 'sedentary'. By this date the Queen had become ruddy of complexion and obese of figure, with round bulging cheeks, more than one chin and exopthalmic eyes. Her lethargic days were regulated by a strict routine and a round of large meals interlarded with pralines, fondants and dainties ever to hand. Her life was one of self-indulgence and her idiosyncratic view of the world coloured her relationships with people. She did not welcome visitors gladly and became irritable if jolted from her daily habits. Her crankiness increased if she was not constantly attended by familiar faces – her daughters, her German dresser Emilie Dettweiler, her Scots wardrobe-maid Annie Macdonald and the ubiquitous John Brown. Some evenings she would sit at her spinning wheel in pure contentment with her favourite minister, the Revd Dr Norman MacLeod, reading to her from Scott or Burns. For those around her it was a life of relentless boredom; the one person who truly thrived on this humdrum existence was John Brown, content in his own 'kingdom'.

At Balmoral the Queen often went to Glassalt Shiel ('cottage of the grey burn'); the 'cottage' was really a fifteen-roomed house at the western end of Loch Muick, on Abergeldie land, which she had had built in 1868. The housewarming for Glassalt Shiel was a bittersweet occasion for the Queen. Amid the reels and merrymaking, the 'whisky toddy' and the oatcakes, the Queen 'thought of the happy past and my darling husband'.[59] She called the building 'the first Widow's House', but brightened up when John Brown begged her to drink a toast to the 'first fire kindling'. This was in accord with the old Highland superstition that a well-tended and toasted first blaze in the hearth of a new house would assure 'long life' to all who dwelt therein.

At Glassalt Shiel the Queen kept house with just a few familiar servants to look after her and with her reluctant family to entertain her. All were guarded at night by a single policeman. Her secretary, Sir Henry Ponsonby, actively deplored her retirement to this secluded place, where the Glassalt Burn tumbled down the White Mounth of Prince Albert's favourite wild spot. But regularly the Queen would issue from it with her tiny entourage to picnic in the hills with Brown fussing over the tea kettle or watching from a knoll with his telescope for the possible approach of unwelcome ramblers or – most hated of all – journalists. While muttering over the inconvenience of contacting the Queen on state business when she was at Glassalt Shiel, Ponsonby admitted she was brighter and more approachable after staying there. In the year she built Glassalt Shiel, the Queen was to give the world a remarkable insight into her private life.

CHAPTER FOUR

ALL THE SECRETS
OF THE UNIVERSE

Queen Victoria trusted John Brown to be discreet, as she said, with 'all the secrets of the universe', her daily routines, highs and lows, arguments and happy events, Court intrigues and confidences, yet she herself was to hand to her nation titbits about her personal life, sanitised of course by her own romantic imagery. Not since the publication in 1832 of the volume *Secret History of the Court of England*, by Lady Anne Hamilton, had the curtains been parted on Court life.[1]

In 1867 Queen Victoria published privately her *Leaves from the Journal of Our Life in the Highlands, From 1848 to 1861*, dedicated to Prince Albert, and circulated it to selected friends. Recipients like Dean Gerald Wellesley urged her to make her writings available to a wider readership. With some hesitation, the Queen handed over her holograph manuscript to Arthur Helps, Clerk of the Privy Council. An accomplished writer, Helps had already assisted the Queen with the preparation of *Speeches and Addresses of the Prince Consort*, which appeared in 1862. Helps produced an edited manuscript, without 'references to political questions, or to the affairs of government', and this persuaded the Queen to go ahead with general publication, in 1868, including additional material on 'Earlier visits to Scotland, and Tours in England and Ireland, and Yachting Excursions'.

The clincher for a wider publication of her writings is further thought to have come from a visit to Sir Walter Scott's old home at Abbotsford, as part of a tour of the Scottish Borders during 20–4 August 1867. She was staying at the time at Floors Castle, near Kelso, the home of the 6th Duke and Duchess of Roxburghe. At Abbotsford the royal party was hosted by James Hope-Scott and his second wife, the Queen's god-daughter Lady Victoria Fitzalan-Howard. In Sir

Walter's old study the Queen signed her name in the great man's journal 'which I felt it to be a presumption for me to do', she later wrote.[2] A press report of the time noted: 'The royal party then proceeded to the dining-room, where fruits, ices, and other refreshments had been prepared, and Her Majesty partook only of a cup of tea and "Selkirk bannock".'[3]

Queen Victoria had been introduced to the works of Sir Walter Scott by her German governess Baroness Lehzen, and included in her large collection of dressed dolls some inspired by his *Kenilworth* (1821). Reading aloud from Scott was very much a part of Balmoral evening pastimes. Sir Walter had met the Queen on 19 May 1828, during the festivities for her ninth birthday; Scott had dined at Kensington Palace at the invitation of the Duchess of Kent, and later wrote of the Princess Victoria: 'She is fair, like the Royal Family, but does not look as if she would be pretty.'[4]

Scott's descriptions of Scottish scenery greatly appealed to the Queen's romantic sensibilities and his portrayal of the noble, independent, loyal Highlander, in books such as *Rob Roy* (1818), echoed the Queen's opinions. For her, John Brown was the epitome of a Scott character. So taken was she by Scott's way of looking at all things Scottish, and so interested in his life, especially after reading his son-in-law John Gibson Lockhart's *Narrative of the Life of Sir Walter Scott* (1848), that she was determined to have a Border Terrier dog like Scott's own. So in 1850 two pups were delivered to the Queen at Windsor by the Lockhart family friend Sir Edwin Landseer from the kennels at Abbotsford.

Bound in embossed moss-green covers, decorated with antler motifs in gold, Queen Victoria's *Leaves* appeared in January 1868 and rapidly sold 20,000 copies; it was to run through several editions, notching up 100,000 sales and several translations. The Queen dedicated the work to Prince Albert with the words: 'To the dear memory of him who made the life of the writer bright and happy.' The considerable royalties accrued were donated to various charities. On 1 January 1869 she wrote to Theodore Martin:

The Queen thanks Mr Martin very much for his two letters and for the cheque which she has sent this day to Mr Helps. She quite

approves of what he intends doing with the remaining £4016 6s. Of
this the Queen would wish him to send her a cheque for £50, which
she wishes to give away. £2516 she wishes absolutely to devote to a
charity such as she spoke of, and the remaining £1450 she wishes to
keep for other gifts of a charitable nature, at least to people who are
not rich. Would Mr Martin just keep an account of sums he sends
her so that we may know how and at what time the money has been
disposed of? The Queen will keep a copy of the names which she
does not wish others to know . . .[5]

Among the 'names' mentioned were local Balmoral and Crathie folk
brought to her notice by John Brown. Brown was in regular contact
with his relatives around Crathie and had regular letters from them
informing him about events at home. Snippets of gossip from these
letters he related to the Queen.

General readers – and in the Britain of the mid-nineteenth century,
this meant the middle classes – were fascinated by the Queen's
revelations of her life in Scotland from 1842 to her widowhood in
1861, and were particularly interested in what she wrote in the
footnotes, which included a range of gossipy details about her servants.
The most controversy was caused by twenty-one separate references to
John Brown, describing what she saw as his strong points – all 'peculiar
to the Highland race'. The Prince of Wales complained to his mother
that Brown and other Highland servants were mentioned but he was
not. He received a terse reply from the Queen listing the pages on
which he was mentioned.

The Queen attributed the success of her 'simple record' of family life
to the artlessness of its narrative, its obvious representation of married
life and the cordial relationship with her Highland servants. Its
popularity, she believed, was an endorsement of her way of life, which
she was determined not to change. For these reasons Sir Howard
Elphinstone suggested that the book should be issued in an inexpensive
edition 'to clinch the Queen's love affair with the middle classes'.[6]

The book's aristocratic detractors, such as the Whig peer Antony
Ashley-Cooper, 7th Earl of Shaftesbury, far outnumbered Elphinstone.
Ashley-Cooper, a former junior minister, rubbished it at every
opportunity at his London club. The royal family were appalled by such

public comment and Lady Augusta Stanley summed up the feelings of most of the aristocracy. In particular they were dismissive of the book's numerous footnotes detailing the lives of servants and giving them credibility as gentlefolk. The comment in the magisterial Tory literary and political magazine *Quarterly Review* singularly stung Lady Augusta; it had noted that 'only with <u>Scottish servants</u> [sarcastically underlined] one could be on such blessed terms!' Lady Augusta wrote: 'These ignorant stupid remarks are calculated to do great harm to our Dear One . . .'[7]

Punch noted that the book was nothing more than the clash of tea trays. Because it dwelt mainly on her leisure moments the volume led to a public belief that Queen Victoria had little to do. In truth, a glance at John Brown's daily schedules reveals that a large part of the Queen's day was spent at her desk, with interludes for meals and exercise. Even her leisure time was rigorously organised, as 'Dear Albert' would have wished no moment to be idly spent.

Although there were numerous references to John Brown in the *Leaves*, certain incidents, all well known to the Queen, were left out. For example, during the autumn tour of the Scottish Borders in 1867, the growing national regard for John Brown did not go unnoticed. One journalist made it his particular brief to monitor the Highland Servant's movements. As the royal train puffed into the 'prettily decorated' Kelso station, on the Berwick–Kelso branch of the North British Railway, the reporter noticed how John Brown leapt with great speed from his reserved railway compartment and 'But for the intervention of the Duke and Duchess of Roxburghe, the Duke of Buccleugh, and other distinguished company on the platform, the stalwart Highlander would have conducted his sovereign across the platform and through the triumphal arch to the royal carriage at the outside of the station.' Pushing his way through the crowd, the reporter kept his eye on John Brown: 'John, who was dressed in full Highland costume, seemed immensely proud of his position; and it was certainly amusing in the extreme to see him now and again, with a broad grin, bowing his acknowledgements for the cheers raised for Her Majesty, some of which he probably thought were intended for himself.'[8]

To the consternation of the 'duty' courtiers Sir Thomas Biddulph, Keeper of the Privy Purse, equerry Lord Charles Fitzroy, and Colonel

Charles Gordon, two prominent banners were stretched across the
Wool Market. They proclaimed: 'WELCOME TO THE BORDERS –
JOHN BROWN' and 'GOD SAVE THE QUEEN – JOHN BROWN'.
A quick conversation with the Provost of Kelso elicited the fact that
the said 'John Brown' was a local shopkeeper bent on opportunistic
publicity. But the 'real' John Brown was now seen as good newspaper
copy and when the Queen visited the nearby ruins of the medieval
Cistercian Abbey of St Mary at Melrose, the journalists ignored the
royal party and threaded their way through the tombstones in the
wake of Brown who was getting 'a good view of the abbey's
architectural beauties'. Queen Victoria's *Leaves* was to be parodied the
year after John Brown's death. In 1884 a 77-page satirical version
appeared in New York under the pseudonym of 'Kenwood Philp' an
Irish Land League member. Supported by a series of cartoons, the
paperback volume was entitled *John Brown's Legs or Leaves from
a Journal in the Lowlands*. The publication carried the dedication:
'To the memory of those extraordinary Legs, poor bruised and
scratched darlings . . .' as a direct sneer at Queen Victoria's numerous
mentions of John Brown's legs being injured as he jumped down from
her carriage.

The volume offered to the public a mockery of all that Queen
Victoria held dear about her Highland servant, composed in the style of
her own writings:

> We make it a point to have breakfast every morning of our lives . . .
> Brown pushed me (in a hand-carriage) up quite a hill and then ran
> down again. He did this several times and we enjoyed it very much
> . . . He then put me in a boat on the lake and rocked me for about
> half an hour. It was very exhilarating.

The text reverses John Brown's political views and has him declare: 'I'm
a Leeberal in politics.'[7] It shows him swearing in the Queen's presence,
making her cry with his rudeness, and denouncing Benjamin Disraeli
with the racist comment 'd——d Sheeny'. Here too is Queen Victoria
sending a command to the Poet Laureate, Lord Tennyson, to compose a
sonnet commemorating Brown's legs as 'no nobler theme ever inspired
the pen of genius'.

Picking up on Queen Victoria's carriage accident in 1863, the author has Brown tending the Queen's staved thumb. When he grows a wart on his own thumb, the Queen, escorted by forty-two Highlanders, processes to his cottage to give succour in 'fine old whisky'. Brown's excesses of familiarity are rewarded with a beating from the Prince of Wales. At last a missive is received from New York noting that the Fenian leader, one 'O'Donovan Rossa', is sailing to Britain to assassinate John Brown. Thus the Highland Servant – 'The Legs' – are seen scampering away from 'Windsoral', never to be seen again.

Despite her courtiers' disparaging remarks, Queen Victoria continued to promote what she saw as the nobility of her Highland staff. Prior to the appearance of *Leaves*, she had commissioned the Royal Scottish Academician Kenneth Macleay Jr to produce a series of watercolours of her Balmoral retainers. This series developed into the published portfolio *Highlanders of Scotland: Portraits illustrative of the principal Clans and followings, and the Retainers of the Royal Household at Balmoral*. The text was written by the 6th Duke of Atholl's cousin Miss Amelia Murray MacGregor, long-time companion and friend of Duchess Anne; the Queen had met Miss MacGregor on her jaunts to Blair Atholl.[9]

Herein John Brown is shown among the denizens of the great clans of Scotland, depicted in 'the grey jacket, kilt and hose of half-mourning instituted for him by Queen Victoria after the death of the Prince Consort'.[10] Sporting a royal blue cravat, gold watch and fob, a dirk in his right stocking and a folded plaid over his right arm, Brown looks more like a mannequin than a hard-working gillie. His brothers William and Archibald appear on other plates, both similarly dressed. If the volume raised eyebrows in royal circles because of its blatant promotion of Queen Victoria's Highland servants, more was to come.

For some time before the publication of *Leaves*, Queen Victoria had been anxious to show her family and his detractors at Court that John Brown, with what she saw as his noble mien, was not of common stock. To this end she instructed her Commissioner at Balmoral, Dr Robertson, to prepare a biographical memorandum on Brown.

Dr Andrew Robertson knew John Brown well and crossed swords with him on a number of occasions. Dr Robertson had practised medicine in the Crathie area for many years and was probably the best-known individual within a radius of 50 miles from Balmoral.[11] Originally from the Aberdeenshire village of Tarland, some 7 miles north of Aboyne, Dr Robertson had actually delivered John Brown as well as a generation of Crathie babies before his appointment as Queen's Commissioner at Balmoral in 1848. Through the Shaws of Badenoch it is likely that the Robertson and Brown family trees shared a branch or two.

Dr Robertson's memorandum survives in a fine four-page copperplate edition.[12] It is dated 'Balmoral, June 2nd, 1865', when Dr Robertson began his researches, and is written in the third person. Dr Robertson fashioned the content to appeal to the Queen's sensibilities. This is what it says:

> The following is a brief outline of the Ancestry of John Brown –
>
> Dr R. is unable to extend this *history* beyond the G.G.Father of *John*
>
> James Shaw, better known on Deeside by the cognomen of Captain Shaw, was the second son of a small proprietor in Badenoch. The paternal Acres were not very numerous, but they were deemed sufficient to allow him to rejoice in the title of *Laird Shaw* – The family consisted of two sons and one daughter – The second son James, was the G.G.Father of John Brown, and Janet the Daughter, was the Maternal Grand Mother of Dr Robertson.
>
> James Shaw was a remarkably handsome man, and in his younger days, was celebrated for his prowess in all the Athletic Games and Exercises of the day. He was of a warm generous disposition, possessing all the high and chivalrous feelings of the Highland Gentlemen. It was said of him, that he was never known to desert a 'friend or turn his back on a foe'.
>
> Dr Robertson when very young remembers seeing him, and he retains to this day a vivid recollection of his fine *Aristocratic* appearance.
>
> Dr R. has also seen many of his letters which displayed much shrewdness, high intelligence, and knowledge of the world – yet with all these noble qualities he was always in difficulties, he would direct his best energies to the business and interests of *others*, but neglected his own.

It is from the blood of this man, that *John* has derived those qualities which have recommended him to Your Majesty – he is every inch *a Shaw*.

Captain Shaw when a young man obtained a commission in a Highland Regt, he was present in most of the actions during the War of Independence, in America, was taken prisoner by the rebels, but broke out of Prison, and after many hardships, and adventures, made his escape. On his arrival in England, the Regt was disbanded and he retired to his native glen, upon the half pay of a Lieutenant. He soon after married a Miss McDonald, a Woman of good Family and considerable personal attractions, as famous for attention and good management of her domestic concerns, as her husband was neglectful. They had a family of four children, three sons and a daughter. The sons were all handsome, fine looking men – Two of the sons entered the Army, the eldest Lieut. Alexdr. Shaw was killed in a duel in Aberdeen – the second Hugh, died a Captn in the 73rd Regt. The third son Thomas died young – Janet the daughter, married Donald Brown who lived for many years in the Croft of Renachat [*sic*], opposite Balmoral Castle.

Mrs Brown, Dr Robertson knew well, a shrewd sensible woman, she had two sons John and James Brown. The former married M. Leys – daughter of Charles Leys in Aberarder, who became the Mother of John Brown.[13]

Dr Robertson was clearly struggling to promote John Brown into a higher social class than that to which he actually belonged. Robertson ignored the Brown family tree, which he clearly knew, and concentrated on his own, and better, Shaw connections. The key words 'handsome', 'prowess', 'noble', 'Highland Gentleman' were all the Queen wanted to read. The memorandum managed to get Robertson out of an awkward position, and copies of it were circulated to members of the Royal Household and to the Queen's friends and family. The Prince of Wales tore his copy to shreds; his rage seethed until the Queen's autumn visit to Balmoral in 1868. On that occasion John Brown was inexplicably missing for a whole week. When he did appear his face was battered and bruised. The explanation, said the other staff, was not hard to find.

A few months before, the Prince of Wales had arrived at Windsor to see the Queen. On walking into the royal sitting room he encountered John Brown:

'What dae ye want?' Brown had asked in his usual bluff manner.

'I wish to see the Queen,' the Prince of Wales had replied equally brusquely.

'Ye're no' seein' yer mother till five o'clock,' Brown commented rudely; the Queen was having her afternoon nap. 'Ye'll need to gang an' amuse yersel' for twa hours', Brown suggested, sitting down with newspaper raised in front of the dressing-room door where the Queen napped. Purple with rage the Prince of Wales left. The incident, gossip averred, caused the Prince (and maybe a few others) to hire an Aberdeen bruiser to give Brown a 'going over' in a discreet part of Balmoral estate.[14]

As the years passed Queen Victoria's interest in events at Balmoral never dimmed and John Brown encouraged her to share every aspect of estate life. Her *Journal* entries are full of such incidents. On 21 October 1868 she went to The Bush Farm, then the residence of John Brown's brother William, to witness the 'juicing' of the sheep. It was the practice in the Highlands, before the sheep went off to their low country winter quarters, to 'juice' – or dip – the sheep in a mixture of liquid tobacco and soap. Queen Victoria witnessed the process, with Princess Louise and Prince Leopold, as John Brown's elder brother James and William dipped the sheep. Sheep clipping was done in due season by the womenfolk of the shepherds' families and Queen Victoria greatly admired their expertise.

Such events were mixed with more personal occasions. Three days after the 'juicing', the Queen, with Princesses Louise and Beatrice, was taken by John Brown to the home of forester John Thomson for the christening of his three-week-old baby, named Victoria, by the Revd Dr Malcolm Taylor. Queen Victoria considered the simple ceremony 'impressive', and added: 'I gave my present (a silver mug) to the father, kissed the little baby, and then we drank to its health and that of its mother [Barbara] in whisky, which was handed round with cakes. It was all so nicely done, so simple, and yet with such dignity.'[15]

Queen Victoria knew the names of all her estate workers and their families and visited them regularly, particularly if there was illness in the house. Yet she was selective in her generosity and tended to favour individuals for her bounty rather than being broadly munificent of spirit. John Brown had a great deal of the latter in his character. At the turn of the year 1868/69 the winter brought hardship to many and unemployment with its accompanying social distress had not been as severe since 1842 – the so-called 'Year of the Locust', when twenty-one manufacturers were declared bankrupt in a month and five thousand hands were thrown out of work.[16]

Not far across the Solent from Osborne House, some six thousand dockyard employees, from shipwrights to mechanics, were thrown on the unemployment scrap heap when the Admiralty, under the First Lord, Liberal Hugh Culling Eardley, closed the dockyard at Portsmouth. Queues formed at the pawn shops and beggars lined the streets of Southampton and Portsmouth in order to raise a few pence to buy relief.[17] At Osborne John Brown set up a fund of moneys collected from below stairs staff. Under the headline 'HER MAJESTY'S SERVANTS AND THE DISCHARGED DOCKYARD WORKERS', *The Times* published an item about the fund: 'The Committee of the Portsmouth Dockyard Discharged Workmen's Relief Association thankfully acknowledges through the medium of *The Times* the receipt of £22 16s 6d subscribed by Mr John Brown and the Queen's servants at the Royal establishment now at Osborne, and forwarded to the chairman of the committee.'[18]

As John Brown's fame spread, a number of anecdotes, imagined and real, sprang up concerning his activities, and over the years dozens of Deeside folk have added their 'memories' of him. One such was Mary Henderson who lived at Crathie, and remembered the Queen's visits with John Brown to her family's cottage. She recalled one occasion:

I am afraid that as children we had little appreciation of the honour of the Queen's visits and the Queen's interest in our life and doings. Not seldom if when playing about we spotted the distant approach of the grey horses, did we bolt and hide behind a stone dyke lest royal eyes should see us. The carriage was stopped and we were called, grubby and reluctant, to the royal presence.

And of John Brown:

I recall clearly that John Brown, who apparently had been sent into [our] cottage on some errand, came suddenly out behind us, and snatching my brother's tam-o'shanter from his head, demanded what he meant by standing before the Queen with his bonnet on. The truculent youngster, nothing daunted, turned round and grabbed his tammy back, declaring that he had taken it off, as he had done on being greeted by the Queen, but was too young to know he should have kept it off.

It was characteristic of the Queen that she should at once interpose – 'Yes, Brown, he did take it off,' and to my brother – 'Put it on again, my dear, you might catch cold.'

So we rather scored off the great John Brown that day, and the more so that when the Queen told him who we were, he replied, 'Damn it, your Maa-dj-esty, I could 'a'sworn it was twa laddies.'

I was inclined to be a pious young party in those days, and I reported later in shocked tones, that John Brown had sworn before the Queen. Indeed, so horrified was I that (so I was often told after) I did not even say swore, but spelt it, 'S.W.O.R.E.' – it was too awful a word to repeat! One lady-in-waiting was said to have complained that John, having been sent to fetch her, happened to meet her on the staircase and remarked, 'Ye're the very wumman I want.' Much on her dignity, the outraged lady complained to the Queen that John Brown had called her a woman, on which Her Majesty replied: 'Well, aren't you a woman?'[19]

On 1 September 1869 the Queen set off with Princesses Louise and Beatrice, her Lady of the Bedchamber, Jane, Lady Churchill, John Brown and a staff of fifteen, by train, for a five-day visit to Invertrossachs House near Callander, Perthshire. The house was lent to her for her visit to The Trossachs by Mr and Lady Emily Macnaghten. Invertrossachs House had previously been known as Drunkie House, but this was changed because 'Drunkie' was not considered a suitable name for a dwelling in which the Queen was to spend some time.

Queen Victoria and her entourage, with John Brown leading the way, embarked on what was to prove a pioneering tour. News of the Queen's adventures led to the creation of 'The Trossachs Tour', which was to see thousands of visitors from the south following in the Queen's carriage ruts to see what she had seen. The travellers on the tour were introduced to a region of spectacular scenery, made famous in the Queen's mind by episodes in Sir Walter Scott's poem *The Lady of the Lake* (1810) and the novel *Rob Roy* (1818). The tour would take its own 'traditional form', leading from Callander via The Trossachs ('bristly country' in Gaelic) at Loch Achray to Loch Katrine and thence by steamers on Loch Katrine and Loch Lomond to Balloch at the lower end of Loch Lomond. Aboard the little steamer *Rob Roy* – on which the Queen and Prince Albert had travelled when they opened the Glasgow Waterworks in 1859 – the royal party viewed the majestic scenery and the Queen dipped into Scott's prose as she went. Tears were shed when the Queen boarded the steamer *Prince Consort* at Loch Lomond; 'that that dear name should have carried his poor little wife', she grieved and indulged bittersweet memories of her trips aboard the *Winkelreid* with Prince Albert on Lake Lucerne. Refreshed, though, by Ben Lomond and the varied scenery, the Queen prepared to return home after meeting a Highland woman, Mrs Ferguson, who had become 'quite rich' on the sale of whisky.[20]

In November 1870 a piece of gossip circulated at Balmoral that John Brown had secretly married Miss Ocklee, the personal maid to Princess Beatrice. Certainly at this point in his life Brown was broody and, although still devoted to his growing circle of nieces and nephews, he seems to have been thinking that his chances of marrying and fathering children were receding: in fact he was only forty-four. In the event he did not marry Miss Ocklee, who, if she was enamoured of Brown, wasted no time in fastening her attentions on another and in 1873 she married an estate steward called Lawson. John Brown was to remain a bachelor.[21]

The parish kirk of Crathie, in which John Brown worshipped man and boy, was the 'old church' of 1804. Up to 1878 Crathie and Braemar were a large single parish. Presbyterianism and Sabbatarianism still loomed strongly in the area where the Kirk Elders, imbued with the legacy of severe discipline of the eighteenth-century church, had great influence. Queen Victoria was by no means conventional in her religious beliefs; disliking both Evangelicals and

High Church elements in the Anglican communion she followed the
'simple piety' of her Lutheran mother. The fact that Prince Albert
had found parallels in the church service at Crathie with the
Lutheranism of his childhood also influenced the Queen to attend
Crathie Church. She did, however, find Presbyterians 'tiresome' in
their narrow-mindedness and bigotry. Yet although she was head of
the Church of England, she had no such status in Calvinist Scotland
and was largely free to worship as she pleased in her northern realm.
In years to come the Queen's visits to Crathie Church became fewer
as the pews became crammed with visitors bent on seeing the Queen
at prayer. Instead she worshipped in a private chapel set up at
Balmoral.

John Brown invariably preceded the Queen into the church to
shoo away any, including her suite, who might crowd the Queen as
she prepared to sit in the royal pew. Those selected to sit with the
Queen were often gripped firmly by the elbow, irrespective of their
rank, as the Highland Servant directed them to their positions. From
her seat in the gallery, which was raised round three sides of the old
kirk, the Queen listened to a range of prominent Scots divines,
invited to preach by the incumbent from 1840, the Revd Archibald
Anderson. Communion was enacted only twice a year at the kirk by
the 1870s and it was only after 3 November 1873 that the Queen
took the Scots Sacrament.[22] From her perch the Queen was able to
observe her neighbours. On Communion Sunday, 13 November
1871, she wrote of the scene and mentions various members of John
Brown's family, describing how his uncle, Francis Leys, an Elder,
assisted with the communion elements, and how she saw John
Brown's parents – 'he eighty-one and very much bent, and she
seventy-one' – his father dressed in the 'large' plaid of the old-time
Highlander.

From late September 1870 Queen Victoria was in a depressed state
again. Within seven months she lost several old friends: Countess
Blücher, formerly lady-in-waiting to Augusta of Saxe-Weimar, Queen
of Prussia; General Charles Grey, Prince Albert's old secretary; Sir
James Clark, her Physician-in-Ordinary, and Baroness Louise Lehzen,
her old governess. European events also depressed the Queen. In 1870
France had declared war on Prussia; in Britain the royal family were

attacked as a 'pack of Germans' by republicans, and in Germany her daughter Vicky, along with the royal family, was denounced in Berlin by the Prusso-German statesman Prince Otto von Bismarck as pro-French. It was all very unsettling. At length, on 2 September 1870, Queen Victoria's brother-monarch, Napoleon III Emperor of the French, with whom she had enjoyed reciprocal state visits, was captured at the Battle of Sedan. Within days his Second Empire gave way to the Third Republic. Gloom descended on Queen Victoria, not because she supported French activities, but rather because she feared for her own throne. Yet she put forward no protest either to the exile in Britain of Napoleon III's Empress Eugénie and the French Prince Imperial and their suites, or to them being joined by the Emperor on his release.

All this time the Queen's health was deteriorating: she had difficulty in swallowing; she had an abscess which was tardy in healing; and she had been suffering for months from painful gout, and all her joints ached: 'Never . . . have I felt so ill,' she wrote in her *Journal* on 22 August 1871. Her illness, news of which was not communicated to her subjects, made her more reclusive and subject to increased attacks in the press for her 'invisibility'.

Even though she was unwell the Queen did not send for her children. Courtiers like Sir Thomas Biddulph were aware that her children's presence and opinions irritated the Queen, and like Sir Henry Ponsonby, he noted how much more dependent on Brown she had become. The fact that Brown was a kind of messenger-cum-nursemaid-cum-guardian was bitterly resented by her children. At length the powder keg exploded at Balmoral.

The quarrels between John Brown and various members of the Queen's family were often extremely complex in origin. The latest one, between John Brown and Prince Alfred, can be explained in this way. The Gillies' Ball of 1870 had been extremely noisy and bibulous. When the dancing and jollities seemed likely to get out of hand, Prince Alfred ordered the music to stop. Brown was furious, and made his opinions known in no uncertain terms. Brown was reported to have barked at the prince – 'I'll not take this [order] from you or from any other man.' He disliked Prince Alfred, whose head gillie John Grant refused to take orders from Brown, and the Prince now

> *Of John Brown*
> After watching John Brown perform his duties as MC at a Balmoral
> Gillies' Ball, Cairns said: 'What a coarse animal that Brown is . . . of
> course, the ball couldn't go on without him . . . Still, I did not
> conceive it possible that anyone could behave so roughly as he does to
> the Queen.'
>
> **1st Lord Cairns,**
> **Lord Chancellor**

openly started to ignore Brown and deliberately to snub him because
of his outburst at the Ball. It is certain that John Brown complained
to the Queen when Prince Alfred refused to shake hands with him
on his arrival at Balmoral in September 1870. Summoning Ponsonby
to her sitting-room, Queen Victoria insisted that the quarrel with
Brown be 'patched up' immediately and that Ponsonby should
arrange it.

Prince Alfred reluctantly deferred to his mother, but insisted that he
would resume conversation with Brown but only with Ponsonby as
witness. This irritated the Queen further when she was told that the
Prince had insisted on a witness. In the Royal Navy, when he was
commander of the cruiser *HMS Galatea*, he explained, he always saw
inferior ranks in the presence of an officer witness. 'This is not a ship,
and I won't have naval discipline introduced here,' the Queen retorted,
on hearing her son's comment.

In a letter to his wife, Sir Henry Ponsonby recounted the resultant
exchange between the Prince and the servant at the subsequent
interview:

JOHN BROWN: Am I right, Sir, in thinking that you are annoyed
with something I have done in the past? If so, please tell me, for it is
most painful that any of Her Maa-dj-esty's children should be angry
with me.
PRINCE ALFRED: It's nothing you have done in the past. But
I must confess that I was surprised at the extraordinary language you
used at the Gillies' Ball last May.

JOHN BROWN: Her Maa-jd-esty put the whole arrangements for
the Ball into my hands . . . At first I did not know that it was Your
Royal Highness who had stopped the music, and I was very angry
and lost my temper. I cannot think it possible that I used any nasty
words, but if Your Royal Highness says so then it must have been so,
and I must humbly ask your forgiveness.
PRINCE ALFRED: Thank you, I give you my forgiveness. [To
Ponsonby] I am satisfied with the outcome of this meeting.
JOHN BROWN: I'm quite satisfied too.[23]

As a fragile calm descended once again on Balmoral, Queen Victoria's
tender sensibilities were to be assailed by a more poignant worry.
On 9 November 1871 the Prince of Wales returned to Sandringham
from a pheasant shoot at Londesborough Lodge, Scarborough, where
he and a 'fast group' of his cronies from his 'Marlborough House Set'
had been the guests of William Henry Forester Denison, Earl of
Londesborough. While at the insanitary lodge – the drains were in a
fearful state of neglect – several of the guests had complained of
stomach upsets and had been treated for diarrhoea by the earl's
physician Dr George Dale. As he prepared to host the visit of
Maharajah Dhuleep Singh, the Prince of Wales was stricken with
typhoid. A week later another of the Londesborough guests, George
Philip Stanhope, 7th Earl of Chesterfield, died, as did the Prince's
groom.
    As soon as the Prince of Wales's condition was deemed life-
threatening the royal family descended on Sandringham in their usual
squabbling mass. Never before had a royal illness stirred up such fear and
anguish in the nation. An observer of the age, Joseph Irving, wrote in
Annals of Our Time, 1837–91:

  Bulletins were posted up in all places of resort; newspapers were
  eagerly bought up, edition after edition, as they were hourly brought
  out; and whenever two or three friends met, the condition of the
  Prince was not only the first but the single topic of discussion . . .

The public anxiety grew as the tenth anniversary of the death of Prince
Albert approached. From the *Reynolds News* ('an epidemic of typhoid

loyalty') to the *Daily Telegraph* ('the dreaded approach of death'), the press stirred up a public panic which brought huge sympathy and increased popularity for the royal family.

Slowly the Prince of Wales rallied and the nation rejoiced with a great service of Thanksgiving for his life on 27 February 1872 at St Paul's Cathedral. Round the corner, though, lurked a greater danger for the Queen.

Full-length portrait of John Brown by Carl Rudolph Sohn. (Christie's Images)

Margaret Leys, John Brown's mother, pictured with her eldest son James Brown in the 1860s. This was one of several pictures of John Brown's family in Queen Victoria's possession; the picture is from an album presented to Mrs Brown by Queen Victoria with her signature above the date 28 August 1871. (Aberdeen Museums)

John Brown (centre) with his brothers Hugh (left) and Archie. (Aberdeen Museums)

Balmoral gillies, photographed in 1857 by George Washington Wilson. Left to right: D. Kennedy, J. Smith, Willy Stewart, John Brown, F. Farquharson, Gillie Morgan, Charlie Coutts, P. Robertson and John Grant. (National Portrait Gallery)

John Brown, aged about forty-two. Controversially, this etching appeared as an illustration in Queen Victoria's second volume of Scottish writings, More Leaves from the Journal of a Life in the Highlands. The etching is dated 1868. (Author's Collection)

John Brown in Highland dress, from the photograph by Cornelius Hughes, probably taken at Osborne House some time after 1864. (Aberdeen Museums)

John Brown with his dogs at Windsor, pictured by Robert Hill and John Saunders soon after they opened their Oxford Photographic Gallery at Eton in about 1863. (National Portrait Gallery)

Queen Victoria in her 'widow's weeds'. While she clung to her depressive seclusion at Osborne and Windsor, John Brown was summoned from Balmoral to attend her and to remind her of happier days when she visited Scotland with Prince Albert. (Purves Papers)

John Brown with Queen Victoria on 'Fyvie', photographed at Balmoral on 20 October 1863 by George Washington Wilson. This is the final cropped version of the picture – it originally also included Head Keeper John Grant – and was published by Marion & Co. at a time of increased public interest in Queen Victoria and John Brown. The original photograph was commissioned by Queen Victoria and entered in her personal album with the caption 'A Highland Widow'. (Scottish National Portrait Gallery)

Sir Robert Peel (1788–1850), twice Conservative Prime Minister, made the arrangements for Queen Victoria's first visit to Scotland in 1842. Steel engraving by W. Holl, from a portrait by Sir Thomas Lawrence. (Author's Collection)

William David Murray, 4th Earl of Mansfield (1806–98), hosted Queen Victoria at Scone Palace on 7 September 1842. He was the oldest and longest-serving Lord Lieutenant (for Clackmannanshire) in Scotland in Victoria's reign. (The Earl of Mansfield)

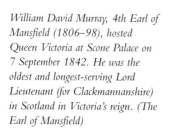

THE QUEEN'S FIRST TOUR IN SCOTLAND

FROM AUGUST 29TH 1842
TO SEPTEMBER 17TH 1842

THE LIBRARY, TAYMOUTH CASTLE.
The seat of the Earls of Breadalbane.

DALKEITH PALACE.
The residence of the Dukes of Buccleuch.

DALMENY PARK
The seat of the Earls
of Rosebery.

Montage of 1901 illustrating 'Queen Victoria's First Tour of Scotland' in 1842. (Author's Collection)

A typical aristocratic family who attended and served at Queen Victoria's court and were shocked by John Brown's behaviour. On the right is William Henry Walter Montague-Douglas-Scott, Earl of Dalkeith (and later 6th Duke of Buccleugh and 8th Duke of Queensbury); on the left is his wife Lady Louisa Jane Hamilton. They are seen here with their two sons, John Charles and Walter Henry, entertaining relatives at Langholm Lodge, East Dumfriesshire, in 1879. Lady Louisa served as Mistress of the Robes to Queen Victoria, and Lord Dalkeith was Captain-General of the Royal Company of Archers. (The Estate of the late Rt Hon. Lord Home of the Hirsel)

Old Balmoral Castle, built in 1834–9 by Sir Robert Gordon. This photograph by George Washington Wilson shows the castle shortly before it was demolished in 1854 to make way for Queen Victoria's new Highland home. (Purves Papers)

Balmoral Castle from the north. On the left is the ballroom. The foundation stone for the new castle was laid on 28 September 1853 and the royal family took possession on 7 September 1855. (Author's Collection)

Abergeldie Castle from the south. Set on the banks of the River Dee some three miles from Balmoral, Abergeldie had been a stronghold of the Gordon family. Prince Albert acquired it on a long lease but the 40,000 acre estate did not come into royal ownership until after his death. The castle became the home of Queen Victoria's mother, the Duchess of Kent, and later the Prince of Wales came here to avoid John Brown's presence at Balmoral. To his great annoyance, John Brown would regularly be sent to Abergeldie with messages – usually terse – from the Queen. (Author's Collection)

Prince Albert, the Prince Consort, in Highland dress with the new Balmoral Castle in the background, painted in 1858 by Aberdeen artist John Philip, the Prince is wearing the ribbon of the Order of the Thistle, while on his left leg is the Order of the Garter. (Purves Papers)

Albert Edward, Prince of Wales, with his brothers Prince Alfred, Duke of Edinburgh and Saxe-Coburg-Gotha, Prince Arthur, Duke of Connaught, and Prince Leopold, Duke of Albany, pictured at Abergeldie Castle on 1 September 1881 by the London Stereoscopic Co. All four brothers crossed swords with John Brown at various times. (Robert Milne)

This popular parlour print was taken from Carl Haag's painting of Queen Victoria's ascent of Lochnagar with family and gillies. The Queen made her first ascent in 1848. (Purves Papers)

Queen Victoria and Prince Albert take luncheon at Cairn Lochan on 16 October 1861, during the last Expedition before Albert's death. Again taken from Haag's painting, this print shows John Brown offering a plate of food to the Queen. On such occasions John Brown was meticulous in checking that the hampers contained the delicacies that the Queen enjoyed. (Purves Papers)

Alfred Brannon's drawing of Osborne House, dated 7 June 1849. Osborne was built to Prince Albert's designs during 1845–51 as a country retreat for the royal family. John Brown took up service at Osborne in December 1864; his lodgings were to the left of the clock tower. (Author's Collection)

Queen Victoria, accompanied by Princesses Helena and Beatrice, prepare for a carriage ride from Balmoral in the early 1860s. John Brown is on the box with coachman Smith. The print is from the original by William and Daniel Downey. (Aberdeen Museums)

A group of courtiers at Balmoral in 1886. All knew John Brown well and had been several bossed about, irritated, mortified and frustrated by his behaviour. Left to right: Captain Fleetwood Edwards, Equerry and Advisor to the Queen; Sir Henry Ponsonby, Private Secretary; Viscount Bridport, Permanent Lord in Waiting; Dr Francis Laking, court physician; Dr James Reid, court physician; the Earl of Cranbrooke, Conservative Lord President of the Council. Seated: Amelia, Countess of Erroll, Lady in Waiting to the Queen; the Hon. Rosa Hood, daughter of Lord Bridport; Fraulein Caroline Bauer, German governess. (Purves Papers)

General Charles Grey (1804–70), Private Secretary to Prince Albert from 1849 to 1861 and then Private Secretary to Queen Victoria from 1861 to 1870. He became skilled at biting his tongue when he was irritated by John Brown's interference. (Lord Ponsonby)

During his several decades of royal service John Brown accumulated a large collection of gifts from Queen Victoria. Here is a representative sample of tie-pins, cuff-links and shirt studs. Note the gold and enamel portrait stick-pin of John Brown dated 27 March 1883 and presented to him a few months before his death, and the portrait mourning stud of John Brown's father, 'Old John', with his dates 1789–1875. (Sotheby's)

Queen Victoria sits at her spinning wheel. A regular guest at Balmoral was the Revd Dr Norman McLeod who read to the Queen from the works of Scott and Burns as she sat spinning local Aberdeenshire flax. During their travels John Brown always looked out for spinning wheels to add to the Queen's collections. (Aberdeen Art Galleries)

Queen Victoria, Princess Louise, Duchess of Argyll, and John Brown pose by the terrace wall near the ballroom at Balmoral in the 1860s. (National Portrait Gallery)

John Brown stands with the gillies in full Highland dress at the ball at Balmoral given by Queen Victoria to celebrate the twenty-second birthday of Princess Helena, 25 May 1868. Helena had married Prince Christian of Schleswig-Holstein in 1866. (Purves Papers)

CHAPTER FIVE

TO KILL THE QUEEN

By the early 1870s John Brown had taken to sleeping with a loaded revolver under his pillow.[1] One of his self-imposed duties was to patrol the immediate precincts of wherever the Queen happened to be, as dusk fell, to root out possible assassins. Throughout her reign the safety of the Queen's person was not considered a very high priority by the succeeding Secretaries of State for the Home Department. At Balmoral the only security measure was a single policeman. From time to time the police monitored the two perceived sources of danger for the Queen as represented by the loosely organised 'republican movements' and the Fenians. Surges of republicanism were noted when events abroad stirred up anti-monarchist feelings. The Franco-Prussian War (15 July 1870–10 May 1871), which toppled Napoleon III, was a stimulus to the founding of republican clubs. Queen Victoria was upset and concerned about the 'disloyalty' of the movement rather than fearful for her life.[2]

On 5 November 1871 the left-wing MP for Chelsea, Sir Charles Wentworth Dilke, stirred up radical republican beliefs with an attack on the monarchy, highlighting what he saw as the Queen's 'dereliction of duty'.[3] He incited his audience at a public meeting at Newcastle to rise up and establish a republic. The wind was rather taken out of his rhetorical sails by the upsurge of national sympathy over the Prince of Wales's illness. Republicanism continued to huff and puff, mostly among the Liberal Parliamentarian cadres, until the end of the reign. The most dangerous group conspiring against the Queen was the fanatical Fenians.

The Fenians formed a secret society of Irish–American revolutionaries whose aims in 1866–7 were to bring about the separation of Ireland from 'English rule', and establish an Irish Republic. Founded by James Stephens in 1858 as the Irish Republican Brotherhood, they had financial and moral support in the United States where many Irish had recently fought in the Civil War.[4] Groups of disaffected Irish families in cities such as London, Manchester and Chester caused regular disturbances. They made much of their stated aim to kill a member of the royal family.

On a number of occasions Victoria's ministers were disturbed by purported Fenian 'plots' to assassinate her, and on 14 October 1867 the police uncovered Fenian plans in Manchester to mount a new attack on the Queen. General Charles Grey wanted to surround Balmoral with troops. Security was accordingly stepped up, and the Queen asserted that it was all 'Too foolish!'[5] Extra warships began patrolling the Isle of Wight in sight of Osborne. It was all 'such a bore',[6] the Queen declared when for the umpteenth time she was warned that out of the lanes near Osborne or the woods near Balmoral Fenians might spring, overpowering the protective John Brown, and carry her off to a dreadful fate. Reluctantly, for a while, she accepted the increased numbers of sentries and outriders.

In all there were seven assassination attempts on the Queen's life, and John Brown was involved with two of them. The first ever attempt on her took place on 10 June 1840, just a few months after her marriage. As her low phaeton climbed London's Constitution Hill, a deranged eighteen-year-old called Edward Oxford fired two shots at her. She was unhurt. Oxford was committed to Newgate prison; found 'guilty, but insane' he was subsequently detained at Bethlehem Royal Hospital, Moorfields, and latterly at Broadmoor. He eventually went under supervision to Australia where he died. On Sunday 30 May 1842, again while driving on Constitution Hill, Queen Victoria was fired at by twenty-year-old John Francis. Found guilty of the capital offence of treason, the Queen reprieved Francis and the death penalty was commuted to transportation for life to Norfolk Island in the Pacific. A few weeks later, on Sunday 3 July 1842, as she drove to the Chapel Royal, St James, John William Bean made an attempt on her life but was thwarted. Bean was given eighteen months imprisonment, under a new Bill which reduced the charge from 'high treason' to 'high misdemeanour'.[7]

The fourth attempt on her life was made on 19 May 1849 when the insane Irishman William Hamilton attacked the Queen with an empty gun. He was transported for seven years. On 27 June 1850 the Queen was attacked by Robert Pate, a retired lieutenant in the 10th Hussars, who struck her across the face with a cane. Pate was tried for assault and sentenced to seven years transportation. John Brown was involved with the sixth attempt on Queen Victoria's life. It occurred two days after the Thanksgiving Service at St Paul's for the recovery of the Prince of Wales, and of all the attempts up to that date it was the one which frightened her most.

The attack took place as the Queen returned to Buckingham Palace following a drive through Regent's Park on 29 February 1872. The would-be assassin was an eighteen-year-old, undersized, scrofulous youth. Arthur O'Connor lived at 4 Church Row, Houndsditch, a district of London that social historian and *Punch* editor Henry Mayhew described as full of 'Jewish shopkeepers, warehousemen, manufacturers and inferior jewellers'. O'Connor worked there for an oil and colour manufacturer.

Armed with a flintlock pistol, O'Connor watched Queen Victoria leave Buckingham Palace at 4.30pm in an open landau with her Lady-in-Waiting Jane Churchill, and Princes Arthur and Leopold. On the box sat John Brown, while her two equerries, the Crimean Veteran General Arthur Hardinge and Lord Charles Fitzroy, rode on either side of the carriage. The escort was completed with Charles Tomkins as outrider at the front and mounted postilion John Cannon at the rear. As the Queen completed her drive O'Connor climbed the 10ft high railings at Buckingham Palace, and, unobserved, sprinted across the courtyard and took up position at the Garden Entrance to the palace, intent on intercepting the carriage. In her *Journal* Queen Victoria took up the story:

It is difficult for me to describe, as my impression was a great fright, and all was over in a minute. How it all happened I knew nothing of. The Equerries had dismounted. Brown had got down to let down the steps, and Jane C[hurchill] was just getting out, when suddenly someone appeared at my side, whom I first imagined was a footman, going to lift off the wrapper. Then I perceived that it was someone unknown, peering above the carriage door, with an uplifted hand and a strange voice, at the same time the boys [Princes Arthur and

Leopold] calling out and moving forward. Involuntarily, in a terrible fright, I threw myself over Jane C. calling out, 'Save me,' and heard a scuffle and voices! I soon recovered myself sufficiently to stand up and turn round, when I saw Brown holding a young man tightly, who was struggling, Arthur, the Equerries, etc., also near him. They laid the man on the ground and Brown kept hold of him till several of the police came in. All turned and asked if I was hurt, and I said, 'Not at all.' Then Lord Charles Fitzroy, General Hardinge, and Arthur came up saying they thought the man had dropped something. We looked, but could find nothing, when Cannon, the postilion, called out, 'There it is,' and looking down I then did see shining on the ground a small pistol! This filled us with horror. All were as white as sheets, Jane C. almost crying, and Leopold looked as if he were going to faint.

It is to good Brown and to his wonderful presence of mind that I greatly owe my safety, for he alone saw the boy rush round and followed him! When I was standing in the hall, General Hardinge came in, bringing an extraordinary document which this boy had intended making me sign! It was in connection with the Fenian prisoners! Sir T[homas] Biddulph came running, greatly horrified. Then the boy was taken away by the police and made no attempt to escape . . .[8]

During his examination it emerged that O'Connor had endeavoured to deliver a petition to the Queen as she knelt at prayer at the Thanksgiving Service at St Paul's. This is the document the Queen mentions in her *Journal* entry. O'Connor had been discovered lurking in a side aisle in the Cathedral the evening before the service and had been removed by the Virgers (the St Paul's terminology for 'vergers'). The police examination also revealed that O'Connor was the great-nephew of the Chartist leader Fergus O'Connor, and it became clear that the youth had confused Chartism – a movement of the late 1830s seeking parliamentary reform – with Fenianism. Police records showed that Arthur O'Connor came from a family who had been 'reduced' in social circumstances, but that he had been educated at the church school of St-Dunstans-in-the-East, Fleet Street, and that he had obtained indentures as a law stationer. He also had a history of mental derangement. On 26 February he had bought an old and useless flintlock pistol at a pawnshop in Southwark for 4s. Having no ammunition, he had stuffed the barrel with wads of blue paper and leather.

Queen Victoria was more than grateful to John Brown for his gallantry during the episode and caused this public announcement to be written by Secretary Ponsonby:

The Queen, who had contemplated instituting a medal as a reward for long and faithful service among Her Majesty's domestic servants, has inaugurated the institution by conferring on Mr John Brown, the Queen's personal attendant, a medal in gold, with an annuity of £25 attached to it, as a mark of her appreciation of his presence of mind and of his devotion on the occasion of the attack made upon Her Majesty in Buckingham Palace Gardens on 29 February 1872.[9]

On a much-disliked equerry
One of Queen Victoria's equerries, General Sir Lyndoch Gardiner, was held in particular dislike by John Brown. While Gardiner was perfectly polite to Brown, the Highland Servant was irritated by Gardiner's being a stickler for everything being just so before he could write up an order. At the beginning of one duty he enquired of Brown how the Queen was keeping. 'The Queen's very well,' replied Brown. 'It was only the other day that she said to me "There's that dommed old fool General Gardiner coming into waiting and I know he'll be putting his bloody nose into everything that doesn't concern him".' The general's reply is not recorded.

The Prince of Wales was annoyed at his mother's gesture. Had not Prince Arthur been just as gallant? He received only a tie-pin. The Queen once more exhibited her strategic deafness to the Prince of Wales's opinions.

John Brown was the hero of the hour and the public clamoured for news of the incident and to learn what was to happen to O'Connor. It was soon announced that O'Connor was to appear before the Senior Magistrate at Bow Street, barrister Sir Thomas Henry. Huge crowds blocked Bow Street and Long Acre, and the little streets to the east of

Covent Garden, and extra police were called in. A delay in the legal
procedures held up the start of the hearing which added to the tension.
Prince Leopold, summoned as a witness, was cheered when he entered
the court buildings with his party, while O'Connor was hissed. The
crowd reserved its heartiest welcome for John Brown.

The charge against O'Connor was read out by Harry Bodkin Poland,
a leading counsel and adviser to the Home Department. Then he read
out the curious petition written by O'Connor and which he had
intended to force Queen Victoria to sign. John Brown was now called
to the witness box. On the public benches people craned their necks to
get a view of the Queen's personal attendant. Journalists' pencils
scribbled and all was attention when Brown's gruff Scottish voice was
heard for the first time in any court of law:

> I am in the service of the Queen. Yesterday, after the Court, I went
> with her Maa-dj-esty for a drive. It was an open carriage. Lady
> Churchill sat on the right-hand side and the Queen sat on the left.
> Opposite Lady Churchill sat Prince Leopold and opposite the Queen
> sat Prince Arthur. Lord Charles Fitzroy and General Hardinge were
> riding on each side of the carriage. There were two outriders in front
> and two grooms behind . . . We drove through the garden gate, after
> driving through the enclosure. The carriage stopped at the entrance
> for the purpose of allowing Her Maa-dj-esty to alight. The left side
> of the carriage was towards the entrance. I got off to open the door
> when the carriage stopped and the Equerries also dismounted. The
> prisoner was between the Equerries about a yard from the carriage
> door. I shifted him back. The prisoner then ran round the back of
> the carriage to the side where the Queen was sitting. I followed him.
> He reached the door where the Queen was sitting and raised his
> hand. He placed his hand upon the carriage and I seized his neck. He
> dropped a pistol from his right hand. I fancy General Hardinge
> picked up the pistol. I kept the boy in custody until the police
> arrived. The Queen stood up in the carriage during the
> proceedings.[10]

Following the witness testimony of Prince Leopold, General
Hardinge and Charles Tomkins, Sir Thomas Henry committed

O'Connor for trial at the Central Criminal Court. John Brown and the other main witnesses were charged to attend. Against his counsel's advice O'Connor pleaded guilty and although Dr Harrington Tuke of the Chiswell Lunatic Asylum testified to hereditary insanity, the jury found O'Connor fit to plead; judge Sir Anthony Cleasby sentenced him to one year in prison with hard labour, and twenty strokes of the birch.

At an audience with Queen Victoria, Prime Minister Gladstone was assailed by royal disapproval of the 'extreme leniency' of the sentence. She implored Gladstone to set in motion the process that would have O'Connor transported lest he attack her again. The Queen's anxiety was well founded. After he had completed his sentence O'Connor was persuaded to go to Australia, but he soon returned to Britain. On 5 May 1874 he was arrested for loitering with intent outside Buckingham Palace. He was then committed under court order to Hanwell Lunatic Asylum.[11]

Following the excitement of the trial and John Brown's obvious enjoyment of his high public profile, the Highland servant attended Queen Victoria on her fortnight's visit to Baden-Baden, on the Rhine valley slopes of the Black Forest. The Queen visited her ailing half-sister Princess Feodore of Leiningen. Once again she was using the pseudonym 'Countess of Kent' while travelling – no one was fooled – and she stayed at a villa outside the town.[12] John Brown attended while she viewed the casinos of Baden-Baden which were dubbed the second homes of 'the worst characters of both sexes in Europe'. Then it was back to a welter of 'domesticity' and junketing in Scotland.

One afternoon John Brown came to the Queen to tell her that a 'bairn had fallen into the water' and that estate workers and local folk were searching for him along the banks of the River Dee, then in spate. The Queen immediately set off with Princess Beatrice and her Lady of the Bedchamber, Jane, Marchioness of Ely, to help in the search. The Rattray boys, ten-year-old Jemmie and three-year-old Sandy from nearby Cairn-na-Craig, had been fishing when the younger lad had fallen into the Monaltrie Burn that feeds into the Dee. Jemmie had dived in to help his little brother, and both had been swept away. The body of poor Sandy was found next day; his brother remained missing. With John Brown the Queen paid a visit to the grieving family.

Jemmie's body was found a few days later. On the day of the children's funeral Queen Victoria watched the 'very sad sight' of the cortège from her discreetly parked carriage.

On Wednesday 14 August 1872 Queen Victoria and her entourage arrived at Edinburgh from Osborne for an official visit. Escorted by a troop of Scots Greys, and with John Brown on the box, the Queen's carriage made for what she called 'the old, gloomy, but historical Palace of Holyrood'. Accompanied by John Brown, carrying her plaid wrap, Queen Victoria and Princess Beatrice were taken on a tour of the palace and the ruined abbey by Duncan Anderson, Keeper of the Chapel Royal. He related the history of the old palace, built next to the 1128 abbey of the Augustinian canons of Holyrood by King James IV of Scots from 1498. Its place had been etched in history by his grand-daughter Mary, Queen of Scots, whose colourful court had breathed life, murder, skulduggery and mayhem into its stones. Queen Victoria had not stayed at the palace since 1850, when she and Prince Albert were en route to and from Balmoral. This time she included a carriage drive around the old city, and visited St Matthew's Chapel, 7½ miles away at Roslin where she relaxed in the garden and read from a volume of the collected poems of James Hogg, the renowned 'Ettrick Shepherd', a gift from John Brown a few years earlier. After more lengthy drives around Edinburgh and its environs the Queen and her entourage left for Balmoral on Saturday 17 August.

During Friday 6 September a large party of relatives and retainers, with John Brown 'who supervised everything' wrote the Queen in her *Journal*,[13] set off from Balmoral to visit Dunrobin Castle. The thirteenth-century ancestral pile of the Dukes of Sutherland had been extended in 1856 and now sported a new wing and frontage of towers, turrets and extinguisher roofs to delight the eye. Set on a natural terrace by the sea, just to the north of Golspie, the castle was one of the most stunning in Scotland. As the royal train approached Keith, John Brown and two railwaymen disturbed the Queen's peace when they had to break through a jammed carriage interior door. With her ears still ringing from the din, the Queen stepped down at Elgin for a tour of the sights on this 'broiling hot day'. At Bonar Bridge they were met by their Dunrobin host, George Granville Leveson-Gower, 3rd Duke of

Sutherland, who escorted them to Golspie station and thence to Dunrobin, whose approach road was bedecked with banners carrying Gaelic sentiments:

Ar Buidheachas do'n Bhuadhaich
    ('Our gratitude to Victoria')

Na h-uile lath ch's nach fhaic, slainte duibh'is solas
    ('Every day see we you, or see we not, health to you and happiness')

Ceud mile failte do Chattaobh
    ('A hundred thousand welcomes to Sutherland')

Failte do'n laith Buidhe
    ('Hail to the lucky day')

Better lo'ed you canna' be
Will ye no come back again?

These were translated by Brown, who added his usual gratuitous comment: 'Aye, they're pleased to see you.'

The visit lasted until Monday 9 September, the day they visited Monument Hill, where the huge statue of George Granville Leveson-Gower, 1st Duke of Sutherland, still gazes out over his vast estates. The duke, dubbed the 'great improver', was a hate figure for decades as a result of the infamous 'Highland Clearances'.[14] En route John Brown ordered the royal carriage to stop when he spotted a clump of white heather; he jumped down and picked a spray for the Queen. Knowing her companions' irritation at John Brown stopping the royal progress at will, Queen Victoria wrote in her *Journal* for that day: 'No Highlander would pass by [white heather] without picking it, for it is considered to bring good luck.' On this trip the Queen was to sample the Highland delicacy of boiled sheep's head – 'really very good', she commented. A somewhat pushy host, the Duke of Sutherland had invited the Welsh explorer and journalist Henry Morton Stanley to meet the Queen; some years before, Stanley had 'found' the explorer Dr David

Livingstone at Ujiji, Tanganyika. At the time Stanley was in some bad odour for his presumed opportunistic 'self-advertisement', and the Queen was annoyed that she was forced to greet Stanley. The tour ended on a sour note.

For some time Queen Victoria had been contemplating emulating her relatives in the courts of Prussia and the Grand-Duchy of Hesse by awarding a special medal to her servants. She now gave attention to the creation of a Faithful Service Medal. Her main aim was to reward John Brown for his devotion to her, and to honour his *de facto* superior Rudolph Löhlein. Both Ponsonby and Princess Alice, who represented the opinions of the Queen's children, thought the idea set a dangerous precedent. They feared that she would hand out the medal willy-nilly to her beloved Highlanders to the detriment of the morale of her English servants.

After due reflection Queen Victoria decided that acts of bravery by servants should be marked with a higher honour than a basic Faithful Service Medal, and the Devoted Service Medal was introduced. John Brown was thus awarded the silver Faithful Service Medal for his twenty-one years in Queen Victoria's employment, to which in 1881 a 'bar' was added for another ten years' service. His gold Devoted Service Medal, designed and engraved by Joseph Shepherd Wynn, chief engraver of seals, bore the inscription: 'To John Brown Esq, in recognition of his presence of mind and devotion at Buckingham Palace, February 29, 1872.' This was awarded in recognition of the O'Connor attack. The Faithful Service Medal was to survive as the Royal Victoria Medal for royal service, but the latter, dismissed by courtiers as 'The Greater Order of Brown', seems to have lapsed.[15]

On John Brown

'To my regret I had no personal acquaintance with Mr John Brown, but my valet often told me of pleasant evenings in his company. He appeared to be a favourite and Mr Brown invited him to his room, where over whisky and tobacco, they went into committee on the state of the nation.'

4th Lord Ribblesdale,
Lord-in-Waiting and Master of Buckhounds

For those in society who paid attention to such things – most of the County Set and London Club members and Salon devotees – the steady elevation of John Brown Esq. was an eyebrow-raising event. Even the *Almanac*, first published by the bookseller and editor Joseph Whitaker in 1868, lists 'John Brown, Her Majesty's Personal Servant' as a member of the Royal Household, hob-nobbing on the page with the Queen's relatives, such as Count Albert Edward Gleichen. Brown's privileges also included not only the organisation of shoots at the royal estates, but also the right to take part; this also applied to salmon fishing on the Dee where Brown would proprietorially restrict the best beats to himself.

Brown's duties had expanded greatly in the preceding ten years. He was now overseer of all below-stairs work and management and he acted as personnel officer when servants' personal problems tipped over into their royal service. Brown monitored the servants' lives from appointment to death. His keenness to know all that was going on meant that he was also message-bearer not only to the Queen but to her equerries, too. It led to a gruelling day. The Queen wrote tersely to Lady Biddulph, wife of the Master of the Household, on this subject with underlined emphasis:

It is, that my poor Brown has so much to do that it wd be a gt relief if – the Equerries received hint not to be constantly sending him at all hours for trifling messages: he is often so tired from being so constantly on his legs that, he goes to bed with swollen feet and can't sleep from fatigue! You see he goes out twice with me – comes then for orders – then goes with messages to the pages, and lies [ladies]. – & often to the Equerries & then comes up with my bag twice . . . he must not be made 'a man of all work' – besides it loses his position . . . [One of the Equerries is] an extra fidget, but some of the others do the same & it must be put a stop to . . .[16]

All this was to take its toll. Wherever he went John Brown was a source of great interest to high and low alike, and those who were closest to the Royal Household began to see a decided physical change in him. From time to time his face swelled up, adding to the gossip that he was an alcoholic, and both his face and legs were subject to blotching. He was growing old and grey in his royal mistress's service; his muscular leanness was now turning to fat and his famed thighs and legs, which had so set off the kilt he always wore, were causing him problems. Brown, who could once easily stride up hills with the Queen's bag of paints and her easel, now tired more quickly, and he found difficulty in sleeping because of his swollen limbs and aching joints. It is certain that John Brown repeatedly jarred his legs jumping down from the royal carriages. From now on Brown's health became a factor in the Queen's planning of future jaunts and state visits.

Yet life went on, with the Queen's mood swinging between melancholy and cheerfulness. The year 1873 was another bittersweet one. There was great sorrow for the Queen on the death of her brother-sovereign Napoleon III in English exile on 9 January, although she maintained her friendship with his Empress Eugénie. Brown was to accompany the Queen on the first visit to the Empress's home at London's Camden Place soon after the Emperor's death. The Queen was also to share her sister-in-law's grief after the tragic death of her son, the Prince Imperial, killed on 19 June 1879 while on scouting duties during the Zulu War. Brown broke the news to her at Balmoral and the Queen travelled south to comfort in person 'the Poor, poor, dear Empress! her only, only child – her all gone!'[17]

This tragedy, however, lay in the future. Queen Victoria continued her regular pattern of life. Now that she suffered more from rheumatism, John Brown pushed her in a wheelchair around the gardens of Balmoral, Osborne and Windsor, with the patient Princess Beatrice chatting to her as they negotiated the flowerbeds. On Tuesday 9 September 1873 they were off to Inverlochy. Again Brown accompanied the Queen with her usual large retinue as they travelled from Ballater station on the main Aberdeen line south to join the Highland Railway. On such jaunts there was a respectful informality between sovereign, servants and courtiers; for instance, the Queen's German maid Emilie Dittweiler shared a carriage with Henry Ponsonby, while Brown sat next to the Queen on the train.

Carriages awaited them at Kingussie. At Laggan Bridge they changed horses, and a little girl presented the Queen with a nosegay. This was a common occurrence on royal progresses, and 'the innkeeper gave Brown a bottle with some wine and a glass'.[18] People turned out along the way to cheer the Queen amid triumphal arches of heather, Gaelic inscriptions and pipers. The gentry, too, turned out, standing at the gateways of their estates to greet the Queen. At Ardverikie, an estate and deer forest not far from Loch Laggan, the new owner Sir John Ramsden, MP for Monmouth and erstwhile Under-Secretary for War 1857–8, stood at the roadside with his family and servants to salute the Queen.[19]

The Queen's base for exploring this part of Inverness-shire was the then modern Inverlochy Castle, some 3 miles from Fort William. Not far away were the ruins of the old Inverlochy Castle made famous by Sir Walter Scott in *The Legend of Montrose* (1819). Each day was to bring extensive and tiring excursions in the area known as Lochaber. At Loch Arkaig the Queen was hosted aboard a screw steamer owned by Cameron of Lochiel, chief of the Clan Cameron. His presence recalled a story that was to be often repeated in the 'Brown anecdotage'. It seems that one day Cameron of Lochiel was making his way to a 'drawing-room' at Buckingham Palace, when his carriage, which had been delayed in the horse traffic, was surrounded by urchins clamouring "Ooray! 'Ere's John Brown!' Indignantly the chieftain lowered the sash-window of the carriage, brandished his glengarry bearing the eagle's feather of his clan position and shouted: 'I'm no John Brown. I'm Cameron o'Lochiel!'[20] Many a Highland gentleman in full dress was similarly accosted on the streets of London.

The Inverlochy jaunt, which ended on 16 September, took in hundreds of miles of Inverness-shire, and the long days were spent soaking up Highland and Jacobite history and culture. The trip also resulted in another of John Brown's encounters with the hated press. The royal party was at a location some 10 miles from Ballachulish on Loch Linne. While the Queen viewed the peaks known in Gaelic as *Na tri Peathrraichean* ('The Three Sisters'), John Brown and his cousin Francie Clark set out the luncheon on plaids. After setting up the Queen's sketching board, Brown saw in the distance a group of 'inquisitive reporters' from the 'Scotch papers' approaching. One had already taken up position and was watching the Queen, Princess Beatrice and Lady Jane Churchill through a telescope. John Brown made his way over to them and told them to move away. 'I've as good a right as the Queen to be here,' replied the reporter with the telescope. Brown, quite politely for him, indicated the Queen's distress at the reporters dogging her steps. Again the reporter refused to move and so Brown threatened him with violence. On his dignity, the reporter challenged Brown to repeat the threat to the rest of the reporters who were now moving over to the arguing men. Brown said he would repeat the threat, and an argy-bargy of 'strong words' ensued. At length his companions advised the reporter with the telescope to move away. The Queen was indignant when Brown reported what had happened; it was an increasing type of occurrence on her jaunts for the press to openly follow her: 'Such conduct ought to be known,' she said.[21]

Another of Queen Victoria's family was married in 1874. Her second son and fourth child Prince Alfred, Duke of Edinburgh and Saxe-Coburg and Gotha, had become engaged in July 1873 to the Grand-Duchess Marie of Russia (1853–1920), the only daughter of Czar Alexander II. Queen Victoria was not enthusiastic about the match as she looked upon the House of Romanov as 'half-oriental', but the marriage of Alfred and Marie took place on 23 January in St Petersburg. The year 1874 was also to be remarkable in the history of John Brown with the arrival at Balmoral of Dr Alexander Profeit.

In 1874 Queen Victoria's Commissioner at Balmoral, Dr Alexander Robertson, finally decided to retire and the Queen approved the appointment of Dr Profeit in his place. Born in 1833 at his father's farm at Nether Towie, in the Aberdeenshire parish of Towie on the River Don, north-west of Balmoral, and some 8½ miles from the railway terminus at Alford, Profeit had attended Towie parish school, Aberdeen Grammar School, and King's College, Aberdeen University, where he graduated MA in 1855.[22] In 1857 he graduated LRCS at Edinburgh.[23] He married Miss Anderson (d. 1888) of Tarland, and by her had seven children; he practised medicine at Towie and Tarland, where he became a firm friend of Dr Robertson. At the latter's suggestion Profeit went to Crathie as parish doctor, creating for himself a reputation for respect and efficiency.[24] Alexander Profeit's royal career started when he was engaged as medical resident at Balmoral in 1874; he became Commissioner of Balmoral and Overseer of Abergeldie on 22 November 1875.[25]

While Profeit's independence of character, energy, zeal for his job and devotion to her won him Queen Victoria's regard, he and John Brown were enemies from the start, with neither willing to yield to the other. Profeit now knew Crathie and its people better than John Brown, a point that the latter resented. Profeit was permanently on hand at Balmoral and in medical practice at Crathie ministered to royal servants, estate tenants and locals alike. He was also a tireless organiser of the Braemar Gathering, of which the Queen was frequently hostess. John Brown resented Profeit's involvement. Before Profeit arrived at Balmoral, John Brown had had a prominent role in the hiring and firing of estate workers and gillies. When Profeit was appointed he was disturbed by the fact that Brown was so influential and endeavoured to scale down the Highland Servant's importance. The situation led on one occasion to a useful employee being sacked.

In the mid-1870s Queen Victoria decided that she would like to have a 'boy piper' as a part of her permanent Balmoral staff and Dr Profeit was dispatched to Corgarff, in Strathdon parish, where the Machardy boys were winning a reputation for themselves as prominent pipers. Edith Paterson, the daughter of one of the boys, Jamie Machardy, remembered:

> Come an autumn day in 1877 [Jamie and his brother] climbed into a box cart with grandfather for the journey to Balmoral, their pipes cushioned in the straw at their feet. The day was hot and the pipes mute when Jamie would fain try a tune before the final descent on the Castle. 'Ach,' said grandfather, 'there'll be pipes there.' And they trundled on again. The Queen heard them play in the rose garden. There were no other pipes [but their own]. And Jamie won [with his test piece 'Whaur the Gadie rins'].[26]

Backed by his own skill and Dr Profeit's recommendation Jamie MacHardie entered royal service for training under Pipe Major Ross of the 42nd Regiment.

Edith Paterson went on: 'My father stayed with Queen Victoria for five years, 1877 to 1882.' John Brown was always off-hand with him, as he was not a 'Brown appointment', and the boy was warned by the Highland Servant to keep his 'eyes open and his mouth shut' about life at Balmoral. At length, said Mrs Paterson, Jamie 'streeve' ('quarrelled') with John Brown, who refused to have him any longer on the staff. In his usual manner John Brown complained about him to the Queen, and despite Dr Profeit's protestations, the young man had to go. His customary reference was terse: 'James MacHardy left. Gave no offence. Signed, John Brown.' Said Mrs Paterson: 'My father with youthful impatience tore it up.'[27]

On 17 September the Prince of Wales said goodbye to his mother before setting off on an important tour of India. The royal family, together with Henry Herbert, 4th Earl of Carnarvon and Tory Secretary of State for the Colonies, dined at the Prince's quarters at Abergeldie. Rudolph Löhlein and John Brown were there to say goodbye to the Prince. Shaking him by the hand Brown said: 'God bless your Royal Highness, and bring you safe back.' This sentiment added to the Queen's distress at the parting. Even so she urged her 34-year-old son to watch what he ate [he ate too much], attend a Sunday service [always a great reluctance on his part], and to go to bed before ten o'clock each night [a forlorn hope].[28]

Four days later Queen Victoria set off by rail and carriage for Inverarary Castle, the home of George Campbell, 8th Duke of Argyll, and his Duchess Elizabeth Georgina. The Campbells were the in-laws of Princess Louise, who met the royal party with her husband the Marquess of Lorne and led them to the castle. Through an arch bearing the Gaelic welcomed *Ceud mille Failte do'n Bhan Rhighinn do Inerara* ('A hundred thousand welcomes to the Queen to Inveraray'), the Queen drove into the heart of Campbell country.

The Queen was to spend a week at Inveraray, with customary jaunts into the local hinterland. She treated the castle as if it were a hotel, and usually dined in her room separately from the Duke's family but always attended by Brown. As Henry Ponsonby was to write: 'Evidently she considered herself as paying a visit to Princess Louise' and the other members of the household were 'merely accidental'.[29] Princess Louise took the opportunity to complain to her mother that her permanent quarters 'were not good enough' and that her husband's family did not give her the respect due to a royal princess. The Duke's staff were astounded to have to take orders from Brown.[30] The Duke and Duchess held a ball to celebrate the royal visit, and John Brown danced a reel or two with Princess Louise and Lady Churchill. There was much adverse comment from the Queen and Brown that the band hired by the Duke, from Glasgow, could not play reels and pipers had to supply the required music. On the royal party's return to Balmoral, John Brown was to receive some bad news.

For some time John Brown's father had been ailing and he died on 18 October 1875, aged eighty-one. On the morning of the funeral the Queen drove out alone after breakfast for the first time in years, while Brown went over to Wester Micras to finalise the funeral arrangements.[31]

The day of the funeral was wet. Queen Victoria stood with the Brown family in the stone-flagged kitchen of the Wester Micras farmhouse and tried to comfort the newly widowed Margaret Brown. Outside, a hundred or so neighbours and Crathie folk waited for the funeral party to appear. As was the custom at a Highland funeral, since the Reformed Church of Scotland forbade any set burial service, the minister Dr Campbell intoned impromptu prayers while the chief mourners John Brown and his four brothers (Hugh was then in New Zealand), the Queen, Princess Beatrice and Lady Jane Ely, the Hon. Mortimer West (later Lord Sackville) and the three doctors, Marshall, Profeit and Robertson, stood around the 'kist' (coffin). According to custom, too, only the male mourners attended the actual burial, and the Queen and Princess Beatrice watched the interment from a distance. The Queen returned to the farmhouse with Mrs William Brown and gave the grieving widow a mourning brooch. Queen Victoria remained for the customary oatmeal cakes, cheese and whisky repast before returning to Balmoral, leaving the family with their grief.[32]

In early 1876 John Brown's legs were causing him great pain once more, and for this reason Queen Victoria postponed her planned trip to Germany. Even when the royal party were installed on the royal yacht *Victoria and Albert*, some doubts remained whether Brown would be well enough to sail. But pronounced fit to travel John Brown thus accompanied the Queen, this time travelling as the 'Countess of Rosenau', to Coburg where his temper developed an increased illness-produced acerbity.

On 1 May 1876 Queen Victoria was promulgated Queen-Empress and proudly signed herself 'Victoria Regina and Imperatrix' for the first time. By 2 August John Brown was grief-stricken once more by the death of his 77-year-old mother at Craiglourican Cottage on the Balmoral estate.[33] After her funeral he was soon back at the Queen's side to prepare for the next engagements.

The year 1876 was to see the unveiling of an equestrian statue by Sir John Steell of Prince Albert in field-marshal's uniform at Charlotte Square Gardens, Edinburgh. Staying at Holyrood Palace on 17 August the weather was hot enough for the Queen to sit in the gardens to write her letters, with John Brown blotting and stacking them ready for posting. After lunch Princess Beatrice and Prince Leopold accompanied the Queen to the statue unveiling with Brown, in full dress Highland uniform, and Collins, Prince Leopold's valet, on the box; Prince Arthur commanded the sovereign's escort of 7th Hussars. The Queen noted that John Brown was delighted with the reception he received from the crowd.[34]

Ceremonially the year was rounded off at Balmoral with the presentation of colours to Queen Victoria's father's former regiment, the Royal Scots, of which he had been Colonel. On this occasion John Brown's brothers William and Hugh, with their wives, were included in the 'viewing party' near the Queen.

The slow deterioration of John Brown's health caused him to be more accident-prone. On 11 August 1877 he accompanied the Queen on a tour of one of the first British sea-going masterless warships HMS *Thunderer*; on this occasion he clumsily fell through an aperture in a gun turret, sustaining severe bruising to his shins. It is certain, too, that he was suffering from recurrent erysipelas of the face and cellulitis of the legs, and his feeling of unwellness contributed to his increased alcoholism and shortness of temper. Heavy drinking among the estate workers at Balmoral was an accepted fact; with so many whisky distilleries in the area the liquor was readily available so in this Brown was not acting out of character in any way.

Still John Brown soldiered on, embarking with the Queen on a six-day journey to Loch Maree, between Gairloch and Kinlochewe, Ross-shire. His workload was heavy, and largely self-regulated; for instance, on this occasion he helped the Queen to pack a number of large boxes with state papers and the documents she had to attend to while away. The entourage made the uneventful journey to Loch Maree Hotel, but a gruelling pace of visits and sightseeing was maintained, with John Brown jumping up and down from the box to run errands for the Queen. Writing about the trip Arthur Ponsonby opined: 'Having a picnic luncheon, sketching, talking to old women in cottages and making purchases in the village shops, the Queen thoroughly enjoyed herself. She genuinely liked associating with humble people in the villages. This led to many stories which were pure fabrications.'[35] To the sovereign all was *gemütlich*, but it was exhausting for everyone else, especially Brown.

On his own drunkenness
More than once a maid was sent to John Brown's room to enquire about his non-appearance to attend the Queen. On one occasion a maid went to Brown's room in the Clarence Tower, Windsor Castle, with just such a query from the Queen. Brown, fully clothed, addressed the startled woman from beneath a pile of bedclothes: 'She'll no be seein' me the day. She kens damned well I'm fu' [drunk].'

During Queen Victoria's autumn visit to Balmoral in 1878 she spent a few days, from 24 to 26 August, at Broxmouth, just over a mile from the east coast town of Dunbar in East Lothian. Broxmouth was a seat of the Duke and Duchess of Roxburghe. On 26 August, the anniversary of the birthday of Prince Albert, the Queen dispensed presents in memory of her husband to her ladies and gentlemen and servants. 'After breakfast,' she wrote, 'I gave my faithful Brown an oxidised silver biscuit-box, and some onyx studs. He was greatly pleased with the former, and the tears came to his eyes, and he said "It is too much." God knows, it is not, for one so devoted and faithful.'[36]

John Brown's perceived 'interference' in all 'Balmoral matters' reached its peak of irritation for both courtiers and servants in the 1870s. An example was the 'Great Pony Row'. It seems that Brown complained to the Queen that the small mountain ponies were being ridden too hard and too often by her visitors and courtiers. He cited particularly the Revd Canon Robinson Duckworth, a royal chaplain and Prince Leopold's former tutor; Herr Hermann Sahl, her librarian and German secretary; and the sculptor Edgar Boehm (Brown's 'Mr Bum'). Each received a terse note from the Queen. All they could do was stand at the windows of Balmoral and fume at Brown riding out whenever he wished. Not even the intervention of the Prince of Wales on their behalf had much effect. It was an all-too-typical scenario.

Yet Queen Victoria's children as well as her courtiers found it convenient to get John Brown to broach matters with the Queen which they themselves dare not, and for him to break bad news to her. For example, he was asked to tell the Queen that her daughter Princess Alice had died of diphtheria at Neue Palais, Darmstadt, on 14 December 1878.

As John Brown's health continued to worsen, Queen Victoria's enthusiasm for travel increased, with Highland jaunts in particular. The logistics for each journey, be they simple picnics in the Scottish hills or lengthy tours, were vast, with John Brown playing a major role in organising the packing and transportation of the large amount of personal impedimenta which the Queen considered basic requirements, from her desk, easel and paints, photograph collections and bric-à-brac to carriages and ponies. For serious jaunts an entourage of some sixty people was the norm. One such visit was her spring tour of Italy in 1879. This was her first trip to the country and she ensconced herself in the Villa Clara, Baveno, on the eastern shores of Lake Maggiore, as the 'Countess of Balmoral'. Even the youngest Italian urchins correctly identified the elderly woman dressed in black, accompanied by the kilted Brown, a Maid of Honour (Miss Cadogan), a piper and numerous *carabinieri*, and hailed her with cries of '*Bravissima . . . La Regina d'Inghilterra*'.

During this holiday John Brown suffered his first severe bout of erysipelas, which clearly discomfited the Queen. Her state of mind was already disturbed by news received when she stopped for a night at the British Embassy in Paris en route for Italy, that her eleven-year-old grandson Prince Waldemar of Prussia, the sixth child of Princess Victoria, Empress of German. Henry Ponsonby was to remember the Baveno trip: 'John Brown was insufferably bored and made himself intensely disagreeable. He generally managed to prevent the Queen going out till after four o'clock as was her custom at home.' He continued, describing a trip 'to a lovely place', where the Queen remained in her carriage. 'We believed it was because Brown would not allow her to get out. He is surly beyond measure and today we could see him all the way – a beautiful drive – with his eyes fixed on the horses' tails refusing to look up.'[37] Although he was to receive as much attention as the Queen on excursions to places like Milan, John Brown remained 'surly' and the Queen 'saw nothing' as she remained in her closed carriage. Although Ponsonby stopped the carriage to point out particular features of the scenery to the Queen, his efforts were 'coldly received' as she mirrored Brown's ill-temper.[38]

Early 1879 was to bring the Queen news of a plethora of important personal events. On 13 March Prince Arthur, Duke of Connaught, married Louise of Prussia (1860–1917); on 12 May the Queen received news that Princess Charlotte of Saxe-Meiningen, still in mourning for her brother Prince Waldemar, had given birth to her first great-grandchild, Princess Feodora; and on 24 May the Queen celebrated her sixtieth birthday. Yet, the Queen's writings also mentioned the deaths of several people who had played a prominent role in her life. Her Keeper of the Privy Purse, Sir Thomas Biddulph, was among them, while deaths at Balmoral included John Grant, her Head Keeper, and her former Commissioner Dr Andrew Robertson.

'Packed my boxes with Brown,' the Queen wrote on 20 June as she set out on her way to comfort Empress Eugénie on the death of her son the Prince Imperial. The Queen's miserable state of mind was hardly lifted as she passed 'over the marvellous Tay Bridge'[39] as the 'Scots papers' brought her news of the Zulu War, the result of the British annexation of the Transvaal in 1877.

A poignant highlight of the autumn Balmoral visit that year was a drive which the Queen took with Empress Eugénie to Glen Gelder Shiel, bynamed in Gaelic *Ruidh na Bhan Righ* ('Queen's Shiel'). The Queen had invited the Empress to stay at Abergeldie after her tragic bereavement. It was a fine interlude and the Queen wrote that she had walked with the Empress by the Gelder Burn, and:

When we came back to the little Shiel, after walking for an hour, we had tea. Brown had caught some excellent trout and cooked them with oatmeal, which the dear Empress liked extremely, and said would be her dinner. It was a glorious evening – the hills pink, and the sky so clear.[40]

But for the Queen the skies were soon to darken again in a way they had not done for twenty years.

CHAPTER SIX

SICKLE OF THE REAPER

In the 1880s Queen Victoria suffered a series of blows which deeply disturbed her state of mind. The first came in April 1880 when Prime Minister Benjamin Disraeli, whom she had made Earl of Beaconsfield on 12 August 1876, was thrown out of office. The Queen received the news at Baden-Baden, and the prospect of having the Liberal statesman W.E. Gladstone as Prime Minister filled her with gloom. She wrote to Henry Ponsonby on 4 April that she would 'sooner abdicate than send for or have any communication with that half-mad fire-brand who would soon ruin everything & be a Dictator'.[1] On 27 April Disraeli paid a personal farewell as Prime Minister to his monarch in sad audience, and 'she presented him with statuettes of herself, John Brown, the royal pony and the dog "Sharp"'.[2]

At Christmas 1880 Queen Victoria gave John Brown a silver pipe case. He used it daily for his well-worn pipe. The case was engraved with the monogram 'JB', and the legend: 'FROM VR CHRISTMAS 1880'.[3]

Despite a great deal of unconstitutional jockeying on Queen Victoria's part, Gladstone did form a Liberal ministry and confirmed her worst fears. At Windsor Castle she wrote in her *Journal* for 1 January 1881:

> Another year past, and we begin one with heavy clouds. A poor Government, Ireland in a state of total lawlessness, and war in the Cape [the Transvaal Boers had risen under Paul Kruger] of a very serious nature. I feel very anxious and have no one to lean on.

To Disraeli she wrote: 'I often think of you – indeed constantly – and rejoice to see you looking down from the wall after dinner. [Disraeli's portrait by Heinrich von Angeli, 1877, hung in the dining room at

Windsor Castle.] Oh! if only I had you, my kind friend and wise counsellor and strong arm to help and lean on.'

John Brown also missed Disraeli and sent him gifts of salmon from the Dee. Disraeli expressed to the Queen his feelings about Brown's generosity: 'No man has been more faithful to me in my fallen fortunes . . .'[4]

The Queen particularly felt the loss of Disraeli's sympathetic male support; after all, he and John Brown had between them filled the vacuum in her life left by Prince Albert's death. But worse was to come. On 19 April Disraeli died at his home at 19 Curzon Street, London. The Queen penned the death notice for the *Court Circular* herself and her wreath of wild primroses with the words 'His favourite flowers; from Osborne, a tribute of affection and regret from Queen Victoria' was placed on his coffin as it travelled to burial in the private vault on his estate of Hughenden, Buckinghamshire. On the bier rested another wreath from his old friend John Brown.[5]

Queen Victoria always took an interest in the development of the Royal Infirmary in Edinburgh, which establishment Lord Provost George Drummond had pressed for in 1721. By 1870 the infirmary's third phase was completed, the foundation stone laid by the Prince of Wales; enlargement had taken place in 1879. In the autumn of 1881 the Queen visited the infirmary to review progress. Among those invited to view the proceedings was the deaf and almost blind Dowager Lady Ruthven, who had met the Queen on her first visit to Scotland in 1842. Lady Ruthven had a piercing stentorian voice, and during a moment when the waiting dignitaries fell silent she bellowed: 'Tell me Bailie Mucklewaite, why is she so tardy?' Oblivious to the Bailie's reply she went on: 'I love the Queen – I long to see the Queen – but I came to see John Brown.'[6]

At Windsor station, on 2 March 1882, there waited a more sinister interested party. Queen Victoria, Princess Beatrice and the Duchess of Roxburghe were greeted with the 'huzzahs' of a crowd of boys from nearby Eton College as the royal party arrived on the 5.30pm train from London. They kept up their greeting until the royal group, including Henry Ponsonby and with John Brown on the box, made to depart. The royal carriage had hardly gone two dozen paces when the Queen heard an explosion which she thought came from the royal

> *On John Brown*
> 'Brown was a commonplace rather coarse type of man with little of
> the shrewdness and humour usually found in the Scottish character in
> the humbler classes, although on occasions he showed good sense. His
> head was naturally turned by the attention the Queen paid him and by
> her employment of him in a peculiarly privileged position. To his
> rudeness, his overbearing manner and his contributions to quarrels and
> altercations in the Household there are several references in the
> correspondence [between Sir Henry Ponsonby and Queen Victoria].'
> **Arthur Ponsonby,**
> **after reading the 'Ponsonby Papers'**

train's engine. The report was to mark the seventh and final attempt
on the Queen's life, and came from a six-chambered rapid-fire
revolver.[7]

Luckily, the bullet missed the Queen and before the putative assassin
could reload, two Eton boys rushed forward and belaboured him with their
umbrellas. For once John Brown was upstaged and stared bemused
watching the events. He rather languidly opened the carriage door to
announce to the Queen: 'That man fired at your Maa-dj-esty's carriage . . .'
The culprit was arrested and subsequently revealed to Superintendent
George Hayes of the Windsor police that he was a starving Scots poet called
Roderick Maclean.

Next day Brown brought the revolver, which had been delivered from
the police station, for the Queen to see. Three days later Queen
Victoria received the nine hundred Eton scholars in their college
quadrangle and thanked her young 'protectors' personally. In due course
Roderick Maclean was tried at Reading Assizes in Berkshire for High
Treason. His attack on the Queen seems to have been the result of his
disaffection with the Liberal government for not subsidising him as a
poet. In his effects a letter was found summing up his grievances.
Addressed to the government, it said:

I should not have done this crime, had you, as you should have done,
allowed me the 10s per week instead of offering me the insultingly

small sum of 6s [probably parish relief] per week and expecting me to live on it. So you perceive the great good a little money might have done, had you not treated me as a fool and set me more than ever against those bloated aristocrats ruled by the old lady, Mrs Vic, who is a licensed robber in all senses. Roderick Maclean. March 2nd, 1882. Waiting Room, G.W.R.[8]

The court learned that Maclean had suffered a brain injury following a fall in 1866, and that he had been discharged from the Bath and Somerset Lunatic Asylum in 1881. Dressed in a green greatcoat with a worn velvet collar, Maclean was defended by barrister Montague Stephen Williams QC, who recalled: 'With a vacant, imbecile, expression he kept glancing hither and thither about the crowded Court.'[9] Maclean was found 'not guilty on the ground of insanity' and was ordered to be detained. Once more the Queen was enraged by the verdict: 'If that is the law,' she berated the hapless Prime Minister, W.E. Gladstone, 'the law must be altered.'[10]

On 15 March 1882 the Queen and her entourage were off to Menton, the former Italian and now French town in the department of Alpes Maritimes on the Riviera. As usual John Brown had packed for her, as usual making sure that her travelling case of medicines was included. As she grew older this case was the Queen's constant companion and John Brown was delegated to be apprised of sources of supplies should she run out of opiates, or *vin marianne* (a wine laced with *cannabis sativa*), among the bottles of spirits of rosemary (for hair loss), tincture of arnica (to rub on bruises) and belladonna (for her irritable bowels) that the case contained. But there was more than the salving of the royal bowels to disturb Brown on this trip.

The British policemen travelling with the Queen received a message that three members of the Irish Republican Brotherhood were on their way to Menton to assassinate the Queen. The police thought the message a hoax; the Queen, too, made light of it when John Brown told her of the message's receipt. Brown, who was loathing Menton, not least because his presence in the town in full Highland dress was causing great interest, agitated for special precautions to be taken. Safety measures were put in place and the Queen wrote to Henry Ponsonby about her sympathy for Brown's apprehensiveness:

The Queen thanks Sir Henry Ponsonby for his kind letter which has much reassured her tho' she cannot say <u>she</u> felt so much alarmed but it gave her a great shock as she was forgetting the 2nd of March [when she was shot at by Maclean] & she trusts Sir Henry will also reassure Brown who was in such a state heightened by increasing <u>hatred</u> of being 'abroad' which blinds his admiration of the country even. The Queen thinks that one principal cause of all this (wh. was <u>not</u> the case in Switzerland) is that he can communicate with <u>no</u> one when out, nor keep anyone off the carriage nor the coachmen either. At Lucerne we always had Hoffman & <u>now</u> when Greenham [one of the London policemen] is not with us [when we are out] walking we have <u>no one</u> and that is what puts Brown so out and makes him so anxious.[11]

On 27 April 'the Scot of the family', Prince Leopold, who sported Duncan among his Christian names, was married at St George's Chapel, Windsor, to Helena of Waldeck and Pyrmont. The radical weekly paper *The World*, whose journalists had monitored John Brown since his first appearance in public, added to the accounts of the wedding by reporting that among the guests were 'a good many local tradesmen who were known to be John Brown's friends'.[12] Over the years many tradesmen sought to curry favour with John Brown in the hope that this would bring them to a useful connection with the Queen. One assiduous practitioner of such flattery was Sir John Bennett, watchmaker and jeweller in London's Cheapside from 1846 to 1889. After showing cases of jewellery to the Queen on one occasion, although she bought nothing, Bennett was advised by an equerry that he should share his lunch, which the Queen had authorised in the Stewards' Room at Windsor Castle, with John Brown and do a little marketing. So Bennett invited Brown and during the meal he obsequiously expressed his love for Deeside and all things Scottish. For his part John Brown supplied wine from the Queen's cellars to accompany the meal and a convivial afternoon resulted. Thereafter courtiers noted that the Queen became a good customer of Bennett's.[13]

In the autumn of 1882 Queen Victoria continued her round of Balmoral activities with visits, picnics, walks and sketching trips, her mind taken up with the war in Egypt, where revolution had been

> *On John Brown*
> 'Brown understood the Queen. But even he could not always have his
> way or satisfy her whims and fancies. One winter when she was angry
> because her sleigh stuck in the snow he told Ponsonby that it did not
> matter what sleigh you had, six large people must weigh heavily and
> "ye canna go like lightning as she wants to do".'
>
> **Arthur Ponsonby,**
> **after reading the 'Ponsonby Papers'**

sparked off in September 1881. Arabi Pasha, the Egyptian soldier and
nationalist leader, overthrew the Khedive, Tewfik Pasha, and helped to
establish a nationalist government with himself as Minister of War. The
British intervened to protect their interests in the Suez Canal area. On
11 September John Brown brought the Queen a Reuters telegram, in
which she read about the recent events in Egypt in the words of Major-
General Sir John McNeill, an Equerry in Ordinary, who was serving in
the campaign.

The Queen was anxious about Prince Arthur, Duke of Connaught,
who was in command of the Brigade of Guards in the Egyptian theatre.
On such occasions she asked Brown to rummage among her music
scores to find something soothing for her to play. This time she chose a
song by Karl Theodor Körner which Prince Albert used to sing: *Gebet
vor der Schlacht, 'Vater, ich rufe Dich'* ('Prayer before battle, 'Father I call
to Thee'). On 13 September Arabi Pasha was defeated at Tel-el-Kebir
and the war came to an end. This was followed by a happy visit to
Balmoral by Prince Leopold and Princess Helen, just returned from
their honeymoon. After meeting the royal couple at Ballater station,
John Brown and the kilted gillies led the Queen's entourage back to
Balmoral for an alfresco toast in whisky, proposed by John Brown. He
intoned: 'Ladies and gentlemen, let us join in a good Highland cheer
for the Duke and Duchess of Albany; may they live long and die
happy!'[14] Brown's hopes were not fulfilled: Prince Leopold died at
Cannes in March 1884, just one year later.

March 1883 was one of the worst on record for inclement rainy
weather. Those who were out walking in Windsor Great Park began to

notice how John Brown was greatly slowing in his reactions to the sudden showers of rain. No longer did he jump with alacrity from the box to offer umbrellas to the Queen and her usual companion Princess Beatrice. They were usually soaked before he finally unfurled the umbrellas and tugged the rugs over the royal knees. John Brown was entering the last months of his life but did not shirk his duties and the Queen was about to encourage him in the role of detective. But first there was an accident.

On Monday 17 March Queen Victoria descended the stairs from her private apartments at Windsor Castle to prepare for her afternoon ride. For a moment her attention strayed and she stumbled on the last step. In trying to save herself she twisted her knee. She wrote: 'I could not move for a moment. Then Brown came, and helped me with great difficulty into the carriage.'[15] When she arrived back at Windsor Castle her leg was too sore to support her so John Brown, with the assistance of Lockwood, the footman on duty, half carried and half walked her back to her room. While this was going on, some 3 miles away a strange scenario was purportedly taking place involving one Lady Florence Dixie.

Whether or not Queen Victoria knew Lady Florence Dixie personally before 2 March 1883 is not clear, but on that date a rather hysterical letter to the Queen arrived at Windsor Castle from Lady Florence. Now in her twenty-sixth year, Lady Florence had written to the Queen to express her rising dismay at how the peasants of Western Ireland were starving. The subject was one about which Lady Florence, as an absentee Irish landlord herself, had made a particular study. Her penchant for such pursuits set her apart from other aristocratic women of her day in the intensity of her eccentric notions, such as taking up such causes as sex equality and the reform of fashion. Lady Florence and Queen Victoria were at opposite ends of the scale of opinion – the Queen looked upon gender parity as a 'mad, wicked folly', and was outraged by the idea of women wearing trousers and monocles to copy men.

Certainly the Queen had 'heard' of Lady Florence. She was the sister of John Sholto Douglas, 9th Marquess of Queensbury. (His son Lord Alfred Douglas, 'Bosie', was the notorious friend of Oscar Wilde, and caused the latter's downfall.) Like her brother, Lady Florence was an excellent hunter, earning herself the nickname 'female Nimrod'; she regularly walked around Windsor Castle Great Park with a jaguar which she had captured on a hunting trip to Patagonia with her husband Sir Alexander Beaumont Churchill Dixie, whom she married in 1875.[16]

About the time Brown and Lockwood were carrying Queen Victoria to her boudoir, Lady Florence Dixie arrived back at her Windsor House, The Fishery, with her clothes dishevelled and spattered with mud and her hands bleeding from several wounds. According to her testimony, while she was walking her St Bernard dog Hubert in the rough ground that bordered her estate, she had been set upon by two transvestites. Lady Florence told the press:

> One of them seized me roughly by the neck, pushed me backwards, and threw me to the ground with great violence. The other man, his confederate . . . was standing over me . . . I saw in his hand a sort of dagger . . . I saw a momentary flash of steel, and then I felt the blade go through the upper part of my dress . . . Luckily the blade came in contact with one of the steel stays of my corset and glanced off . . . the wretch withdrew it, and plunged at me again with the dagger. As it descended I caught hold of the blade with my left hand, and held it for a moment. The weapon cut through my glove, and inflicted a deep but clean cut. He wrenched the weapon from me, and as it slipped from my left I caught it with my right hand . . . Then I lost my hold upon the knife . . . He was about to deliver the third [stab] when the dog must have pulled him off . . . Then I became unconscious . . . When I regained consciousness I found myself quite alone.[17]

When the story broke it created a sensation. Yet Lady Florence's account of what happened, and her subsequent assertion that the perpetrators were Fenians, did not stand up to close scrutiny. As the pressmen investigated the story each of its strands was contradicted by a number of eye-witnesses only too willing to talk. Private Bates of the Scots Guards, the regiment then on guard duty at Windsor, was one. He was walking in nearby Maidenhead Road and had kept his eye on Lady Florence because of her noteworthy dog. Bates had seen nothing of the assailants. A gardener on the nearby estate to Lady Florence's, one Mr Groves, had been working close to where she had passed but heard nothing of Lady Florence's purported cries for help. An Eton

College schoolmaster averred that he had had Lady Florence in sight during the whole of her walk, and had seen her return to The Fishery unhurt. Why was Lady Florence lying? Queen Victoria was intrigued. She also shared Lady Florence's fear of Fenian assassination and suspected that a gang of Irish terrorists were forming in the area of Windsor. She sent John Brown to gather evidence.

On 18 March John Brown braved the bitter cold and drove to The Fishery in an open dog-cart. There he met Sir Henry Ponsonby, engaged in making his own investigations. Lady Florence seemed perky enough after her supposed ordeal and infused tea for her guests with a gusto that belied her injured hands. After making a fuss of Hubert, and demanding of Lady Florence that he have a photograph of the magnificent beast – at his own expense of course! – John Brown set off to examine the circumstances of the crime that Lady Florence had recounted to him just as she told it to the journalists.

John Brown had noted from the newspaper reports that the slashes on Lady Florence's outer clothing did not correspond with tears on her under garments. There was no mud on the back of her clothing, which one would have expected if she had been thrown to the ground. Despite a minute investigation of the scene of the supposed crime John Brown could come up with nothing original; he reported his failure to his royal mistress. 'The whole case so puzzled Mr Brown that he spent considerable time in the open air making his enquiries, thus exposing him to the bitter cold,' reported a journalist.[18]

On 30 March 1883, in replying to a question in the House of Commons, the Liberal Home Secretary, Sir William Harcourt closed the case by stating that none of Lady Florence's assertions had been corroborated. What did it all mean? The Queen remained puzzled and studied closely the usual distillation of the news on the subject prepared for her by Sir Henry Ponsonby.

One paper commented that Lady Florence had been beset by 'sturdy beggars' and that fear of Fenian assassination had affected her 'imagination' and coloured 'her narrative of events'.[19] A medical paper used the case to talk about examples of 'hallucination' and the work done on the subject by Professor Legrand du Saulle of the Salpêtrière Hospital in Paris.[20] Yet the whole business was summed up for the Court gossip network by Louisa, Countess of Antrim, who opined that

Lady Florence had been under the influence of alcohol at the time of her supposed attack. After all, said the Countess, it was common knowledge that Lady Florence and her husband were referred to in Court circles as 'Sir Sometimes and Lady Always Tipsy'.[21]

The brouhaha engendered by Lady Florence soon died away, but the chilling he had received as a consequence of his open air investigation of her case caused John Brown to develop a severe chest cold. His devotion to royal duties kept John Brown out of a sick bed. The Queen needed him. Her twisted knee was followed by rheumatic twinges that kept her carriage and chair-bound, but she still insisted on daily 'walks'. On Saturday 24 March the Queen declared herself well enough for a longer drive and Brown and footman Lockwood carried her down to the pony-chair which had been a favourite conveyance at Balmoral. Wrapped in 'a huge assortment of wraps, known to her ladies as "the White Knight's paraphernalia",' as the Countess of Antrim recalled, Queen Victoria and John Brown set out down the Long Walk at Windsor Castle. It was the last time.[22]

That Saturday evening, press reports noted, John Brown was seen around the castle 'apparently in fair health, although still suffering from a cold'.[23] But his condition declined and Dr Sir William Jenner was called by Brown's anxious brother Archie. By the morning of Easter Sunday, 25 March, erysipelas had extended over the right side of John Brown's face and he developed a high fever. In those days of no antibiotics, his condition deteriorated fast and by the evening he had lapsed into delirium tremens.

The Queen was enjoying her Easter, but wrote with a slightly petulant undertone: 'Had a good night. Vexed that Brown could not attend me, not being at all well, with a swollen face, which is feared is erysipelas.'[24] It is clear that Queen Victoria did not realise the gravity of John Brown's illness. On Monday 26 March, leaning heavily on footman Lockwood, she went to the private chapel at Windsor Castle to attend the christening of Princess Alice Mary Victoria Augusta Pauline, born to the Prince and Princess Leopold on 25 February. This Princess Alice was to be the longest-surviving of Queen Victoria's thirty-seven grandchildren; she died in 1981.

During the morning of Tuesday 27 March, Dr James Reid, who had been constantly monitoring John Brown's condition at the request of

Queen Victoria, was handed a telegram from his father's medical partner, Dr Andrew Fowler, informing him of his own father's serious illness. Dr Reid senior died shortly afterwards. As John Brown was so ill, Queen Victoria deemed herself unable to allow Dr Reid to leave his bedside.

By Tuesday afternoon John Brown had sunk into a deep coma from which he never regained consciousness. According to the death certificate signed by Dr Reid, John Brown died at Windsor Castle at 10.40pm that night.[25]

Who was to tell the Queen of Brown's death? Her family shirked the task until Prince Leopold reluctantly agreed. The Queen wrote of the event:

> Leopold came to my dressing-room and broke the dreadful news to me that my good, faithful Brown had passed away early this morning. [sic] Am terribly upset by this loss, which removes one who was so devoted and attached to my service and who did so much for my personal comfort. It is the loss not only of a servant, but of a real friend.[26]

Prince Leopold conveyed his feelings in a letter to his brother-in-law Prince Louis, Grand Duke of Hesse-Darmstadt: 'I have deep sympathy with [the Queen]. We can feel for her, & her sorrow, without being sorry for the cause. At least I can't be a hypocrite.'[27]

As the Queen wept alone at Windsor Castle, Prime Minister Gladstone prepared a letter of condolence at Downing Street:

> Mr Gladstone presents his humble duty and presumes to lay before Your Majesty the expression of sincere concern with which he had learned that Your Majesty has been deprived, by a sudden and fatal illness, of the services of Mr J Brown. He is able in some degree to understand how the aid and attention of an attached, respected, and intelligent domestic prolonged through many years, and naturally productive of an ever-growing confidence, must, when withdrawn thus abruptly, leave a sense of serious loss, and this most of all in Your Majesty's elevated sphere, and closely occupied life. Even in his own contracted circle of personal relations, he has had occasion to feel

how much more of proximity may be the natural growth of such services than the outer world would readily suppose.

Mr Gladstone trusts Your Majesty may be able to select a good and efficient successor, though it would be too much to hope that anyone, however capable, can at once fill the void.[28]

This was typical of the pedantic twaddle that Queen Victoria expected of Gladstone. The Prime Minister's hope that a 'successor' be selected to replace the 'intelligent domestic' grated with the Queen, whose low opinion of Gladstone descended a further notch or two. Benjamin Disraeli would never have made such a 'pitiless' blunder. Nevertheless in due course Queen Victoria appointed John Brown's cousin Francie Clark to his former position. She had moulded John Brown into the servant she required and would endeavour to form Francie Clark in his image.

Laid out by the royal undertakers, John Brown's body rested in state in his 'untidy room' in a temporary 'shell' while a 'handsome State coffin was constructed'.[29] The Queen's hand was undoubtedly behind the entry in the *Court Circular* reporting John Brown's death. After detailing a short comment on Brown's royal service it went on:

This melancholy event has caused the deepest regret to the Queen, the Royal Family, and all members of the Royal Household. To Her Majesty the loss is irreparable, and the death of this truly faithful and devoted servant has been a grievous stroke to the Queen . . . An honest, faithful, and devoted follower, a trustworthy, discreet, and straightforward man, and possessed of strong sense, he filled a position of great and anxious responsibility, the duties of which he performed with such a constant and unceasing care as to secure for himself the real friendship of the Queen.[30]

The Queen's emotions as reported in the official announcement were not shared by the Prince of Wales and his siblings. Searching out 'social items' in the *Court Circular*, author E.E.P. Tisdall noted that the Prince and Princess of Wales and Prince and Princess Alfred, among others, embarked on a flurry of theatre trips and after-theatre parties to an unprecedented extent.[31] Sadly, the Prince of Wales's reaction to the

Queen setting out in her pony carriage the day after John Brown's death went unrecorded, but teeth must have been on edge when Francie Clark was seen walking in his cousin's usual place.

On Tuesday 3 April all the preparations were completed for John Brown's funeral. His body, still in its inner lead 'shell', was lifted into a polished oak coffin, with layers of charcoal placed between the two containers. Unsealed, the coffin was laid upon the bed in which he had died and a short service was conducted by the Revd Thomas Orr, the Independent Minister at Windsor, attended by Queen Victoria and Princess Beatrice.[32] Following this private service, the coffin was sealed and carried down to the visitors' reception area in Clarence Tower, where the Revd Orr repeated the service in the presence of a gathering of the Royal Household.

Queen Victoria placed her wreath of myrtle and arum lilies on the coffin, where it was joined by another floral tribute from the Empress Eugénie. The Queen then retired to the Oak Room, from the window of which she watched the hearse bear John Brown to Windsor station. The town's streets were quiet, the shops closed in respect. The bells of the parish church of St John, Windsor, and the bell in the Curfew Tower, were tolled as Brown's coffin made its last journey. For once, at the Queen's command, the pipers did not play under the castle walls.[33] John Brown's body was conveyed by train from Windsor to Ballater and thence by hearse to Baile-na-Coile, the house Queen Victoria had given him for his retirement and in which he had never lived.

Some five hundred people turned out for John Brown's funeral at Crathie cemetery on Thursday 5 April. His bier was flanked by a guard of honour made up of Colonel Farquharson's men from Invercauld and the Earl of Fife's retainers from Mar Lodge. Over the coffin, at the Queen's instruction, was draped a worn plaid. It was a swathe in which she had been wrapped many times for the John Brown 'walks' at Balmoral. Another instruction, on deep mourning paper and in the Queen's own hand, went direct by royal messenger to John Brown's sister-in-law. It read: 'To tell Mrs Hugh to place a wreath of flowers in dear Brown's room [at Windsor Castle] on his bed on the day.'[34] The Queen had already poured out her grief to Brown's sisters-in-law, Mrs William Brown and Mrs Hugh Brown, a few days earlier. Her letter reads:

Dear Lizzie and Jessie,

Weep with me for we all have lost the best, the truest heart that ever beat! As for me – my grief is unbounded – dreadful – & I know not how to bear it, – or how to believe it possible. We parted all so well and happy at dear Balmoral – and – dear, dear John! My dearest, best friend, to whom I could say everything and who watched over & protected me so kindly and who thought of everything – was well and strong & hearty, not 3 or 4 days before he was struck down. And my accident worried him. He never took proper care, would not go out the whole time (a week) I was shut up & would not go to bed when he was ill.

'The Lord gave, – The Lord hath taken away! Blessed be the name of the Lord.' – His Will be done. – He, dear, excellent, upright, warmhearted – strong! John – is happy, blessing us – while we weep. God bless you both! You have your husbands – your support – but I have no strong arm to lean on now. Dear Beatrice is my great comfort.[35]

The floral tributes at Crathie graveyard on the day of Brown's funeral were legion, spilling over other graves and lining the paths of the old ruined pre-Reformation church. A regular stream of mourners, curious and voyeuristic, crowded the graveside for days afterwards and read the sentiment the Queen had written on the main wreath: 'A tribute of loving, grateful and everlasting friendship and affection from his truest, best and most faithful, friend, Victoria. R & I.' Her words were long pored over: 'loving', 'affectionate' – what *could* they mean?

In the days following John Brown's death Queen Victoria was what Brown would have called 'aff the legs'. She found it difficult to stand on her swollen and painful legs, made worse by her state of grief. She refused to have any male members of the Royal Household at dinner for weeks after Brown's interment because of her incapacity; she grumbled to Henry Ponsonby at not having Brown's strong arm to lean on: 'How can I see people at dinner in the evening? I can't go walking about all night holding on to the back of a chair.'[36]

For a while, too, after the official announcements of John Brown's death in the *Court Circular*, Queen Victoria scoured the papers for mentions of him. Many of Britain's national daily newspapers, from the

Daily Telegraph to the *Manchester Examiner*, carried obituaries. Curiously, Scots newspapers, such as the *People's Journal for Glasgow & Edinburgh* descended to doggerel verse to describe him, with such couplets as:

> He's gane at length, though lo'ed by a'
> John Brown's deid![37]

To the snippets that her maids pasted into the Queen's scrapbooks a final encomium was added from the Braemar correspondent of the Press Association:

> On Deeside [Brown] was universally esteemed for his manly straightforwardness. To many his manner may have appeared abrupt, if not brusque, but that only illustrated the simplicity of his character. He never affected an artificial polish, nor sought to soften the native harshness of the Highland dialect; and he never made any distinction of persons. Brown was implicitly trusted by the Queen, and it is evident that her confidence was not misplaced.[38]

For a while, as she had done after the death of Prince Albert, Queen Victoria made herself as inconspicuous as possible when travelling to and from Osborne and Balmoral. As she embarked on her spring journey to Balmoral the Queen was transferred to her railway carriage by closed chair, and at Perth station she insisted that when her coach came to rest she was to be hidden from inquisitive eyes by a bower of evergreens. She explained to Sir Theodore Martin: 'As if it were pleasant for any lady to be carried in and out of a carriage before crowds of people.'[39] On this particular occasion, too, the Queen was agitated because she was to visit John Brown's grave for the first time.

Missing her 'faithful, kind friend and constant companion' greatly, Queen Victoria arrived at Balmoral on 26 May. Minutes after she had arrived at the castle she went in her pony-chair to inspect John Brown's as yet unmarked grave, the environs of which had been picked clean by souvenir hunters bearing off wreath clips, tie-ribbons, labels and flower holders. Writing to his wife, Henry Ponsonby described the Queen's graveside visit, adding opinions of his own:

The Deeside looked very pretty with the bright green birches and the sun was bright if not warm . . . It was a day that we could easily understand would make the Queen low and she was low . . . Wreaths from Princesses, Empresses and Ladies in Waiting are lying on Brown's grave. He was the only person who could fight and make the Queen do what she did not wish. He did not always succeed nor was his advice always the best. But I believe he was honest, and with all his want of education, his roughness, his prejudices and other faults he was undoubtedly a most excellent servant to her.[40]

The headstone for John Brown, which the Queen had ordered in Aberdeen granite with its thistle motif pediment, was set in place, within railings to deter vandals, by the time she visited Balmoral in the autumn of 1883. It stood alongside the one John Brown had erected to his parents and siblings who had predeceased him. She viewed it with approval.[41] The wording of the headstone again came from her own hand, forming a rather indifferent sentiment above a quotation from *Matthew* XXV:21:

THIS STONE IS ERECTED
IN AFFECTIONATE
AND GRATEFUL MEMORY OF

JOHN BROWN
PERSONAL ATTENDANT
AND BELOVED FRIEND
OF QUEEN VICTORIA
IN WHOSE SERVICE HE HAD BEEN
FOR 34 YEARS

Born Crathienaird December 8th 1826
Died WINDSOR CASTLE 27th March 1883

That friend on whose fidelity you count,
that friend given you by circumstances
over which you have no control, was GOD's
own gift.

WELL DONE, GOOD AND FAITHFUL SERVANT; THOU
HAST BEEN FAITHFUL OVER A FEW THINGS, I WILL MAKE THEE
    RULER OVER MANY THINGS; ENTER
THOU INTO THE JOY OF THE LORD

The stone drew an increased number of visitors to Brown's grave. In conversation with Lord in Waiting Viscount Bridport, Mrs Campbell, wife of the Minister of Crathie, observed that 'a hundred pilgrims visited a day'; sardonically Lord Bridport replied: 'You ought to charge them a shilling a head.'[42]

Just as she had permitted a plethora of memorabilia after the death of Prince Albert, ranging from Worcester pottery busts to commemorative medals and from belt clasps to music covers, the Queen embarked on a set of 'Brown memorials'.[43] These included statuettes and plaster of Paris busts, gold tie-pins set with diamonds around John Brown's head and funeral brooches designed by the royal jeweller Mr Collingwood. These were handed out by Queen Victoria with largesse. Funeral brooches were given to John Brown's relatives and tie-pins to courtiers. Sir Frederick Ponsonby recalled that the recipient of one of the tie-pins, Dr Profeit, the leader of the anti-Brown camp, 'realised that if he wore this everyone at Balmoral would laugh at him. He therefore hit upon the idea of keeping it in his coat pocket so that when he had to see the Queen he could take it out and put it in his tie, returning it to his pocket when he came away.'[44]

The most contentious of the memorials, and certainly the largest, was the life-size bronze statue the Queen commissioned from Edgar Boehm. When completed it was erected near the garden cottage on Balmoral estate where Queen Victoria had sat al fresco to complete her state dispatch boxes while John Brown handed her the documents for consideration. The statue shows John Brown in Highland garb, with the medals Queen Victoria gave him on his left lapel, and his lucky threepenny piece and pipe on his fob; he is bareheaded, holding his bonnet in his right hand. Queen Victoria went to great lengths to get the inscription just right on the supporting plinth. As she had done for the gravestone epitaph, she consulted Alfred, Lord Tennyson.

Lord Tennyson replied, suggesting a few possible lines. The Queen chose this from what the Poet Laureate called an 'anonymous hand':

> Friend more than Servant, loyal truthful, brave
> Self less than duty, even to the Grave.

In her letter of thanks of 15 September the Queen added: '[Are the words] not perhaps by yourself?'

The statue was duly set in place. While the Countess of Errol likened the statue to the graven image that Nebuchadnezzar, King of Babylon, had placed on the plain of Dura in *Daniel* III:1, the Queen's immediate family preferred to avert their eyes when in its vicinity. After his mother's death King Edward VII ordered that statue to be 'hidden' at a location on the hillside on the north-east side of Craig Gowan where it still rests.[45]

The folk of Deeside had generally liked and respected the gruff John Brown, but to most he remained a man of mystery. Apart from the innuendo about himself and Queen Victoria, after his death a new range of John Brown myths sprang to life, mostly about his supposed influence over the Queen and his purported wealth.

The gossips charged John Brown with using his position to obtain jobs for his family. It is true that John Brown's brothers William, Hugh and Archie were in royal employment, but such an arrangement was hardly unusual. Queen Victoria liked to have around her people she knew, so it was not surprising that members of certain families, related by marriage or blood ties, succeeded one another to royal positions, or worked in parallel. For instance, Sir Frederick Ponsonby (1867–1935), 1st Lord Syonsby, had forty years of court service, in several positions including Equerry and Assistant Keeper of the Privy Purse; his father General Sir Henry Ponsonby was the Queen's Private Secretary and Keeper of the Privy Purse. Louisa Jane, Countess of Antrim, the daughter of another of the Queen's private secretaries, General Charles Grey, became a Lady-in-Waiting and, like Fred Ponsonby, served at the courts of successive monarchs. Again Harriet, the daughter of the court official Receiver-General to the Duchy of Cornwall, the Hon. Sir Charles Beaumont Phipps, became Woman of the Bedchamber and Queen Victoria's personal amanuensis.

More seriously, people began to say that John Brown had made himself rich at royal expense and through various scams. The publication *Truth* averred that John Brown left a fortune of £20,000.

The World noted that John Brown had a fortune in 'plate and pieces of jewellery'. The facts told a different story. Brown died intestate but letters of administration show that his total estate was valued at a few pence over £7,198. This was made up of £6,816 19s 11d in cash deposits at banks in Windsor, Ballater and Braemar, and goods at his unlived-in house at Baile-na-Coile, valued for inventory at £379 19s 6d. Certainly it was a considerable amount of money at a time when the average labouring wage was 5s per week, but it was hardly a fortune. In contrast, John Brown's namesake, the Glasgow iron, steel and shipping magnate, had access to several millions. Records show that John Brown had been a generous donor to various charities over the years, in many cases insisting on anonymity. His siblings also received financial assistance and from time to time Brown gave Queen Victoria gifts of puppies he had reared and the use of horses he had bought. For instance, he purchased the Highland pony 'Jessie' in 1874, which was painted for the Royal Collection by Anthony de Bree in 1891.[46]

The biographer Clare Jarrold repeated a more serious allegation against Brown. She averred that Brown had extracted bribes: '[Brown] was said to take large percentages from the tradesmen, and in return would, when possible, give them his help.'[47] No such allegations have ever been substantiated. Both those outside and within royal circles attested to John Brown's honesty, and the ordinary people who knew him best scorned the idea that he had in any way fiddled the royal books.[48] Nevertheless for many decades John Brown's probity has been assailed by common gossip.

CHAPTER SEVEN

TRIAL BY GOSSIP

In understanding Queen Victoria's emotional reaction to John Brown's death the recollections of one man are of particular interest. Randall Thomas Davidson, later ennobled as Baron Davidson of Lambeth, and future Archbishop of Canterbury (1903–28), became Dean of Windsor and Queen Victoria's domestic chaplain in the year of John Brown's death. From his first audience with the Queen on 9 December 1882, he struck a chord of sympathy with her. Of the 35-year-old Scottish cleric she wrote: 'Was seldom more struck than I have been by his personality . . . I feel that Mr Davidson . . . may be of great use to me.' She began immediately to consult him on ecclesiastical matters.[1]

The tasks facing the new Dean were some of the most fraught he had ever undertaken. His interviews with the Queen were 'most touching, solemn and interesting, but terribly difficult,' he averred.[2] Nothing in his experience as chaplain-secretary to his father-in-law, Archbishop Campbell Tait, could prepare him for the eccentric caprices of his sovereign. On 14 December 1883, the twenty-second anniversary of Prince Albert's death, Queen Victoria required Davidson to prepare a special memorial service at the royal mausoleum at Frogmore. The prayers, said the Queen, should couple the names of Prince Albert and John Brown, as well as Davidson's newly deceased predecessor Dean Gerald Valerian Wellesley, not forgetting blessings for the current travels being undertaken in India by Prince Arthur, Duke of Connaught. The whole was to be 'a very difficult task' wrote Davidson in his diary, 'but . . . it must be done'.[3]

This was to be Davidson's first introduction to Queen Victoria's curious notions about the dead. As he met with more experienced courtiers he heard and witnessed the strange rituals surrounding Prince Albert's memory. He observed in disbelief the dead Prince Consort's room at Windsor Castle which had been left to the last detail just as the

> *On the Queen's Grief*
> After paying his first visit to Prince Albert's tomb at the royal
> mausoleum at Frogmore in attendance with the royal family, John
> Brown had been much moved and had said to Queen Victoria:
>
> I didn't like to see ye at Frogmore this morning. I felt for ye – to see
> ye coming there with your daughters and your husband lying there
> – marriage on one side and death on the other. No, I didn't like to
> see it. I felt sorry for ye. I know so well what your feeling must be –
> ye who had been so happy. There is no more pleasure for you, poor
> Queen, and I feel for ye but what can I do for ye? I could die
> for ye.
>
> **John Brown**

prince had used it in life; he witnessed how hot water was set out in the
Prince's former dressing room for morning ablutions; how his clothes
were laid out at certain times of the day . . . all as if the Prince was still
alive; and how John Brown's room in the Clarence Tower at Windsor
had been locked after his death and preserved as a living museum. Yet
the Dean was to encounter more trying difficulties during March 1884
as the Queen's mourning for Brown showed no let-up. Davidson's heart
sank when he learned that the sovereign was writing a memoir of John
Brown which she fully intended to publish.

Fresh from the publication of *More Leaves from the Journal of A Life in
the Highlands*, which Smith, Elder & Co. issued in February 1884, with
its boldly displayed 1868 steel engraving of John Brown, Queen
Victoria approached Sir Theodore Martin, Prince Albert's biographer,
to assist with editing her John Brown memoir. Pleading his wife's ill-
health, Sir Theodore demurred, whereupon the Queen consulted Sir
Henry Ponsonby. He suggested that she approach the newly appointed
Bishop of Ripon, William Boyd Carpenter, or Dr Cameron Lees of
St Giles High Kirk, Edinburgh, as editorial mentor. Their hasty refusal
when John Brown was mentioned was dignified but absolute. In the
event the Queen consulted Miss Murray MacGregor, who had helped
her both with *Leaves* and with the *Highlanders* volumes.

A copy of the completed Brown manuscript was passed to Randall Davidson for comment, although not on the Queen's instructions. He read it and decided that its publication should be thwarted. Racking his brains for a plausible excuse, he thanked the Queen for sending him a copy of *More Leaves*, and opined that further writings would be unwise because of the adverse comments about her widowed jottings which had appeared in certain broadsheets. Although the book had been received by the public to great acclaim, the prominence of John Brown's name and details of his health and welfare had caused fervid gossip at all levels of society. The royal family had cringed at the dedication to: 'My Loyal Highlanders and especially to the Memory of My Devoted Personal Attendant and Faithful Friend John Brown, these records of My Widowed Life in Scotland are Gratefully Dedicated.'

Queen Victoria was unimpressed by Davidson's opinions; she cared not for the press outpourings and made it known that she still intended to publish. The Dean determined that he would do his utmost to persuade her otherwise. Through her lady-in-waiting, Jane Ely, Queen Victoria expressed her dismay at Davidson's opposition, which had caused her 'pain'.

Bracing himself, the Dean refused to apologise for ruffling the royal feathers and made it known that he maintained his opposition, and backing this up with threats to resign his position. Unmoved, the Queen sent the John Brown manuscript to Montague Corry, Baron Rowton, Benjamin Disraeli's former secretary. Having read it, he suggested to Ponsonby that it should be set up in type and then shown to the Queen.

On John Brown

'[*The Royal Household*] gets on better since John Brown's disappearance from the scene. He was all powerful – no servant had a chance of promotion except through him, and he favoured no man who didn't like his glass [*of whisky*]. Some of the courtiers were full of attention to J.B., gave him presents, etc – and he despised them for it. He was however . . . devoted in his attentions to the Queen.'

**Sir John Clayton Powell,
Master of the Queen's Household**

Seeing it in print, averred Corry, the Queen would see the folly of linking her name so publicly and intimately with John Brown.[4]

For a while Davidson was out of favour with the Queen, but his disagreement with the monarch was soon over. Summoned to the royal presence he found the Queen 'more friendly than ever'; she had decided not to publish the tome on Brown and the whole matter with Davidson was dropped.[5]

WHAT WAS IN THE MEMOIR TO DISCONCERT QUEEN VICTORIA'S HOUSEHOLD?

Assessing Queen Victoria's other writings, it seems likely that the memoir would have contained a collection of anecdotes featuring John Brown's wit, philosophy and activities, which probably included robust comments on her staff. Sir Henry Ponsonby left one clue to the tone of the memoir. In his letter to the Queen advising non-publication, he concluded: 'Your Majesty's innermost and most sacred feelings [contain] passages which will be misunderstood if read by strangers . . .'[6]

Queen Victoria habitually expressed her feelings of devotion for friends in a fervent way that was easy to misconstrue. She dotted her writings with 'dearest', 'darling', 'beloved' and 'darling one'. To the Victorians, 'darling' was expressive of 'great kindness' and 'tenderness'. At his death John Brown's papers included many greetings cards from Queen Victoria which were expressed in ardent terms. One for instance, dated 1 January 1877, bore the picture of a parlour maid and the verses:

> I send my serving maiden
>> With New Year letter laden,
>> Its words will prove
>> My faith and love

> To you my heart's best treasure
> Then smile on her and smile on me
>> And let your answer loving be,
>> And give me pleasure.

In the Queen's own hand were added the words: 'To my best friend J.B. From his best friend. V.R.I.' This card is now in the Royal Archives at

Windsor.[7] The Queen also sent Valentine cards, it should be remembered, to Benjamin Disraeli.

The extant John Brown papers show that Queen Victoria did address John Brown as 'darling one'. In a rather formal letter to Brown, dated October 1874, the Queen suggested that he should send for his brother Hugh, then in New Zealand, as their mother's health was deteriorating: 'I hope darling one that you will do this,' she wrote.[8]

There were more deep-felt expressions of 'love'. In an undated letter to Hugh Brown occurs this passage, with certain words underlined by the Queen:

> I found these words in an old Diary or Journal of mine. I was in great trouble about the Princess Royal who had lost her child in '66 [the Queen's grandson Prince Sigismund] and dear John said to me: 'I wish to take care of my dear good mistress till I die. You'll never have an honester servant.' I took and held his dear kind hand and I said I hoped he might long be spared to comfort me and he answered, 'But we all must die.'
>
> Afterwards my beloved John would say: 'You haven't a more devoted servant than Brown' – and Oh! how I felt that!
>
> Afterwards so often I told him no one loved him more than I did or had a better friend than me: and he answered 'Nor you – than me . . . No one loves you more.'[9]

Queen Victoria's definition of love in the phrase 'no one loved him more' meant sincere friendship; her expression of it was naively innocent and open to misunderstanding by anyone who did not comprehend the Queen's character. This is what Ponsonby was afraid of when he destroyed the Memoir, and what Dean Davidson was trying to protect when he put his career on the line in opposing its publication.[10]

WAS THERE ANYTHING IMMORAL IN QUEEN VICTORIA'S RELATIONSHIP WITH JOHN BROWN?

The naive innocence of Queen Victoria's character is a key factor in assessing this question. Had there been anything of an immoral nature in the famous relationship, would common sense not have indicated that they take steps to mask it? Both were well aware of public gossip. Yet far from keeping it dark, in letters and cards here was Queen Victoria proclaiming her 'love' for John Brown quite openly for all to read. Further she was actively hoping to publish all these thoughts in a publicly printed memoir. *She* knew it was all innocent but it was only the persuasive coercion of her closest advisors that caused her to abandon her plans to go public.

Queen Victoria's relationship with John Brown could not have been sexual for a number of reasons, both physical and social. When Dr James Reid examined her cadaver he found that she 'had a ventral hernia and a prolapse of the uterus'.[11] Reid is probably commenting on a complete procidentia which the Queen probably had for many years. This would have made sexual intercourse not only uncomfortable but distasteful, as the prolapsed uterus would have to be regularly pushed back into place. The Queen never had, nor would even have contemplated, any treatment for her condition. Moreover, she would never have seriously considered having sexual relations with a man not of her own class, however deeply she may have felt. Her powerful sense of morality and social propriety would have forbidden it.

WHAT WAS THE SIGNIFICANCE OF QUEEN VICTORIA'S ATTRACTION TO JOHN BROWN?

Despite having several women around her who devoted their lives to her service, such as her Lady of the Bedchamber Jane, Marchioness of Ely, and Maids of Honour such as Lady Caroline Courtney, Queen Victoria never formed an intimate friendship with a woman. Brown supplied deep personal fellowship, and, as Dean Davidson put it, 'friendly remonstrance and raillery'.[12] Queen Victoria suffered abnormal grief after the death of Prince Albert. She had lost someone who seemed irreplaceable. She weathered the bewilderment that comes in the first stage of grief, then the anger, but then became caught in the depressed stage. All this was manifest in her behaviour. She hardly spoke, and when she did she was irritable; she ate sparingly; she lost interest in affairs of state; and she could not be roused to go out and about on her estates. John Brown's determined interference 'brought the Queen back to normality at a time of acute and dangerous stress'.[13]

Another key factor was that John Brown 'dedicated his life to Queen Victoria' and 'was never indifferent' to her neurotic troubles.[14] From his point of view Queen Victoria gave him something useful to do. And it should be remembered that both Queen Victoria and Prince Albert adored the work of Sir Walter Scott; John Brown was to be a *cavaliere servente* from Scott's novels. John Brown was thus Queen Victoria's 'only real friend'.[15]

In her *Journal* for 19 September 1838 Queen Victoria speaks of her feelings as 'naturally very passionate'. Modern commentators have interpreted this in an erotic sense, pointing out her sexually degenerate Hanoverian uncles. This is totally misleading. Queen Victoria had a fiery temper and her emotions were robust – but her passions were not lustful. Yet it is hardly startling that Queen Victoria found John Brown an attractive man: As biographer E.E.P. Tisdall put it:

Brown was a splendid specimen of manhood and eight women out of ten with the true instincts of femininity in them, who had the privilege to be served by Brown as intimately as he served Queen Victoria, would not be blind to the fact that he was a man.[16]

As to the well-attested 'familiarity' evident between John Brown and Queen Victoria, her biographer Giles Lytton Strachey made the significant observation that 'it is no uncommon thing for an autocratic dowager to allow some trusted indispensable servant to adopt towards her an attitude of authority which is jealousy forbidden to relatives and friends . . .'[17]

Only one man was ever privy to all aspects of Queen Victoria's relationship with John Brown and that was her discreet Private Secretary Henry Ponsonby. He realised that Brown's perceived arrogance and general rude demeanour was rooted in the 'Queen's marked and sustained infatuation' for him.[18] Yet he 'knew there was no danger whatever in Brown's relations with the Queen and neither publicly nor domestically was the Highland attendant of any real consequence'.[19] Yet the rumours persisted and formed themselves into four principal pieces of gossip about the Queen and John Brown that have survived in the public memory. The first speculation was:

1. The Queen has gone mad and John Brown is her keeper.
The Queen and her courtiers, from the Ministers of the Crown to her physicians, believed that she had inherited from her Hanoverian ancestors the proclivity to madness.[20] Her grandfather King George III, now known to have suffered from the metabolic disorder Variegate Porphyria, slipped in and out of mental derangement in the latter years of his life. Queen Victoria's household scrutinised her discreetly for signs of emotional extremities which might lead to incipient insanity. Yet although her father the Duke of Kent had suffered from symptoms of Hemato Porphyria, Queen Victoria escaped the dreadful affliction.[21]

Her real problem was what the 4th Earl of Clarendon dubbed her 'morbid melancholy', which assailed her during times of stress. When Cabinet Minister Clarendon called on her at Windsor in June 1862 to discuss ministerial changes, the Queen's mood at the audience altered rapidly and she indicated her fear of change by tapping her head with the words 'My reason! My reason!'[22] Fearing for her mind, the Queen's ministers and Household were easily blackmailed into doing what she wanted in order to avoid upset. John Brown came to understand what was wrong with the Queen and his determined interference in her life was a help to tackle this 'morbid melancholy'. In this, and this alone, was he her 'keeper'.

As their relationship as monarch and retainer became closer, the second speculation gained ground:

2. The Queen is married to John Brown
The curious assertion that John Brown was the morganatic husband of Queen Victoria was first given publicity by the Scottish socialist republican nationalist Alexander Robertson in his curious pamphlet *John Brown, A Correspondence with the Lord Chancellor, Regarding a Charge of Fraud and Embezzlement Preferred Against His Grace the Duke of Athole K.T.*, which was published from 37a Clerkenwell Gardens, London, in 1873.

Robertson was obsessed with the idea that the seven-arched bridge across the River Tay at Dunkeld in Perthshire, completed in 1809 to the designs of Thomas Telford and largely paid for out of the funds of John

Murray, 5th Duke of Atholl and his family, had a 'fraudulent' set of tolls set by the 6th Duke.

Robertson, who hailed from nearby Doundounadine, ranted on every possible occasion against the half-penny (return) fee charged to foot passengers across the bridge. Local feelings ran high and in 1868 people loudly complained that they had to pay tolls to cross the bridge to church, and the toll gates were consequently broken and thrown into the Tay. A detachment of the 42nd Royal Highlanders was called in to quell the 'toll-gate riots'. Robertson identified the chief 'fraudsters' in this matter as George Murray, 6th Duke of Atholl, and his wife Duchess Anne, both good friends of Queen Victoria and members of her Court. Although his pamphlet was written after the 7th Duke had succeeded to the title in 1864, Robertson saw the Queen as a person who supported all the Murrays in their 'banditry' and regarded her as ripe for exposure.

The pamphlet, addressed to the Lord Chancellor, 1st Lord Selborne, detailed several outrageous accusations against the Queen and John Brown. Quoting Charles Christie, 'House Steward to the Dowager Duchess of Athole at Dunkeld House', Robertson averred that John Brown obtained regular 'admittance' to the Queen's bedroom when 'the house was quiet'.[23] He asserted that John Brown 'acts as master and more' with Queen Victoria who was easy to lead, being 'weak-minded, or semi-imbecile'.[24] Robertson repeated the general gossip that John Brown kept Ministers of the Crown waiting 'a whole day' to deliver their dispatches to the Queen and would not allow Her Majesty to undertake journeys to places he did not approve of.[25]

Warming to his subject, Robertson noted that Duchess Anne was in Lausanne, Switzerland, in 1868, and in that place stood witness to Queen Victoria's marriage to John Brown. Queen Victoria *was* in Switzerland at that time, but she was at Lucerne, not Lausanne; even so, the Dowager Duchess was later quizzed on the matter and poured scorn on Robertson's assertion.[26]

There was yet more, which led to the third assertion:

3. Queen Victoria gave birth to John Brown's child
This was Robertson's *coup de grace*, as he saw it, in undermining the Queen's reputation, her throne and her friendship with the Murray

'fraudsters'. Robertson named as his informant concerning the juiciest
bit of gossip one John McGregor, Chief Wood Manager on the Atholl
estates. He said that McGregor had told him that John Brown and the
Queen had set out one day for a trip to Loch Ordie and along the way
'Hochmagandy' – the old Scots word for sexual intercourse – had taken
place. Nine months later in Switzerland the resulting child was born,
but, said Robertson, he was not suggesting that the Dowager Duchess
'acted as *howdy* ['midwife']'.[27] Noting that what he recounted was well
known 'at various Courts of the continent', Robertson added this for
good measure: 'A gentleman recently informed me that there is at
present a thumping Scottish laddie in charge of a Calvinist pastor in a
retired valley in the Canton of Vaud; but he would not mention the
name of either parent although by his gesticulations I could easily
understand to whom he referred.'[28]

These stories were so ridiculous that no one could credibly
perpetuate them to the Queen and John Brown's detriment, although
the assertions were officially noted. Robertson was never prosecuted for
his undoubted libel, although the Lord Chancellor and Foreign
Secretary, George Leveson-Gower, 2nd Earl of Granville, did discuss the
implications.[29]

Even though the assertions were foolish in the extreme, the Queen's
detractors, from republicans to disgruntled staff, gave them the oxygen
of publicity and many a similar story circulated with Queen Victoria in
the role of 'Mrs Brown'. So much so that pro-Victoria courtiers began
to put the case for the Queen's 'innocence' in her relationship with
Brown. They pointed out that the Queen was hardly ever alone: a
dresser or maid was always on hand, so no trysts *à deux* with John
Brown were possible. Henry Ponsonby commented in a letter to his
brother that Brown was 'certainly a favourite, but he is only a servant
and nothing more – and what I suppose began as a joke has been
perverted into a libel'.[30]

The nonsense that John Brown made Queen Victoria pregnant never
went away and the gossip re-emerged in the 1970s, when the *Sunday
People* newspaper ran a story under the headline 'Was "Louise Brown"
Love Child of Queen Victoria?'[31] Colin Cross of the *Sunday Observer*
brought to the attention of a wider audience the fact that one Dr
Micheil MacDonald, former curator of the Museum of Scottish Tartans

at Comrie, Perthshire, had said that Queen Victoria had born John Brown a son. MacDonald was in the public eye because he had bought for £1,760 a kilt (and tartan under-breeks) which Queen Victoria had given to John Brown. This Royal Stewart tartan kilt was to be an exhibit in the Tartan Museum. MacDonald told the press that the love child story had 'come from a death-bed statement made by a minister of the Church of Scotland'. As with so many outrageous stories about the royal servant, MacDonald refused to detail his source. The story was taken seriously enough for Buckingham Palace to issue a denial pointing out that there was nothing in the Royal Archives at Windsor Castle to substantiate the claim.[32]

The story stimulated a response from Mr John Stuart who, according to a report in the *Sunday People*, said that when he worked for the royal bankers, Messrs Coutts & Co., The Strand, London, in the years immediately after the First World War, he read ledgers and letters confirming that 'Victoria had a child by Gillie John Brown and that the [*female child*] was sent to live in Paris.' Stuart revealed that the letters he saw were signed by one Louise Brown at a Paris address, where she was sent £250 'paid once a quarter'. Stuart went on: 'The money was debited in the account marked "His Royal Highness Prince Albert Edward, Prince of Wales".'

Studying the correspondence, Stuart further commented: 'At the time I thought she must have been one of King Edward VII's children from the wrong side of the blanket. But what could have happened was that the King ordered the payments to continue after his death in 1910, to prevent a scandal involving his mother.' Stuart was intrigued by the 'tone of the letters and some of their phrases', and added: '[*Louise Brown*] was far from being a begging-letter writer, but she wrote pathetically of her terrible straitened circumstances.' A particular letter referred to how benevolent 'dear generous Bertie' [The Prince of Wales] had been, and how she appreciated the visits to the home of 'dear [Princess] Beatrice'. Following up the story the *Sunday People* reporters were denied access to the Coutts & Co. archives and the assertions remain unconfirmed.[33]

The fourth speculation about Queen Victoria and John Brown has accumulated the largest amount of written material.

4. John Brown was Queen Victoria's spiritualistic medium
Spiritualism is a recognised religion whose fundamental theory emphasises that spiritual and supernatural forces directly intervene in daily life. In its refined form in the nineteenth century it came to represent the dual beliefs that the human personality survived death in some form and that it was possible to communicate with the spirits of the dead. The modern aspects of spiritualism developed in the USA in 1848 as a result of events surrounding the Fox family at Hydesville, New York State, who claimed they had found a way to communicate with the dead. The spiritualist movement came to Britain in 1852 through the medium demonstrations of the American citizen Mrs Hayden, and the visits to Britain of the Scots-born medium Daniel Dunglass Home in the 1850s and 1860s sustained interest through the patronage of such people as the 3rd Earl of Dunraven. After this spiritualist societies sprang up in Britain and in 1873 the British National Association of Spiritualists was founded.

The enthusiasts of Spiritualism were anxious to recruit worthy and credible 'names' to their movement and who better than Queen Victoria. *Tinsley's Magazine*, ever on the trail of a royal 'scoop', spread the rumour that the Queen dabbled in the spirit world, but the *Spiritualist Magazine* was bold enough to use the headline: 'Queen Victoria: A Spiritualist'.[34] Thereafter her name was linked with prominent psychic mediums from Robert James Lees to W.T. Stead, all of whom were deemed to be clandestinely smuggled to the Queen's presence to conduct seances and give 'psychic advice' from beyond the grave as to how she should rule. Not one shred of evidence exists to prove that Queen Victoria had any interest whatsoever in spiritualism, although some members of her circle, such as Lady Walburga Paget, clearly had.

It was only a short step to include the ubiquitous John Brown in the talk of spiritualism; after all, his relationship with the Queen remained a total mystery to many. The art critic William Michael Rossetti was even more direct: 'The real secret about John Brown and the Queen is that Brown is a powerful [*spiritualistic*] medium, through whom Prince Albert's spirit communicates with the Queen: hence Brown remains closeted with her alone sometimes for hours together.'[35]

Not surprisingly, John Brown was linked with a Scottish psychic phenomenon known as *Taibhseadaireachd* – Gaelic for Second Sight – the gift of prophetic vision attributed to certain individuals, usually Highlanders.[36] Queen Victoria was aware of the supposed 'gift' through her Balmoral associations; her daughter Princess Louise married into the family of the Dukes of Argyll who were deemed to possess hereditary 'Second Sight'. The Princess's husband, Lord Lorne, was known to have said that he had had a prophetic vision of being offered the position of Governor-General of Canada, while the Princess's sister-in-law, Lady Archie Campbell, was a prominent spiritualist. Brought up in the country, John Brown naturally had the countryman's affinity with nature's moods and weather lore, so his predictions of bad weather to come, or the imminence of natural disasters such as floods – prognostications all given credence by the Queen – could be built up by idle gossip into tales of supernatural capabilities.

None of these matters, from spiritualism to Second Sight, is reflected in any documents or artefacts held in the royal collection at Windsor. But, say believers, Princess Beatrice sanitised Queen Victoria's papers on the Queen's death and could have destroyed all references. Queen Victoria's letters and journals are littered with her personal opinions and private thoughts. One set of intimate papers which Princess Beatrice had no control over were her mother's letters to her daughter Victoria, Empress of Germany. Many still rest in the Kronberg Archives at Friedrichshof and not one of them hints at any interest in organised spiritualism or John Brown's supposed involvement therein. The fact that the Queen was open with her daughter in her feelings of friendship for Brown would suggest that if he was her medium she would have hinted at it. Queen Victoria was convinced that the 'spirit' of Prince Albert always watched over her, but there is no evidence that she took any steps whatsoever to 'get in touch' with his disembodied presence.

SCENES AT A ROYAL DEATHBED

Following Queen Victoria's death from cerebral failure at Osborne House at 6.30pm on 22 January 1901, there was enacted a death-chamber ritual that would not be spoken of publicly for many decades. It was a solemn occasion in which John Brown, dead for eighteen years, would figure in memory. As the royal family dispersed from around the couch-bed in which the Queen had died in the arms of her grandson, the German Kaiser Wilhelm II, and her physician Dr James Reid, each trying to come to terms with the passing of a monarch who had reigned for sixty-four years and the almost mystical entry of another sovereign, the old Queen's exhausted physician supervised the preparation of her body for interment. A series of coffins, fitting one inside another, were ordered, into which her body would be placed. After the family had said their last farewells in the bedroom, the room was sealed off with bronze gates to act as a family shrine for the next fifty years.

On Wednesday 23 January the royal cadaver was finally embalmed and Sir Hubert von Herkomer painted the death-bed portrait which still hangs at Osborne House. With the preliminary sketches completed, the Queen's Chief Dresser, Mrs Tuck, who had acted as Dr Reid's assistant, had a private meeting with the physician. Mrs Tuck read to Dr Reid the 'Instructions' which Queen Victoria had entrusted to her regarding the things she wanted to be interred in her innermost coffin.[1] Some of these items, the Queen had impressed, 'weren't to be seen by any member of her family'.[2]

The dead Queen's chosen artefacts were privately assembled by Tuck and Reid, and they carefully placed them on a bed of charcoal on the floor of the Queen's innermost coffin, known as the 'shell'. These items formed a set of mementoes, from rings and bracelets to lockets and handkerchiefs, reflecting the sovereign's long life, together with Prince Albert's dressing-gown, his cloak (embroidered by Princess Alice), the alabaster cast of his hand, and relics of her family's childhoods.[3] On top of these was placed an all-enveloping quilted cushion. When the last item was out of sight the new King Edward VII and his brothers were fetched to assist in lifting the cadaver of Queen Victoria into the shell.

This done, Dr Reid requested everyone to withdraw except Mrs Tuck, and the two junior dressers Miss Stewart and Miss Ticking. Certain that the door to the chamber was firmly closed, Dr Reid proceeded with the most secret of his funeral duties. Once the Queen's wedding veil had been spread over her face and upper body, now dressed in a white silk robe and the Order of the Garter, he placed in her left hand a photograph of John Brown. In a sheet of tissue paper he folded a lock of Brown's hair set in a case and hid it under a corsage of flowers which the new Queen Alexandra had laid on the body after its placement in the shell. Herein, too, Reid positioned a pocket handkerchief that had belonged to Brown, and a ring that had been John Brown's mother's and which the Queen had worn constantly for the eighteen years since Brown's death. To these Reid added a few other photographs and letters that had passed between them.[4] Despite further last viewings of the dead Queen by family and court members all the John Brown items remained undisturbed and unseen, until at last the outer coffin lid was finally screwed in place.

Queen Victoria's coffin now lay in state for a while in the dining room at Osborne House, watched over by four Grenadier Guards, their rifles ceremonially reversed. On 1 February her funeral cortège processed through East Cowes to the anchorage of the royal yacht *Alberta*, which took the mourning party across the Solent for the journey by train to London. On Monday 4 February the final ceremony of Queen Victoria's funeral took place with interment of her body at Frogmore mausoleum alongside Prince Albert. When the royal family had filed past the royal coffin and all the ecclesiastical and Court officials had left, Reginald Baliol Bret, 2nd Viscount Esher, Secretary of the Office of Works, who had stage-managed the day's events, watched the workmen lower the coping-stone over the royal vault. Thus were the Queen's last secrets sealed away. Yet just a few yards away from the royal tomb, now topped with effigies of Prince Albert and Queen

Victoria, in the ambulatory of the Chapel of the Crucifixion, lies a clue to their presence. Here Queen Victoria had arranged for a bronze tablet to be affixed, 'In loving and grateful remembrance' of Brown her 'faithful and devoted personal attendant and friend'.[5] The tablet was the sole non-family memorial that the Queen ever allowed in the hallowed shrine she had set up for herself and her beloved husband.[6]

From time to time stories of 'compromising letters', which are said to have passed between Queen Victoria and John Brown, are given the oxygen of publicity. Following the première in 1998 of the film *Mrs Brown*, starring Dame Judy Dench as Queen Victoria and Billy Connolly as John Brown, the British press ran a story under the general heading 'Mrs Brown's love letters revealed: Film-makers discover hoard of mementoes from Queen Victoria to gillie John Brown.'[7] The article said that a 'secret cache' of compromising letters had been located in the attic of a house 'near Ballater'. These had been read by the film's executive producer Douglas Rae and writer Jeremy Brocks, who 'were allowed to use the content of the letters to provide most of the background of the film'. The whereabouts and provenance of the letters is shrouded in mystery and the purported 'owners' are reported to have said that the letters 'will not be made public until the next century'. The fatuous reason given is that the 'owners' 'don't want anything revealed while the present members of the Royal Family, particularly the Queen Mother, are still alive'.[8]

The definition of 'compromising' with regard to correspondence between Queen Victoria and John Brown is open to debate and should be assessed from the point of view of Queen Victoria's character and personality rather than in prurient twentieth-century terms. Anything relating to the friends, especially the Queen's gushing words of familiarity and amity – which is probably the best explanation of the Queen's use of 'love' and 'darling one' to John Brown – would be considered 'compromising' by the paranoid Edward VII who himself was drawn into one episode concerning such letters.

In late September 1904 Dr James Reid was contacted by Edward VII's private secretary, Francis Knollys, who said that the monarch wished to consult Reid on a private matter. The late Dr Alexander Profeit's son George was in the process of threatening the King with blackmail concerning letters written by Queen Victoria to Dr Profeit about John Brown. George Profeit had opened a black trunk of his father's and discovered in excess of three hundred letters, 'many of them most compromising' noted Dr Reid.[9] The King wanted Reid to obtain the letters from George Profeit.

Dr Reid was perplexed about how to proceed. During November 1904 he asked for a meeting with Princess Beatrice at Kensington Palace to talk over the problem. The King was willing to pay for the letters; the important point was that the monarch *must* have them. Shortly after the interview with Princess Beatrice, George Profeit met Reid to negotiate the sale. It took several visits from the difficult vendor to complete the negotiations, but on 8 May 1905 George Profeit handed over the letters for an undisclosed sum. Reid personally gave them to the King.[10] The 'compromising' letters thereafter disappeared, adding one more twist to the mystery surrounding the relationship between Queen Victoria and John Brown, the fine detail of which is unlikely ever to be known for certain.

Holograph letter from Queen Victoria, expressing her grief at the death of John Brown, addressed to his sisters-in-law 'Lizzie' (Mrs William Brown) and 'Jessie' (Mrs Hugh Brown). [See p. 142]

not how to bear it,
— or how to believe
it possible. We parted
all so well & happy
at dear Balmoral — my
— dear, dear John!
my dearest, best
friend - to whom I could
say everything and
who watched over &
protected me so
kindly and who thought
of every thing, -
was well & strong
& hearty, but 3 or 4
days before, he was
struck down. And my

accident worried him
he never took pro-
per care, would not
go out the Dode time
(a week) I was kep-
up I would not go
to bed when he was
ill.

"The Lord gave, —
The Lord hath taken
away.' Blessed
be the name of
the Lord." — His
will be done. —

He, dear, excellent

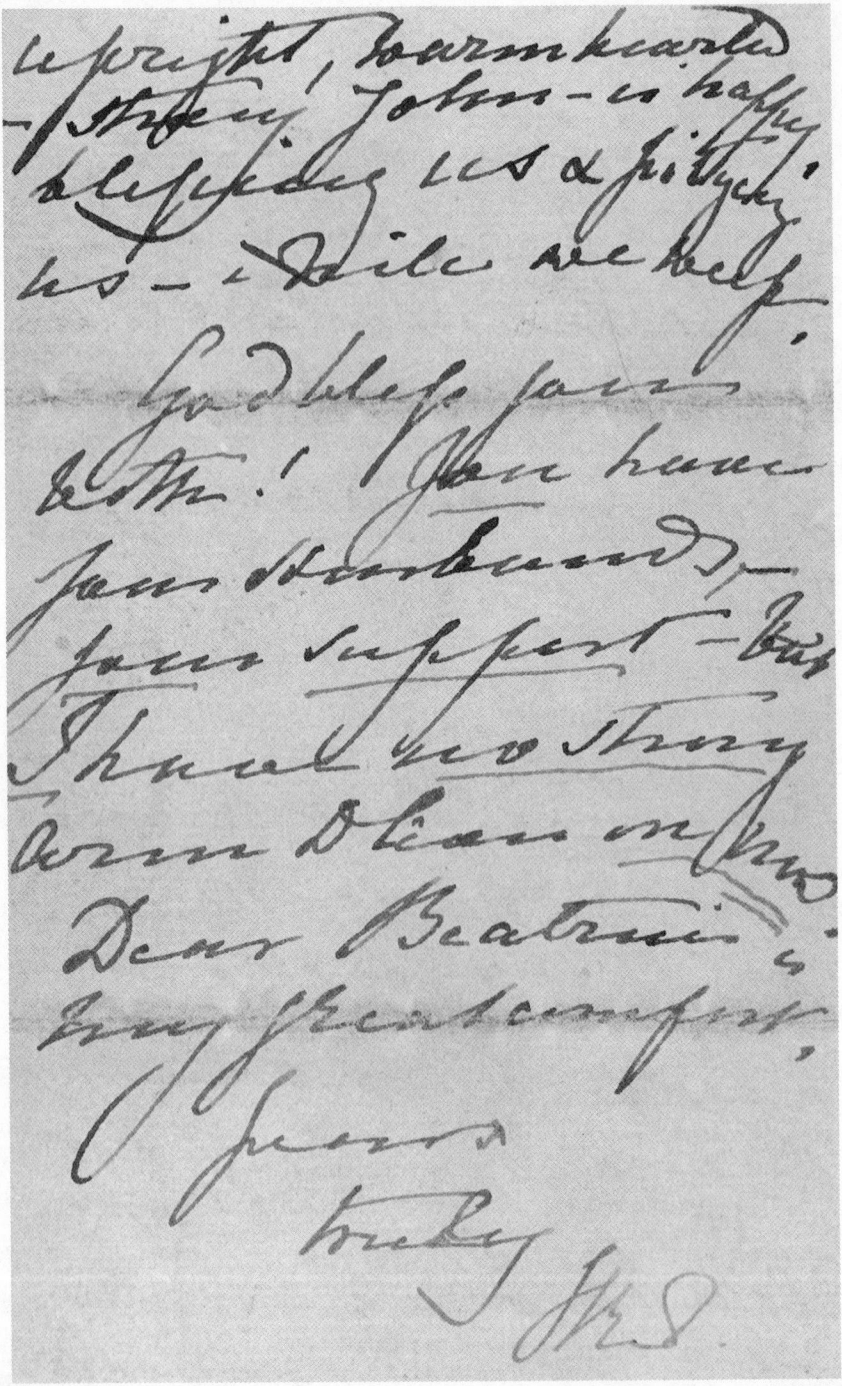
upright, warmhearted
& strong! John – is happy
blessing us & pitying
us – while we weep.
God bless you
both! You have
your husbands –
your support – but
I have no strong
arm to lean on now.
Dear Beatrice is
my great comfort.
Ever
yours
lovingly
V.R.I.

APPENDIX 2:
QUEEN VICTORIA'S CHILDREN AND THEIR ANTIPATHY TO JOHN BROWN

1. VICTORIA ADELAIDE MARY LOUISA, Princess Royal.
Born 21 November 1840. Married: 1858, Prince Frederick William of Prussia (1831–88). Became Crown Princess of Prussia and Empress Frederick of Germany. She had eight children including the autocratic and mentally unstable Wilhelm II (1859–1941), 'Kaiser Bill' of the First World War. She died 5 August 1901.

Princess Victoria was embarrassed and resentful over gossip at the German court regarding Queen Victoria and John Brown. She sent the queen a 'rather formal message' of sympathy on John Brown's death.

2. ALBERT EDWARD, Prince of Wales.
Born 9 November 1841. Married: 1863, Princess Alexandra of Denmark (1844–1925). They had five children. Died 6 May 1910, having acceded to the throne on the death of Queen Victoria as Edward VII.

Harboured a lifelong hatred of John Brown, substituting the phrase 'that brute' for his name in conversation.

3. ALICE MAUD MARY.
Born 25 April 1843. Married: 1862, Prince Louis IV, Grand-Duke of Hesse–Darmstadt (1837–92). She had seven children. Died 14 December 1878.

Supported her elder brother and sister in trying (unsuccessfully) to get John Brown sacked.

4.   ALFRED ERNEST ALBERT, Duke of Edinburgh and Saxe-Coburg-Gotha.
Born 6 August 1844. Married: 1874, Grand Duchess Marie of Russia (1853–1920). They had five children. Died 30 July 1900.

Resented John Brown's 'power and confidence' at court, and was the centre of many 'Brown rows' with Queen Victoria.

5.   HELENA AUGUSTA VICTORIA.
Born 25 May 1846. Married: 1866, Prince Frederick Christian of Schleswig-Holstein (1831–1917). She had five children. Died 9 June 1923.

Admitted to being 'wholeheartedly' German and was irritated by 'John Brown gossip' in Prussian imperial circles.

6.   LOUISE CAROLINE ALBERTA.
Born 18 March 1848. Married: 1871, John Douglas Campbell, 9th Duke of Argyll (1845–1914). No issue. Died 3 December 1939.

Looked upon John Brown as a 'mischief-maker' and believed that he 'tittle-tattled' about her private life to Queen Victoria. Gave her an aversion to Highland gillies.

7.   ARTHUR WILLIAM PATRICK ALBERT, Duke of Connaught and Strathearn.
Born 1 May 1850. Married: 1879, Princess Louise Margaret of Prussia (1860–1917). They had one son and two daughters. Died 16 January 1942.

Shared his siblings' distaste for John Brown's 'interference'.

8.   LEOPOLD GEORGE DUNCAN ALBERT, Duke of Albany.
Born 7 April 1853. Married: 1882, Princess Helena Frederica Augusta of Waldeck and Pyrmont (1861–1922). They had two children. Died 28 March 1884.

As a child he seems to have been on fairly friendly terms with John Brown, who took him and his brother Arthur fishing. Hatred of

Brown (and his brothers) was demonstrated in the 'Stirling Dismissal' episode.

9.   BEATRICE MARY VICTORIA FEODORE.
Born 14 April 1857. Married: 1885, Prince Henry Maurice of Battenberg (1858–96). She had four children. Died 26 October 1944.

To her John Brown was 'the ever present faithful servant' and when he was around 'one was safe'. Princess Beatrice and Prince Arthur were the executors to Queen Victoria's will, and as her mother's literary executor Princess Beatrice 'edited' her personal papers and vast collection of correspondence, deleting and destroying any mention of John Brown that might be construed as 'compromising' and open to misinterpretation.

APPENDIX 3: GENEALOGICAL CHART OF JOHN BROWN, HIS PARENTS AND SIBLINGS

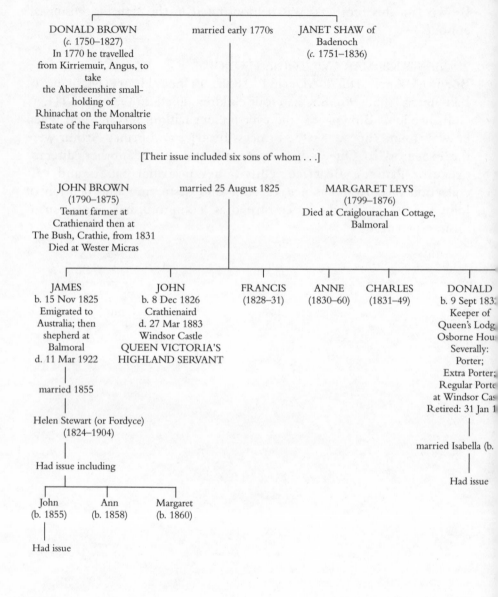

DONALD BROWN   married early 1770s   JANET SHAW of
(c. 1750–1827)   Badenoch
In 1770 he travelled   (c. 1751–1836)
from Kirriemuir, Angus, to
take
the Aberdeenshire small-
holding of
Rhinachat on the Monaltrie
Estate of the Farquharsons

[Their issue included six sons of whom . . .]

JOHN BROWN   married 25 August 1825   MARGARET LEYS
(1790–1875)   (1799–1876)
Tenant farmer at   Died at Craiglourachan Cottage,
Crathienaird then at   Balmoral
The Bush, Crathie, from 1831
Died at Wester Micras

JAMES	JOHN	FRANCIS	ANNE	CHARLES	DONALD
b. 15 Nov 1825	b. 8 Dec 1826	(1828–31)	(1830–60)	(1831–49)	b. 9 Sept 183:
Emigrated to	Crathienaird				Keeper of
Australia; then	d. 27 Mar 1883				Queen's Lodg
shepherd at	Windsor Castle				Osborne Hou
Balmoral	QUEEN VICTORIA'S				Severally:
d. 11 Mar 1922	HIGHLAND SERVANT				Porter;
					Extra Porter;
					Regular Porte
					at Windsor Cas
					Retired: 31 Jan 1

married 1855

Helen Stewart (or Fordyce)
(1824–1904)

married Isabella (b.

Had issue including

Had issue

John	Ann	Margaret
(b. 1855)	(b. 1858)	(b. 1860)

Had issue

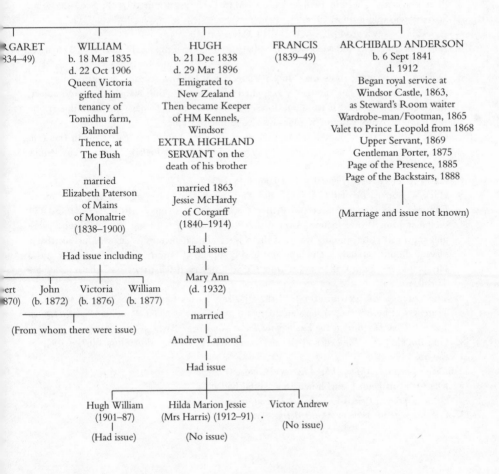

GARET   WILLIAM   HUGH   FRANCIS   ARCHIBALD ANDERSON
34–49)   b. 18 Mar 1835   b. 21 Dec 1838   (1839–49)   b. 6 Sept 1841
             d. 22 Oct 1906   d. 29 Mar 1896   d. 1912
             Queen Victoria   Emigrated to   Began royal service at
             gifted him   New Zealand   Windsor Castle, 1863,
             tenancy of   Then became Keeper   as Steward's Room waiter
             Tomidhu farm,   of HM Kennels,   Wardrobe-man/Footman, 1865
             Balmoral   Windsor   Valet to Prince Leopold from 1868
             Thence, at   EXTRA HIGHLAND   Upper Servant, 1869
             The Bush   SERVANT on the   Gentleman Porter, 1875
                | death of his brother   Page of the Presence, 1885
             married   Page of the Backstairs, 1888
             Elizabeth Paterson married 1863
             of Mains   Jessie McHardy |
             of Monaltrie   of Corgarff
             (1838–1900)   (1840–1914)   (Marriage and issue not known)
                | |
             Had issue including Had issue
                                    |
                                 Mary Ann
 ert   John   Victoria   William   (d. 1932)
870) (b. 1872) (b. 1876) (b. 1877) |
                                     married
(From whom there were issue) |
                                  Andrew Lamond
                                        |
                                    Had issue
                                        |

        Hugh William   Hilda Marion Jessie   Victor Andrew
         (1901–87)   (Mrs Harris) (1912–91) ·
            | (No issue)
        (Had issue)   (No issue)

NOTES

PROLOGUE: BIRTH OF ROYAL RUMOUR

1. Philip Magnus-Allcroft, *King Edward VII*, p. 359.
2. E.E.P. Tisdall, *Queen Victoria's John Brown*, pp. 232–3.
3. Catalogue: *British and Continental Paintings and Watercolours*, Christie's Scotland, 28 May 1998, p. 92. The canvas, signed by Carl Rudolph Sohn (1854–1908) was catalogued as picture 2066 (1884). It was duly sent to William Brown and was stored in a byre for forty-three years; it was sold in 1944 and 1963 and in 1965 was acquired by the Scottish Tartan Society who sold it on in 1998.
4. *Royal Archives*, Vic.Add.MSS.A.4/213, 14 May 1901.
5. *Royal Archives*, Vic.Add.MSS.U32 'Kronberg Letters' to Empress Frederick of Germany, 12 April 1865.
6. *Discreet*: her writings show that Queen Victoria had her own vocabulary of meanings for words she used. For her 'discreet' was applied to anyone thinking as she did on any subject, although she also used it to define foresightedness, unobtrusiveness and bashfulness. She also used the word 'bashful' of gillies who were intoxicated.
7. Queen Victoria's 'published indiscretions were so blatant that they carried with them an aura of innocence'; thus averred Taylor Whittle in *Victoria and Albert at Home*. The Prince of Wales did not see it that way.
8. Christopher Hibbert, *Edward VII: A Portrait*, p. 143.
9. Giles St Aubyn, *Edward VII: Prince and King*, pp. 140–1. On one occasion at Balmoral Edward's sons Prince Albert and Prince George tied a string across a staircase and not seeing it John Brown tripped over it and fell headlong. Cursing the boys (who were giggling nearby) he soundly thrashed them both. The Prince of Wales was furious that a servant should handle his children thus and complained bitterly to the Queen. 'It was a silly prank and I think the boys thoroughly well deserved what they got,' she replied. *See* Tisdall, p. 183.
10. The Duchess of Westminster told the diarist Charles Grenville of Queen Victoria's awareness of her mother's supposed infatuation for Conroy. Cecil Woodham-Smith, *Queen Victoria: From Her Birth to the Death of the Prince Consort*, p. 73.
11. G.E. Buckle (ed.), *The Letters of Queen Victoria*, Series II, 1862–85, 26 July 1867, p. 434; *see also* pp. 449–50.
12. *Elgin Courant and Morayshire Advertiser*, August 1866.
13. *John O'Groats Journal*, established 1836, published at Wick.
14. Giles St Aubyn, *Queen Victoria – A Portrait*, p. 361.
15. E.P. Thompson, *William Morris: Romantic to Revolutionary* . . .

16. Edmund Yates (ed.), 'English Photographs (IX), by 'An American'. *Tinsley's Magazine*, October 1868.

17. Wilfred Scawen Blunt, Unpublished Diaries, within *Blunt Papers*, MS9 4–6–1909.

18. Sir Frederick Ponsonby, *Recollections of Three Reigns*, p. 95.

19. *Gazette of Lausanne*, September 1866.

20. The Foreign Office was somewhat embarrassed by Harris's intervention and officially withdrew the complaint through the Swiss ambassador to the Court of St James.

INTRODUCTION: QUEEN VICTORIA'S
SCOTTISH INHERITANCE

1. David Duff, *Victoria in the Highlands: The Personal Journal of Her Majesty Queen Victoria*, p. 31.

2. *Ibid*, p. 52.

3. *New Edinburgh Almanac*, 1837. Part IV, p. 265.

4. *Ibid*, Census Summary 1831, p. 267.

5. The office of Hereditary Bearer of the Saltire (St Andrew's Cross) was not instituted until 1901 in favour of the 15th Earl of Lauderdale.

6. *New Edinburgh Almanac*, pp. 268–9.

7. Both Dunfermline and Linlithgow were ruined (as they are still), but the latter is listed in the *New Edinburgh Almanac* (1837) as having a 'Keeper' in Sir Thomas Livingstone of Westquarter. In 1837 Falkland was also ruined, but when the Hereditary Keeper, John Crichton-Stuart, 3rd Marquis of Bute, inherited the position in 1877 he laid plans for the palace's rebuilding and restoration.

8. Sir Herbert Maxwell, *Holyroodhouse*, p. 186.

9. The Keepership of Stirling Castle had fallen into disuse with the attainder of the 6th Earl of Mar and Kellie. This family's rights dated from the 1500s when they were foster parents to child sovereigns and heirs to the throne. The office was restored by King George V in 1923 on the 14th Earl. Dunconnel Castle, near Pladda Isle, Firth of Clyde, had been in the hands of the Macleans from before the fifteenth century but they were deprived of it in 1691. The Keepership was recovered in 1980 with Brigadier Sir Fitzroy Maclean of Dunconnel being appointed 11th Hereditary Keeper.

10. Balmoral Estates Factor's Office: figures as at August 1998.

11. *Thüringerwald*: the mountains of East Saxony. On the north side of the Thüringerwald lay Gotha, the capital of the duchy of Saxe-Gotha, the home at Schloss Friedenstein of Prince Albert's mother, Louise of Saxe-Gotha-Altenburg, first wife of Ernest I, Duke of Saxe-Coburg.

12. John Stirton, *Crathie and Braemar: A History of the United Parish*.

13. 'Notes and Queries', *Aberdeen Journal*, Vol. IV, 1911, p. 87.

14. In time Queen Victoria bequeathed Balmoral and its estates to 'the Sovereign of the country', as confirmed on 9 May 1901 in a House of Commons statement by the Chancellor of the Exchequer, Sir Michael Hicks-Beach.

15. Catherine Caulfield, *The Emperor of The United States of America & other magnificent British eccentrics*, p. 128.

16. Queen Victoria bought the furniture which had been in the Old Balmoral of Sir Robert Gordon's day. *See* John Marius Wilson, *Imperial Gazetteer of Scotland*, entry for 'Balmoral'.

17. Arthur Ponsonby, *Henry Ponsonby, Queen Victoria's Private Secretary* p. 124.
18. *Ibid*.
19. Henry Reeve (ed.), *Greville: the Greville Memoirs 1817–60*. Various entries for Balmoral.
20. B. Asquith, *The Lytteltons*.
21. *Ankers*: kegs holding twenty pints.
22. 'Progress of the Queen's Residence', *The Scotsman*, October 1852.
23. Frank Pope Humphrey, *The Queen at Balmoral*, pp. 69–82.
24. *Ibid*, pp. 62, 124.
25. Three messengers were always on duty in London in case papers had to be sent to Balmoral. It cost the Privy Purse £4 19s 6d rail fare to send a messenger in 1855.
26. Queen Victoria's body servants (dressers and so on) included ladies several of German origin like Sophie Weiss, Frieda Müller and Lydia Waetzig. The more staid of her court ladies were stunned on first taking up duties to find the Queen joining in the singing of songs such as *Von meinen Bergen muss klich scheiden* as the servants worked around her.

    A number of Crathie-born servants were to be found on Queen Victoria's permanent staff which moved around with her from the later 1850s to 1901. Besides John Brown's family other Crathie families represented were: McDonalds; Stewarts; Michies; Clarks (John Brown's cousins); Reids; Lamonds; Frasers; and Thomsons. Other Scots servants came from Ayr, Banff, Kelso, Logierait, Montrose, Corgarff, Glencairn and Stonehaven among other places. Sampling, *British Census 1881* for Windsor Castle, RG11.1325.f98, pp. 1–3.
27. Reeve, *Greville*.

CHAPTER ONE

NOTE: The supposed ancestry and early life of John Brown was put together in the first published biography, and issued days after his funeral, by Henry Llewellyn Williams. The 'One Penny Complete', sixteen-page *Life and Biography of John Brown Esq* (British Library Shelf Mark: 10803g6(7)) is so littered with errors as to be a most unreliable source. Alas E.E.P. Tisdall reproduced Williams's errors in his *Queen Victoria's John Brown* of 1938. In Tom Cullen's *The Empress Brown* of 1969, Williams's assertions are dubbed 'controversial'.

1. Margaret Ley's entry in the Registrations of Death for Crathie and Braemar, Ref: 183/19–7 Aug 1876, lists her father as Charles Leys, a farmer. *Scottish Record Office.* Williams Henry *Life and Biography of John Brown Esq*, identifies the father as the 'Aberarder blacksmith', p. 2. Williams also gives John Brown's date of birth as 22 December 1826.
2. Parish Register, Marriages 1820–1854, Crathie & Braemar, Ref: 183/2. *Scottish Record Office.*
3. *Bundling*: Largely a Highland practice, this form of courtship persisted as a tradition into the early twentieth century in such places as the Shetland Isles and the Western Isles.
4. Parish Register, Baptisms 1820–1854, Crathie & Braemar, Ref: 183/2. *Scottish Record Office.*
5. 'Early reminiscences', written by Queen Victoria in 1872, as quoted in A.C. Benson and Viscount Esher, *The Letters of Queen Victoria*, Vol. I, p. 11.

6. *Ibid*, Vol. I, p. 12.
7. *Ibid*, Vol. I, p. 13.
8. This was probably effected after Old John Brown died in 1875 at Wester Micras; the lairs were filled when John Brown's mother, Margaret Leys Brown, died at Craiglourachan Cottage in 1876.
9. His Registration of Death, Crathie Parish, ref. 183/2, describes him as a 'fisherman' and Dr W.G. Mitchell ascribes the cause of death as Alcoholism and Cardiac Syncope. *Scottish Record Office*. Dr James Reid confirmed that he was 'commanded by the Queen on no account to tell the Ladies and Gentlemen [of the court] that Hugh Brown had died of alcoholic poisoning'. Michaela Reid, *Ask Sir James*, pp. 158–9.
10. All relevant entries in the Parish Registers for Births, Marriages and Deaths for the Registration District of Crathie & Braemar. Ref: 183. *Scottish Record Office*.
11. *Bailie*: an officer of a Barony (lands of a baron) or Regality (Crown Land appointment) during the fourteenth to nineteenth centuries; thereafter a town magistrate.
12. Maxwell Gordon, 'The Browns of Crathie', article in *The Scottish Annual & The Braemar Gathering Book*, 1960, p. 251. Williams, *Life and Biography*, avers that Donald Brown farmed at 'Renachat', across the Dee from Balmoral. He also has Janet Shaw as a daughter of Lieutenant 'Captain' Shaw who had fought with British troops during the American War of Independence, p. 2.
13. *Ibid*. Williams (p. 2) opines that Old John Brown claimed descent through the Covenanting soldier Sir John Brown of Fordels (*sic*), Fife. He goes on that one of Sir John's sons secured the Chair of Divinity at Marischall College, Aberdeen, and his large family founded the Browns of Aberdeenshire. Tisdall expands Williams's assertions that Old John Brown had been a schoolmaster, following education as 'a poor student at a Scottish University', and to him is credited authorship of a guide book called *Deeside Guide*. Tisdall, *Queen Victoria's John Brown*, p. 16. A recent search of records of teachers in Aberdeen at this date, and matriculation records of Scotland's oldest universities, St Andrews, Glasgow and Aberdeen, give no substance to these assertions.
14. James E. Johnston, *Place-Names of Scotland*, p. 144.
15. William Watt, *A History of Aberdeenshire & Banff*, p. 16.
16. See entry for Colonel Francis Farquharson (1710–90) in Alistair & Henrietta Taylor, *Jacobites of Aberdeenshire & Banffshire in the Forty Five*, p. 158.
17. *Ibid*, p. 167.
18. Modern Crathienaird farmhouse was built around 1862. Correspondence between owner Dr Alistair Thomson and the author.
19. The Bush Farmhouse was near Bush Crathie on modern Ordnance Survey maps.
20. Benson & Esher, *Letters*, Vol. I, p. 20.
21. *Raithes*: Gaelic for a term at school – really three months of full-time education.
22. Stirton, *Crathie and Braemar*, pp. 324, 326.
23. *Ibid*, p. 327.
24. Act 43: George III, c54. James Scotland, *The History of Scottish Education*, Vol. I, p. 194. Teachers received £16 22*s* per annum at this date.
25. Benson & Esher, *Letters*, Vol. I, p. 48.
26. *Ibid*, Vol. I, p. 49.
27. *Ibid*, Vol. I, p. 188.
28. Marquis of Huntly, *Auld Acquaintance*, pp. 23–4.

29. The Deeside Water Co. Ltd, correspondence with the author. For John Brown's wages see Tom Cullen, *Empress Brown*, p. 54. The Pannanich Wells Hotel has retained its name since the 1760s, but under different spellings.

30. Recollections of Anita Leslie, Jennie, Lady Randolph Churchill's great-niece, and biographer, quoting Peregrine S. Churchill.

31. Tisdall, *Queen Victoria's John Brown*, p. 32. A copy of the *Book of Common Prayer*, given to John Brown by Queen Victoria in 1878, was handed over to Brown's brother Hugh on his death. The volume had been found in Brown's room at Windsor Castle and the Queen added the inscription that Brown was 'a dear and much lamented friend . . . in remembrance of December 14, 1883, by Victoria R.' It is now in the collection of Aberdeen Museums.

32. Story filed on Friday 8 September 1848, for the 11 September columns in the *Illustrated London News*.

33. 'Hours of Idleness', 1807. George Gordon Noel Byron (1788–1824) had been taken by his mother to Aberdeen in 1879 so that she would be near her relatives, the Gordons of Gight, and away from creditors. Byron was educated at the Aberdeen Grammar School and his childhood trips in the area gave him the imagery for his poem.

34. Queen Victoria, *Journal*, Saturday, 6 September 1848, on Lochnagar; 18 September for Ballochbuie. *A royal*: a stag with twelve 'tines' (points) to his antlers.

35. In honour of the occasion she created the Prince of Wales Earl of Dublin, 10 September 1849.

36. Queen Victoria, *Journal*, 30 August 1849.

CHAPTER TWO

1. Queen Victoria, *Journal*, 11 September 1849.
2. *Ibid.*
3. *Herald and Weekly News Press*, Aberdeen, 31 March 1883.
4. St Aubyn, *Queen Victoria*, p. 176.
5. *Ibid*, p. 287.
6. H. Bolitho (ed.), *Further Letters of Queen Victoria: From the Archives of the House of Brandenburg-Prussia*.
7. Sir Theodore Martin, *The Life of the Prince Consort*.
8. Queen Victoria, *Journal*, 13 September 1850.
9. *Ibid*, 16 September 1850.
10. *Ibid*. Footnote added in 1867.
11. *Ibid*, 10 September 1852.
12. Queen Victoria, *Leaves from the Journal of my Life in the Highlands* p. 132.
13. Benson & Esher, *Letters*, Vol. II, p. 394.
14. Queen Victoria, *Journal*, 16 September 1852.
15. *Purves Papers*.
16. Queen Victoria, *Journal*, 10 October 1852.
17. *John Brown Papers*.
18. Queen Victoria, *Journal*, 7 September 1855.
19. Benson & Esher, *Letters*, Vol. III, pp. 146–7.
20. Queen Victoria, *Journal*, 18 September 1858.

21. Roger Fulford (ed.), *Dearest Child*, October 1858.
22. M.H. McClintock, *The Queen Thanks Sir Howard*.
23. Cullen, *Empress Brown*, p. 61.
24. *Sociable*: a double-seated coach for four to six people which could be converted into an open carriage; also known as a 'sociable landau'. John Brown usually recommended the Queen's Cleveland bays for the better surfaced roads around Balmoral.
25. *Praline*: an almond or nut kernel with a brown coating of sugar.
26. Queen Victoria, *Journal*, 4 September 1860.
27. *Ibid.*
28. *Ibid*, 5 September 1860.
29. *Ibid.*
30. *Ibid.*
31. St Aubyn, *Queen Victoria*, pp. 318–19.
32. Queen Victoria, *Journal*, 20 September 1861.
33. *Ibid*, 21 September 1861.
34. *Ibid.*
35. *Ibid*, 9 October 1861.
36. *Ibid.*
37. *Ibid*, 16 October 1861.
38. Benson & Esher, *Letters*, Vol. III, pp. 461–2.
39. Cecil Woodham-Smith, *Queen Victoria*, pp. 504–5, quoting the Queen's diary.
40. 'Diary of Lord Broughton.' Add.MS.43764. xxi, 1861–62, f106v.
41. S.M. Ellis (ed.), *A mid-Victorian Pepys*, p. 70.

CHAPTER THREE

1. Fulford, *Dearest Child*, sequence 1862.
2. Elizabeth Darby and Nicola Smith, *The Cult of the Prince Consort*, pp. 89–90.
3. Tisdall, *Queen Victoria's John Brown*, p. 73.
4. Queen Victoria, *More Leaves*.
5. John W. Dodds, *The Age of Paradox*, p. 444.
6. Barry St-J. Nevill, *Life at the Court of Queen Victoria*, p. 42.
7. *Ibid.*
8. Duchess of York with Benita Stoney, *Victoria and Albert: Life at Osborne House*, pp. 25–6.
9. *Ibid*, p. 178.
10. Cullen, *Empress Brown*, p. 90.
11. *Purves Papers*.
12. Tisdall, *Queen Victoria's John Brown*, p. 66.
13. Benson & Esher, *Letters*, Second Series, Vol. I, p. 255.
14. *Kronberg Letters*, 5 April 1865.
15. McClintock, *The Queen Thanks Sir Howard*.
16. Louisa, Countess of Antrim, *Recollections*.
17. Charlotte Zeepvat, *Prince Leopold*, p. 21.
18. Stirling went on to a colonelcy and a knighthood and is included in *Lists of the Royal Household* as 'Extra Groom'.

19. Zeepvat, *Prince Leopold*, p. 60. Quoting Royal Archives, Add.3p/336.

20. Reid, *Ask Sir James*, pp. 161–2.

21. In a letter to her eldest daughter, dated 5 April 1865 from Windsor Castle, Queen Victoria confirmed John Brown's title as her own device. Fulford, *Dearest Child*, p. 22.

22. Elizabeth Longford, *Victoria R.I.*, p. 407.

23. Fulford, *Dearest Child*, p. 29.

24. Duff, *Victoria in the Highlands*, p. 195.

25. *Esquire*: once a shield-bearer attendant on a knight; later a landed proprietor with the 'title of dignity' below a knight; by the nineteenth century the term went from being a general title of a 'gentleman' to a mark of respect.

26. Longford, *Elizabeth R.I.*, p. 407. Quoting Royal Archives, Vic.Add.MSS. c3/16.

27. Fulford, *Dearest Child*, p. 22.

28. Michael Tyler-Whittle, *Victoria and Albert at Home*, p. 9 and Note.

29. Tisdall averred that John Brown's 'private diaries' were impounded by Queen Victoria's 'private secretary' after Brown's death and burned. Tisdall, *Queen Victoria's John Brown*, p. 13.

30. *Purves Papers*.

31. *Ibid*.

32. Nevill, *Life at the Court*, p. 8.

33. *Purves Papers*.

34. *Ibid*.

35. Mary Waddington, *My First Years as a Frenchwoman 1876–1879*. Ref: John Brown.

36. Tisdall, *Queen Victoria's John Brown*, p. 78.

37. C. Erickson, *Her Little Majesty*, p. 179.

38. Bolitho, *Further Letters*, pp. 153, 156.

39. *Plaid*: from the sixteenth century a term used to describe a rectangular length of twilled woollen cloth, usually in tartan design, formerly worn as an outer garment especially in Scots rural areas. By Queen Victoria's time it was well established as a shawl for women in both town and country.

40. *Morning Post*, March 1866. It has been noted that this is the first recorded reference to John Brown in the popular press.

41. On the 'Scottish run', the royal train was drawn by two engines, with two carriages for the Queen, nine for her Household and two guards and luggage vans. The carriages were a source of public interest in their depot 12 miles away from Balmoral at Aboyne when the Queen was in residence.

42. B. and P. Russell (eds), John Viscount Amberley, *The Amberley Papers*.

43. Princess Marie Louise, *My Memories of Six Reigns*, pp. 26–7.

44. Picture Catalogue, *Royal Archives*, Windsor Castle. PP Vic.7437. 279. Apl, 1867. Provenance and description. Oliver Miller, *The Victorian Pictures in the Collection of Her Majesty the Queen*, text Vol. p. 147.

45. *Saturday Review*, April 1867.

46. *Illustrated London News*, April 1867.

47. Picture Catalogue. PP.Vic.4281. 1869.

48. Miller, *Victorian Pictures*, pp. 13, 28 and 235.

49. Author in conversation with Florence Marian McNeill.

50. F.M. McNeill, *Hallow'en: Its Origins, Rites and Ceremonies in the Scottish Tradition*, pp. 26–7.

51. 'Prologue', note 17.
52. Theo Aronson, *Heart of a Queen: Queen Victoria's Romantic Attachments*, p. 160.
53. *Ibid*, p. 161.
54. *Groom-in-Waiting*: the position of superior page bestowed on young men with Court possibilities; they were usually from genteel families. Bigge was the son of a Northumbrian vicar.
55. Jerrold Packard, *Farewell in Splendour*, p. 32.
56. Ponsonby, *Recollections*, pp. 95–6.
57. Benson & Esher, *Letters*, Second Series, pp. 4532 and 449–50.
58. Queen Victoria, *Journal*, 15 October 1867.
59. *Ibid*, 1 October 1868.

CHAPTER FOUR

1. Lady Anne Hamilton was the sister of the Duke of Hamilton and Brandon and of the Countess of Dunmore. Her *Secret History of the Court of England* was published in 1832 and covered the Court history of Queen Victoria's grandfather King George III and her uncle King George IV.
2. Queen Victoria, *Journal*, 22 August 1867.
3. *Daily Telegraph*, 24 August 1867. *Selkirk Bannock*: a thick, round, flat cake of fruit loaf consistency.
4. John Guthrie Tait (ed.), *The Journal of Sir Walter Scott*, p. 545, ref 5/19/1828.
5. Duff, *Victoria in the Highlands*, p. 15.
6. Longford, *Victoria R.I.*, p. 471.
7. Dean Baillie & Hector Bolitho, *Later Letters of Lady Augusta Stanley*, p. 72.
8. *Inverness Advertiser and Ross-Shire Chronicle*, 24 August 1867, report and editorial.
9. Miss Amelia Murray MacGregor (b. 1829) was a cousin of the 6th Duke of Atholl and a long-time companion of his wife Duchess Anne. Queen Victoria sought her assistance often when composing her prose, and presented her with the Diamond Jubilee Medal in 1897. This was the year Duchess Anne died, making Amelia MacGregor homeless; Queen Victoria made her an 'Extra Sister of St Katherine's Hospital', a medical charity of which she was patron, thus assuring her one of the charity's accommodations and a pension of £100 per annum.
10. *The Scottish Annual & The Braemar Gathering Book*, 1989, pp. 85–6.
11. Patricia Lindsay, *Recollections of a Royal Parish*.
12. *John Brown Collection*.
13. Dr Robertson was confusing 'Captain' Shaw with his eldest son, Lieutenant Alexander Shaw, who was killed in a duel in 1808.
14. Tisdall, *Queen Victoria's John Brown*, p. 141. Writing in 1938 Tisdall added: 'Whether the story was true or not, it is believed on Deeside to this day, and the man who swore he witnessed the epic combat died only a year or two ago.'
15. Queen Victoria, *Journal*, 21 October 1868.
16. Dodds, *Age of Paradox*, p. 82.
17. *Hampshire Telegraph* Series 1868–9.
18. *The Times*, 22 February 1869.

19. From the unpublished memoirs of Mary Henderson, reported in 'Queen Victoria as I remember Her', *Aberdeen Weekly Journal*, 1 February 1934.
20. Queen Victoria, *Journal*, 1–6 September 1869.
21. Cullen, *Empress Brown*, p. 170.
22. Queen Victoria had been incensed by the Roman Catholic Church's declaration in 1870 of 'Papal Infallibility'. Encouraged by Prince Otto von Bismarck's fierce opposition to the Roman Catholic Church in Germany, Queen Victoria decided to show that she was Defender of the Faith in Britain; in a show of independence she decided to take the Crathie Sacrament. Longford, *Victoria R.I.*, p. 505.
23. *Ponsonby Papers*.

CHAPTER FIVE

1. *Purves Papers*.
2. Longford, *Victoria R.I.*, p. 478.
3. *Ibid*, p. 488.
4. The Fenians staged an unsuccessful rising in Ireland in 1867 and the Irish Republican Brotherhood was superceded in the twentieth century by the Irish Republican Army (IRA).
5. Buckle, *Letters*, Series II; Queen Victoria, *Journal*, 14 October 1867.
6. *Ibid*, 31 December 1867.
7. Raymond Lamont-Brown, *Royal Murder Mysteries*, p. 109.
8. Queen Victoria, *Journal*, 29 February 1872. *Fenian prisoners*: which of the rebels mentioned is unclear; in May 1871 the Fenians tried to blow up a statue of the Prince Consort at Leinster Lawn, Dublin, and there had been attempts to rescue Fenian prisoners in Manchester.
9. *The Times*, March 1872.
10. Tisdall, *Queen Victoria's John Brown*, p. 171.
11. For a detailed sequence of the assassination attempts on Queen Victoria's life see: Raymond Lamont-Brown, *Royal Murder Mysteries*, pp. 102–14.
12. Queen Victoria usually used the pseudonyms 'Countess of Rosenau' and 'Countess of Balmoral'.
13. Queen Victoria, *Journal*, 6 September 1872.
14. *Highland Clearances*: the eviction of Highlanders from their traditional homelands during the eighteenth and nineteenth centuries to make way for agricultural development, mainly sheep and deer grazing.
15. In his book *The Empress Brown*, Tom Cullen shows an illustration of Brown's medals which he said were sold in 1965. He also displays a medal bearing the head of Ludwig III of Hesse which he says was presented to Brown. Queen Victoria's daughter Princess Alice married Ludwig III's nephew who became Ludwig IV. H.L. Williams also says John Brown received a medal from the King of Greece.
16. Longford, *Victoria R.I.*, p. 411.
17. Queen Victoria, *Journal*, 19 June 1879.
18. *Ibid*, 9 September 1873.
19. *Ibid*.

20. Cullen, *Empress Brown*, p. 18, quoting a report in *The World*.

21. Queen Victoria, *Journal*, 13 September 1873.

22. *Officers and Graduates of the University & King's College*, Aberdeen, MDCCCLV, p. 307.

23. Records of the Royal College of Surgeons, Edinburgh. Profeit beame Licentiate just before the Medical Act of 1858 tightened regulations on medical qualifications.

24. Obituary in *Aberdeen Journal*, 28 January 1897.

25. Extract: Royal Archives, Windsor. It seems that Queen Victoria was influential in Profeit naming his fifth son Leopold on 7 April 1877; the boy became an actor. In 1883 the Queen acted as sponsor for Profeit's only daughter Victoria.

26. Correspondence between Mrs Edith Paterson and the author.

27. *Ibid.*

28. Duff, *Victoria in The Highlands*, p. 303.

29. *Ponsonby Papers.*

30. St Aubyn, *Queen Victoria*, p. 480.

31. Tisdall, *Queen Victoria's John Brown*, pp. 202ff.

32. The following Christmas Queen Victoria gave John Brown a pocket watch by C.J. Klaftenberger; it was meant to be a 'recollection' present in memory of Old John. It is now in the John Brown Collection of Aberdeen Art Gallery & Museums and is inscribed: GIVEN TO/John Brown/THE DEVOTED PERSONAL ATTENDANT OF/QUEEN VICTORIA/by her/Christmas 1875/After 27th March 1883/IT BECAME THE PROPERTY OF HIS BROTHER/HUGH BROWN.

33. Soon after the funeral of Margaret Brown, Queen Victoria gave a Bible to Hugh Brown and his wife. It is now in the John Brown Collection of Aberdeen Art Gallery & Museums and bears the Queen's holograph inscription: 'To/Hugh Brown & his Wife/In recollection/of their beloved Mother/from Queen Victoria Rg Balmoral Sept 17.1876'. Under the dedication are inscribed four lines of Scripture.

34. Queen Victoria, *Journal*, 17 August 1876.

35. Arthur Ponsonby, *Henry Ponsonby: Queen Victoria's Private Secretary*, p. 123.

36. Queen Victoria, *Journal*, 26 August 1878.

37. Ponsonby, *Henry Ponsonby*, p. 284.

38. *Ibid*, p. 286.

39. Tay Bridge was destroyed in a gale, 28 December 1879.

40. Queen Victoria, *Journal*, 6 October 1879.

CHAPTER SIX

1. Ponsonby, *Henry Ponsonby*, p. 184.

2. Sarah Bradford, *Disraeli*, p. 523.

3. The case is now in the John Brown Collection, Aberdeen Art Gallery & Museums.

4. G.E. Buckle and W.F. Monypenny, *The Life of Benjamin Disraeli, Earl of Beaconsfield*.

5. Robert Blake, *Disraeli*.

6. *Ponsonby Papers.*

7. Lamont-Brown, *Royal Murder Mysteries*, p. 113.

8. *Ibid.*

9. *Ibid.*

10. Following the Queen's tirade the verdict was changed to 'guilty but insane', through the new law of 1883. That law remained on the Statute Books until 1964 when parliament restored the original statutory verdict, 'not guilty on the ground of insanity'.

11. *Ponsonby Papers.*

12. Cullen, *Empress Brown*, p. 195.

13. Emily Crawford, *Victoria, Queen and Ruler.*

14. Duff, *Victoria in the Highlands*, p. 354.

15. Queen Victoria, *Journal*, 17 March 1883.

16. Lady Florence Caroline Dixie (1857–1905), was an author, traveller and big game hunter who won public notice as a correspondent with the *Morning Post* for her dispatches on the Zulu War of 1879.

17. *Press Association*, March 1883.

18. *Central News Agency*, File of Report, March 1883.

19. *Daily News*, March 1883.

20. *British Medical Journal*, March 1883.

21. Louisa, Countess of Antrim, *Recollections.*

22. Elizabeth Longford (ed.), *Louisa: Lady in Waiting* p. 18.

23. *Press Association*, 24 March 1883.

24. Queen Victoria, *Journal*, 25 March 1883.

25. The death was registered by Archie Brown whose address is given as 19 Victoria Street, New Windsor. *General Register Office*, 28 March 1883. Ref: 154.

26. Queen Victoria, *Journal*, 29 March 1883.

27. Extract: Abt D24 No15, 28 March 1883. *Hessisches Staatsarchiv Darmstadt, Großherzogliches Familienarchiv.*

28. Tisdall, *Queen Victoria's John Brown*, pp. 22–4.

29. *Ibid*, p. 224.

30. *Official Court Circular*, 28 March 1883.

31. Tisdall, *Queen Victoria's John Brown*, p. 227.

32. The Revd Orr was a pastor of the Congregational Union of England and Wales; he officiated as there was no Presbyterian Minister at court.

33. *Press Association*, 3 April 1883.

34. *John Brown Collection.*

35. Letter, dated Windsor Castle, 3 April 1883. *John Brown Papers*, Aberdeen Art Gallery & Museums.

36. *Ponsonby Papers.*

37. *People's Journal for Glasgow & Edinburgh*, Series 1882–6.

38. *Press Association.*

39. Sir Theodore Martin, *Queen Victoria as I Knew Her.*

40. *Ponsonby Papers.* Letter, 26 May 1883.

41. The railings were removed during the Second World War and were never replaced.

42. Longford, *Queen Victoria*, p. 577.

43. Elisabeth Darby and Nicola Smith, *The Cult of the Prince Consort*, pp. 96–8.

44. Ponsonby, *Henry Ponsonby*, p. 96.

45. The site of John Brown's statue is not marked on the modern castle and estate guidebook to Balmoral, although memorials to deceased royal dogs are clearly indicated. To arrive at the statue go through the Gate Lodge castle entrance, and turn left off the main drive at the first crossroads. Follow the 'Exit for vehicles' signs towards Easter Balmoral and proceed

to where the road forks past the East Lodge. Just past the fork on the right is Craig Gowan Lodge. Follow the dirt track right of the lodge into the forest. Up the track on the right look for a polished pink granite seat. The statue is beyond the seat in the trees and can be reached by following the path round.

46. Miller, *Victorian Pictures*, Text Vol., p. 38.
47. Clare Jerrold, *The Widowhood of Queen Victoria*.
48. F.P. Humphrey, *The Queen at Balmoral*, quoting unnamed Crathie locals of the 1880s and 1890s.

CHAPTER SEVEN

1. St Aubyn, *Queen Victoria*, p. 451.
2. G.K.A. Bell, *Randall Davidson*.
3. *Ibid*, entries in December 1883.
4. Longford, *Victoria R.I.*, p. 571.
5. The Memoir on Brown, which incorporated excerpts of letters from him to the Queen, was destroyed by Ponsonby. Ponsonby, *Henry Ponsonby*, p. 146.
6. *Ponsonby Papers*.
7. Longford, *Victoria R.I.*, p. 572.
8. Cullen, *Empress Brown*, p. 227.
9. *Ibid*, pp. 224–5.
10. A parallel scandal concerned Queen Victoria's eldest child, the Princess Royal, who became the Empress of Germany and was widowed at the age of forty-eight. Loose tongues wagged that she had a 'relationship' with her Chamberlain, Baron Hugo von Reischach. *See also, Sunday Observer*, 27 May 1979.
11. Reid, *Ask Sir James*, pp. 212–13.
12. Bell, *Randall Davidson*.
13. Tisdall, *Queen Victoria's John Brown*, p. 230.
14. *Ibid*.
15. *Ibid*.
16. *Ibid*.
17. G. Lytton Strachey, *Queen Victoria*.
18. Ponsonby, *Henry Ponsonby*, p. 128.
19. *Ibid*.
20. Ida Macalpine and Richard Hunter, *George III and the Mad-Business*, p. xii.
21. *Ibid*, pp. 261–6.
22. H.L. Kennedy (ed.), *Duchess of Manchester: My Dear Duchess*.
23. Alexander Robertson, *John Brown: A Correspondence with the Lord Chancellor, Regarding a Charge of Fraud and Embezzlement Preferred Against His Grace the Duke of Athole, K.T.*, p. 6.
24. *Ibid*, p. 5.
25. *Ibid*.
26. *Purves Papers*. Ponsonby, *Recollections* notes that the Dowager Duchess of Roxburghe, who was also 'generally supposed to have been present at the marriage' denied that any such thing had ever taken place and that mention of it was anti-royal propaganda, p. 95.
27. Robertson, *John Brown, a Correspondence*, p. 6.

28. *Ibid.*
29. Public Record Office: *Home Office Papers*, 1873. Granville to Leveson-Gower.
30. *Ponsonby Papers.*
31. *Sunday People*, 24 June 1979.
32. *Sunday Observer*, 27 May 1979.
33. *Sunday People*, 24 June 1979.
34. *Spiritualist Magazine*, 1864.
35. Odette Borncand (ed.), *The Diary of W.M. Rossetti*, entries for 1870. Without a hint of the ludicrous nature of the content, modern writers on Spiritualism quote seances with the supposed shade of John Brown. For a recent example see: Neville Randall, *Life After Death*, pp. 161–2.
36. A local Crathie superstition/tradition has it that John Brown also possessed the *Droch Shuil* (Evil Eye), which could blight the health of any upon which it malignantly fell. For this reason Crathie folk avoided passing John Brown's statue at Balmoral lest '*Thuit droch shuil air*' ('An Evil Eye fell upon them').

EPILOGUE: SCENES AT A ROYAL DEATHBED

1. Written on 9 December 1897: 'Instructions for my Dressers to be opened directly after my death and to be always taken about and kept by the one who may be travelling with me.' Reid, *Ask Sir James*, p. 215.
2. Packard, *Farewell in Splendour*, p. 199.
3. Reid, *Ask Sir James*, p. 216.
4. *Ibid. See also* correspondence between Lady Reid and the author; also, *Purves Papers.*
5. St Aubyn, *Queen Victoria*, p. 424.
6. Guidebook: *Frogmore House and the Royal Mausoleum*, p. 47. Opposite Queen Victoria's Tea House at Frogmore is a granite drinking fountain inscribed 'In affectionate remembrance of John Brown, Queen Victoria's devoted personal attendant and friend, 1883.'
7. Inter alia, *Scotland on Sunday*, 27 December 1998, p. 7.
8. *Sunday Post*, 27 September 1998, p. 5. When contacted by the author, Ecosse Films Ltd, makers of the film *Mrs Brown*, refused to cooperate in confirming or denying what data if any had been located.
9. Reid, *Ask Sir James*, p. 56.
10. *Ibid*, pp. 227–8.

BIBLIOGRAPHY

ARCHIVE SOURCES

British Census Records, Public Record Office, Kew, Richmond, Surrey

Royal Household Indexes, Public Record Office

Births, Marriages, Deaths Registers, Scottish Register Office, Edinburgh

Ponsonby Papers, The Lord Ponsonby of Shulbrede

Purves Papers, private collection of unbound leaves, jottings, notes, letters collected by the late Marion Purves

Blunt Papers, 'Secret Diary' of Wilfred Scawen Blunt, Fitzwilliam Museum, Cambridge

John Brown Papers, private collection (location withheld at request of owner)

John Brown Collection, Aberdeen Libraries

Royal Archives, various mss and the *Kronberg Letters*, Windsor Castle

Memorandum, on the life of John Brown by Dr Andrew Robertson, Balmoral, 2 June 1865, private collection

Großherzogliches Familienarchiv, Hessisches Staatsarchiv Darmstadt (former Grand Duchy of Hesse), West Germany

Baron Broughton de Gyfford Papers, British Library

The Amberley Papers, of John, Viscount Amberley (ed. B. & P. Russell and published by L. & V. Woolf, 1937)

SECONDARY SOURCES

John Brown

Cullen, Tom. *The Empress Brown: The Story of a Royal Friendship*, (Bodley Head, 1969)

Philip, Kenwood. *John Brown's Legs or Leaves from a Journal in the Lowlands*, published privately 1884

Robertson, Alexander. *John Brown: A Correspondence with the Lord Chancellor, Regarding a Charge of Fraud and Embezzlement, Preferred Against His Grace The Duke of Athole, K.T.*, published privately, 1873

Tisdall, E.E.P. *Queen Victoria's John Brown*, Stanley Paul, 1938

Williams, Henry L. *Life and Biography of John Brown Esq*, E. Smith & Co., 1883

John Brown's 'Faithful Service Medal' and Bar, and gold 'Devoted Service Medal' were sold at auction in 1965. Details of the awards are to be found in:

Cowell, J.C. *The Victoria Faithful Service Medal: Instituted 1872*, Harrison & Son, 1889

Balmoral, Crathie, Osborne and Windsor

Balmoral: Castle and Estate, Nevisprint, 1998

Brown, Ivor. Balmoral: The History of a Home, Collins, 1955

Clark, R.W. Balmoral, Thames & Hudson, 1981

Farr, A.D. Stories of Royal Deeside's Railway, Kestrel, 1971

Frogmore House and the Royal Mausoleum, Royal Collection, 1998

Humphrey, F.P. The Queen at Balmoral, T. Fisher Unwin, 1893

Lindsay, Patricia. Recollections of a Royal Parish, John Murray, 1902

Osborne, Ken (ed.). Osborne House, English Heritage, 1999

Patchell-Martin, Arthur. The Queen in the Isle of Wight (Brochure II), Vectis, Isle of Wight, 1898

Robinson, John Martin. Windsor Castle, Royal Collection, 1997

Stirton, John. Crathie and Braemar: A History of a United Parish, Milne and Hutchinson, 1925

—— Balmoral in Former Times, Forfar, 1921

Taylor, Alistair & Henrietta. Jacobites of Aberdeenshire & Banffshire in the Forty Five, Milne & Hutchinson, 1928

Tyler, Michael Sidney. Victoria and Albert at Home, Routledge & Kegan Paul, 1980

Watt, William. A History of Aberdeenshire & Banff, William Blackwood, 1900

York, Duchess of and Stoney, Benita. Victoria and Albert: Life at Osborne House, Weidenfeld & Nicolson, 1991

Relevant writings of Queen Victoria

When she was thirteen years of age in 1832, Queen Victoria began a series of journals which she continued to fill until her death in 1901. Those she left passed into the hands of her youngest daughter Princess Beatrice, who, on her mother's instructions, transcribed large passages from the journals into blue copybooks. As she worked Princess Beatrice burned the originals. On her own auspices the princess destroyed much which she did not transcribe and it is thought that many references to John Brown, his background and career, were thus destroyed. Nevertheless Queen Victoria's comments on John Brown can be assessed from the following:

Helps, Arthur (ed.). Leaves from the Journal of Our Life in the Highlands from 1848 to 1861. Smith, Elder, 1868

[With the assistance of Amelia MacGregor]. More Leaves from the Journal of A Life in the Highlands from 1862 to 1882, Smith, Elder, 1884

David, Duff (ed.). Victoria in the Highlands: The personal journal of Her Majesty Queen Victoria, Muller, 1968

Benson, A.C. & Esher, Viscount (eds). The Letters of Queen Victoria, 1st Series, 1837–61, John Murray, 1907

Buckle, G.E. The Letters of Queen Victoria, 2nd Series, 1862–85, John Murray, 1926

—— The Letters of Queen Victoria, 3rd Series, 1886–1901, John Murray, 1930

Bolitho, H. (ed.). Further Letters of Queen Victoria: From the Archives of the House of Brandenburg-Prussia, Thornton-Butterworth, 1938

Dyson, Hope & Tennyson, Charles (eds). Dear and Honoured Lady: The Correspondence Between Queen Victoria and Alfred Tennyson, Macmillan, 1969

Fulford, Roger (ed.). *Dearest Child: Letters between Queen Victoria and the Princess Royal 1858–1861*, Evans Brothers, 1971

Queen Victoria and her Court

Aronson, Theo. *Heart of A Queen: Queen Victoria's Romantic Attachments*, John Murray, 1991
Baillie, Dean & Bolitho, Hector. *Later Letters of Lady Augusta Stanley*, Howe, 1927
Cooke, A.B. & Vincent, J.A. (eds). *Lord Carlingford's Journal*, Oxford University Press, 1971
Crawford, Emily. *Victoria, Queen and Ruler*, Simpkin, Marshall, 1903
Erickson, C. *Her Little Majesty*, Robson, 1997
Hardy, Alan. *Queen Victoria was Amused*, John Murray, 1976
McClintock. *The Queen Thanks Sir Howard*, John Murray, 1945
Marie Louise, Princess. *My Memories of Six Reigns*, Evans, 1956
Martin, Sir Theodore. *The Life of the Prince Consort*, Smith, Elder, 1875–1880
Neville, Barry St-J. (ed.). *Life at the Court of Queen Victoria*, Good Books Ltd, 1984
Packard, Jerrold M. *Farewell in Splendour: The Passing of Queen Victoria and Her Age*, Penguin Group, 1995
Ponsonby, Sir Frederick. *Recollections of Three Reigns*, Eyre & Spottiswoode, 1957
Reeve, Henry (ed.). *Greville: The Greville Memoirs 1817–60*, Longmans Green & Co., 1875–87
Reid, Michaela. *Ask Sir James*, Hodder & Stoughton, 1987
St Aubyn, Giles. *Queen Victoria: A Portrait*, Sinclair-Stevenson, 1991
Strachey, Lytton. *Queen Victoria*, Chatto & Windus, 1921
Victoria, Princess of Prussia. *Queen Victoria at Windsor and Balmoral*, Allen & Unwin, 1959
Whittle, Taylor. *Victoria and Albert at Home*, Routledge & Kegan Paul, 1980
Woodham-Smith, Cecil. *Queen Victoria: From Her Birth to the Death of the Prince Consort*, Hamish Hamilton, 1972
Zeepvat, Charlotte. *Prince Leopold*, Sutton, 1998

General books

Antrim, Louisa, Countess of, *Recollections*, London, 1937
Asquith, B. *The Lyttletons*, Chatto & Windus, 1975
Barncand, Odette (ed.). *The Diary of W.M. Rossetti*, Oxford University Press, 1977
Bell, G.K.A. *Randall Davidson*, Oxford University Press, 1938
Blake, Robert. *Disraeli*, Eyre & Spottiswoode, 1966
Bradford, Sarah. *Disraeli*, Grafton Books/Collins Publishing Group, 1985
Buckle, G.E. & Monypenny, W.F. *The Life of Benjamin Disraeli, Earl of Beaconsfield*, John Murray, 1929
Caulfield, Catherine. *The Emperor of the United States of America & Other Magnificent British Eccentrics*, Corgi/Gransworld, 1982
Dodds, John W. *The Age of Paradox*, Victor Gollancz, 1953
Ellis, S.M. (ed.). *A mid-Victorian Pepys: The Letters and Memories of Sir William Henderson*, London, 1923
Goodman, Jean. *Debrett's Royal Scotland*, Debrett/Webb & Bower, 1983
Hibbert, Christopher. *Edward VII: A Portrait*, Allen Lane, 1976

Huntly, Marquis of. *Auld Acquaintance*, Hutchinson, 1929

Irvine, Douglas H. *The Royal Palaces of Scotland*, Constable, 1911

Irving, Joseph. *Annals of Our Time, 1837–1891*

Johnston, James B. *Place-Names of Scotland*, John Murray, 1934

Kennedy, H.L. (ed.). *Duchess of Manchester: My Dear Duchess*, John Murray, 1956

MacAlpine, Ida & Hunter, Richard. *George III and the Mad Business*, Allen Lane/The Penguin Press, 1969

MacLeay, Kenneth. *The Highlanders of Scotland*, London, 1866

Magnus-Allcroft, Philip. *King Edward VII*, Penguin, 1964

Maxwell, Sir Herbert. *Holyroodhouse*, HMSO, 1923

New Edinburgh Almanac, Oliver & Boyd, 1837

Ponsonby, Arthur. *Henry Ponsonby: Queen Victoria's Private Secretary, His Life from His Letters*, Macmillan, 1942

St Aubyn, Giles. *Edward VII: Prince & King*, Collins, 1979

Thompson, E.P. *William Morris: Romantic and Revolutionary*, Lawrence & Wishart, 1955

Waddington, Mary. *My First Years as a Frenchwoman 1876–1879*, Smith, Elder, 1914

Wilson, John Marcus. *Imperial Gazeteer of Scotland, c. 1866*

Wilson, Dr R. McNair. *Doctor's Progress*, 1938

JOHN BROWN IN DRAMA AND FILM

John Brown appears as a character in one of English novelist and dramatist Laurence Housman's short biographical 'chamber plays' within the series *Victoria Regina*. The series was initially banned by the censor, but was produced at London's Lyric Theatre in 1937. Set in 1877 the scenes in which John Brown appears are entitled *An Episode of Home Life in the Highlands*. Herein John Brown was portrayed as a pawky, genial friend of the Queen, by actor James Gibson.

In 1950 John Negulesco and Nunnally Johnston's film *The Mudlark* was issued by Twentieth Century Fox using a screenplay from the novel by Theodore Bonnet. John Brown, played by Findlay Currie, with Irene Dunne as Queen Victoria, is shown as a haughty, tipsy seneschal, inclined to collapse in a drunken heap.

The best portrayal of John Brown so far on film is Douglas Rae and Jeremy Brock's 1998 Ecosse Films/BBC presentation *Mrs Brown*. The main roles of Brown and Queen Victoria are played by Billy Connolly and Dame Judy Dench. A balanced portrayal of John Brown's character is achieved, but this (and other dramatisations) gives no data on the Highland Servant's background and career.

NOTE: English poet and critic Algernon Charles Swinburn composed a skit-drama 'founded on Her Majesty's [*More Leaves*], called *La Mort du Mari*. In it John Brown is murdered by Albert Edward, Prince of Wales, in vengeance'. *See* Cecil Lang (ed.). *The Swinburn Letters*, Vol. 2, Oxford University Press, 1959.

ACKNOWLEDGEMENTS

SOURCES

The author wishes to acknowledge with particular gratitude the help given by Mrs N. Lamond, widow of John Brown's great-nephew, Hugh W. Lamond, and Mrs Ann Lamond-Webb, great-great niece of John Brown, for assisting with queries about the Brown family of Crathienaird, their extant papers and artefacts. And to Mrs Edith Paterson for family reminiscences regarding John Brown's employment at Balmoral. Important comment on John Brown's birthplace at Crathienaird was supplied by Dr Alistair Thomson. Each has provided original material on John Brown that does not appear in any other source.

A special thank you further goes to the following for supplying answers to queries, advice on sources and providing relevant materials which have helped greatly in the formulation of this book's research: Michael Hunter, Curator, Osborne House; Peter J. Ord, Resident Factor, Balmoral; Dr Elizabeth James, The British Library; Peter Johnston, Berkshire Local History Association; Margo Strachan, Media Resources Manager, Aberdeenshire Council; Catherine Taylor, Central Library, Aberdeen City Council; Martin Simpson, Managing Director, The Deeside Water Co. Ltd; The Countess of Longford; Neil Irvine, Windsor Library; Pamela Clark, the Royal Archives, Windsor Castle; Susan Bellamy, National Library of Scotland; Revd R Taylor, Torphins, Aberdeenshire; and Jane Anderson, Blair Castle. Important field work has been undertaken by Mrs Barbara Swiatek, Berkshire Family History Society, and Margeorie Mekie.

Especial appreciation goes to my wife Dr Moira Lamont-Brown, for her companionship, support and encouragement on many research trips in pursuit of John Brown.

TEXT

Each quotation is identified as to source as it occurs in the text, and copyright heirs and successors are recognised where known. Due acknowledgement is given to Tom Cullen who undertook research on John Brown in the 1960s and published his findings in his book *The Empress Brown* which extended and corrected work done in the 1930s by Evelyn Tisdall who wrote *Queen Victoria's John Brown*. Individual acknowledgements are also due to Michaela, Lady Reid, for the short line quotes from her *Ask Sir James*, and to Lord Ponsonby of Shulbrede for permission to quote from the Ponsonby Papers.

PHOTOGRAPHS

Each photograph is identified as to copyright ownership, and permission to reproduce the images is gratefully extended to all thus identified. Help in researching the images has been gratefully received from Bernard Horrocks, the National Portrait Gallery, Mrs Ann Lamond-Webb and Christine Rew of Aberdeen Art Gallery.

INDEX